DEC. 1973.

JOHN. T. MEADOWS. F.R.I, A.M.A.A.

CANADIAN REAL ESTATE

CANADIAN REAL ESTATE

HOW
TO
MAKE IT PAY

Richard Steacy

Real Estate Press
Willowdale, Ontario

Applications for serialization authority are invited by the publisher.

Design: Brant Cowie

Photos: Ursula Liane

Published by: REAL ESTATE PRESS, P.O. Box 222, Willowdale, Ont.
Canada's most exclusive real estate publishing house.

Printed and bound in Canada by The Bryant Press Limited, Toronto

ISBN 0-9690470-0-2

Library of Congress Catalog Card Number 73-85061

The author sincerely thanks the following, and acknowledges their generous time and patience in helping with my research: H. W. Hignett, President, Central Mortgage and Housing Corporation; Jacques Lapointe, Associate Deputy Minister, Department of Justice, Quebec; Dr. C. B. Ferguson, Provincial Archivist, N.S.; Robert K. Maynard, Lawyers Title Insurance Corp.; Chief Harold Adamson, Metropolitan Toronto Police Force; D. F. Collins, Registrar-General of Deeds, South Australia; Mrs. Helen D. Scott, Manager, Insurance Institute of Ontario; Dean L. Richardson, Deputy Director of Titles (Ontario); R. A. W. Switzer, Dominion Fire Commissioner, Ottawa; Jim McAvoy, Mortgage Insurance Company of Canada; Mr. V. C. Fox; Miss Elaine Charal; and

. . . . *John B. Hudson, F.R.I., for his advice about points to check in leasing office space.*

. . . . *The Insurance Institute of Ontario, for its advice in preparing the chapter on Insurance.*

. . . . *Robert Yeaman, Canadian specialist in interest rates, for his advice in preparing the chapter "Mortgage Repayment Schedules".*

. . . . *Central Mortgage and Housing Corporation for answering ALL my letters, and its help in preparing the chapter "National Housing Act Mortgages".*

. . . . *Mr. Herb Gray, M.P., former Minister of National Revenue, Ottawa, for his patience in correcting me.*

R.H.S.

To my sons,
Charles Richard Graham Steacy
age 5,
William Harold Denham Steacy
age 2,
and their mother, Mary,
my wife.

Contents

Introduction to Real Estate

Mortgages

Buying and Leasing

Selling

Property Protection

General

Foreword

There are about 35,000 real estate agents in Canada. In buying, selling, leasing and mortgaging, these agents can take care of themselves.

But what about the 22,000,000 Canadians who are not real estate agents?

A good method of providing yourself with additional real estate ammunition is to read about it. This book will provide you with helpful information in one volume that would take you weeks of investigation and research to find (if you knew where to look). It will describe short cuts, things you never thought about, pitfalls to avoid, hints on making money, saving money, and using it wisely, and ideas for establishing a firm foothold in the greatest money-making business in the world — REAL ESTATE.

When you lend money to a bank or trust company, with a modest return to you in the form of interest, the borrower uses your money to lend it to somebody else at a higher rate of interest, and that somebody else uses your money to make more money.

A great deal of this money is used to finance real estate, so instead of lending your money to "A" to lend it to "B" to use it to make HIS pile in real estate, eliminate the middlemen and get a piece of the action yourself.

Read this book from cover to cover — study it — and THEN go get yourself a good deal in Canadian real estate.

If I can personally help you, please write. Readers in the Toronto area may reach me at 493-5491 or 493-6037.

> Richard H. Steacy
> c/o P.O. Box 222,
> Willowdale, Ontario.

NOTE: *Since mortgage interest rates are not constant, the sample rates used should be treated as guides only.*

Some also there were that said, we have mortgaged our lands, vineyards, and houses, that we might buy corn, because of the dearth.

From the Old Testament,
Book of Nehemiah,
Chapter 5, Verse 3.

1

Then and Now

In 1881, a *London Truth* editorial writer expressed his opinion about the future of Canada: It was prompted by news that a syndicate had been formed to complete a transcontinental railroad — one of the conditions of British Columbia joining Confederation.

"The Canadian Pacific Railroad Company has begun, I see, to launch its bonds. A group of Montreal and New York Bankers have undertaken to float ten million dollars worth of the Company's land grant bonds, and the Bank of Montreal, with its usual courage, has taken one-fourth of the entire loan.

New Yorkers are keen enough gamblers, and reckless enough at times, I admit, and yet it is impossible to believe that they are such fools as to put their money into this mad project. I would as soon credit them with a willingness to subscribe hard cash in support of a scheme for the utilization of icebergs.

British Columbia is a barren, cold, mountain country that is not worth keeping.

Canada is one of the most overrated colonies we have. As for the country as a whole, it is poor and it is crushed with debt.

This Dominion is, in short, a fraud all through and is destined to burst up like any other fraud. Then, and not I suppose till then, the British tax-payer will ask why we guaranteed so much of this sham Government debt."

This "mad project" went on to become the largest transportation system in the world, and the overrated colony is now the second largest country in the world.

Canada's natural resources and magnitude are staggering and almost incomprehensible to citizens of the world's crowded nations. We have a land area of 3,560,238 square miles — more than one hundred acres of land for every man, woman and child living here. In addition to all this land, nature has provided us with 291,571 square miles of water.

This history of Canadian real estate goes back almost five hundred years.

John Cabot claimed part of North America for Britain and Henry VII in 1497, when he landed on Cape Breton.

In 1534 along came Jacques Cartier who hoisted the flag of France on the Gaspé Peninsula and made his own claims.

In establishing their respective colonies, settlers were recruited and attracted by the thousands, and land holdings in North America began. The French gave large tracts of land to seigneurs, who in turn broke it in pieces and granted rights to individuals, who in turn paid the seigneurs a consideration — money or farm produce — for this favour. The British land grants were outright grants, and the receivers, regardless of whether they obtained them by paying for them or not, owned them.

During the years between the first settlers and the Seven Years' War between France and Great Britain, there was a great amount of territory being captured, recaptured, and ceded between the two countries. The Seven Years' War ended with the Treaty of Paris, 1763.

Under the terms of this Treaty, Franch agreed to cede Canada on condition that England guarantee the inhabitants the right to practise the Catholic religion according to the Roman rite. King George III agreed to this insofar as the laws of Great Britain allowed, and the one chapter in twenty-five of the Treaty of Paris that dealt exclusively with Canada saw Louis XV cede to England all French territory as far as the western plains. The inhabitants could choose to leave the country within 18 months, during which time they could sell their property to British subjects. All the inhabitants remaining in this vast territory became subjects of Great Britain, after being under the flag of France for two centuries.

The King issued a Proclamation, imposing English criminal and civil law on the inhabitants of New France.

The inhabitants, accustomed to French law, were most unhappy about this, and after much representation to George III, the *Quebec Act* (1774) established the Province of Quebec, an area that included part of what is now Ontario, and provided for a Governor and Legislative Council with rights to make ordinances. The Quebec Act revoked the Proclamation of 1763, insofar as it concerned civil rights and property, and re-established the French law as it existed before the Proclamation. It provided for the continuance of the criminal law of England, as introduced by the Proclamation.

When war broke out between England and her American colonies, a large number of British subjects emigrated to the Province of Quebec. They settled chieflly in the west, along the banks of the St. Lawrence river and around Lakes Erie and Ontario. Serious complaints were made by the new British settlers about the state of affairs in the Province of Quebec, and a demand was made for a constitution resembling that to which they had been accustomed.

The result was the *Constitutional Act* (1791) which separated the Province of Quebec into Upper Canada and Lower Canada, each having its own Governor, Legislative Council and Assembly.

English common law was introduced in Upper Canada in 1792, by its first statute, the Property and Civil Rights Act, which stated that the area had been settled principally by British subjects, who were unaccustomed to French law, and repealed the provisions of the Quebec Act regarding civil rights and property, replacing them with English law.

Under the Constitutional Act, Lower Canada retained its French law of real property, except that grantees would be entitled to grants in free tenure if they wished. (Feudal rights and duties were abolished in 1851.)

Conflict ensued between the English and the French. Rebellion broke out in 1837 and the Constitution of Lower Canada was suspended. A High Commissioner was appointed to adjust the relations and government of the two Provinces.

The result of this was the *Union Act* (1840) which united Upper Canada and Lower Canada into the single Province of Canada.

French civil law continued in the area of the former Lower Canada, and English common law continued in the area of the former Upper Canada. English criminal law was in force overall.

The British North America Act of 1867 divided the Province of Canada. Upper Canada was designated as the Province of Ontario and Lower Canada was designated the Province of Quebec, the latter retaining French civil law, which is now the Quebec Civil Code.

When Rupert's Land and the North-West Territories, including the present Provinces of Alberta, Manitoba and Saskatchewan were transferred by the Imperial authorities in 1870 to the administration and control of the Canadian Government, the Department of the Interior was set up to stimulate settlement in this vast area, through immigration and colonization.

In 1872, the Dominion Lands Act was promulgated to govern the manner in which homesteads, pre-emptions and other colonization programs would be carried out, and similar projects were introduced by the various railroad companies to ensure utilization of their vast tracts of subsidy lands.

The Act was a generous one. Entry for a homestead to the extent of one-quarter section (160 acres) could be obtained for a fee of $10. In 1930, the natural resources of Western Canada were placed under provincial jurisdiction.

The record year for Canadian immigration was 1913, when more than 400,000 people were admitted; to-day it is running at less than half that figure.

2

How We Hold Land

Land is a permanent thing. People who live near large bodies of water may disagree with this when they see land erode and disappear. But generally it is considered to be permanent, or *Real*. Thus we have an estate that is real. *Real Estate*.

Pursuant to Section 109 of the British North America Act of 1867, lands, generally speaking, are held by the Crown-in-Right-of the Provinces. When we hold land, we do so subject to the rights of the Crown. This is why expressions such as the following include the word "tenant".

Tenant in Fee Simple: Fee — from feudal term fief (tenure of land subject to feudal obligations). The feudal system was in effect in Europe during the middle ages, based on the holding of lands in return for services to a lord by a vassal. Simple — unaffected. Therefore, this is real estate in its most untrammelled sense. It is an estate granted absolutely to a person and his heirs, forever.

Joint Tenancy: There are four unities here —

(a) Unity of Possession: Each entitled to undivided possession of the whole of the property, and none holds any part separately to the exclusion of the others.

(b) Unity of Time: The interest of each joint tenant must vest at the same time.

(c) Unity of Title: Each person must obtain title under the same instrument.

(d) Unity of Interest: The interest of each is identical. Joint tenancy is land ownership by two or more persons. If one person dies, his interest in the estate passes to the survivor(s). Joint tenancy can be severed and turned into a tenancy in common.

Tenancy in Common: Here we have just one unity, and that is the unity of possession. It is ownership by two or more persons, but if one of them dies, his share passes to his *heirs*, and not to the survivor(s) of the tenancy.

In Britain, from the time of William the Conqueror, all land was owned by the King, who in turn granted it to his nobles. An owner kept all his deeds in his own possession from the time of the original grant from the King, or the patent from the Crown. When he sold or mortgaged, he handed over all the documents.

In the early 1700's, registry offices were set up in each county in Britain. The documents themselves were not registered, but a note or memorandum was registered. These were registered alphabetically under the owner's or mortgagee's name, a system which was found to be most unwieldy.

Canadian land registry offices were established under authority of Upper Canada Statute 35, George III, Chapter 5, passed August 10, 1795, and entitled "An Act for the public registering of deeds, conveyances, wills and other incumbrances which shall be made, or may affect, any lands, testaments or hereditaments within this Province". The choice of registrar and of the place where registrar offices would be established was given to the Lieutenant-Governor. The sureties of the candidates were to be approved by the justices of the peace in the area.

The alphabetical system was changed in most parts of Canada before Confederation, when abstract books were set up as we know them to-day, and documents themselves were registered against lots and plans.

Registration of a deed in a registry office does not imply absolute ownership. Competent persons can examine documents registered, or "search title", and give an opinion as to status of title. But although the opinion may be considered reliable, it may be quite impossible to state definitely that the title is clear.

A government guaranteed system of registration was introduced in parts of Canada in 1885, known as "Land Titles", or the Torrens system, the history of which is covered in the next chapter.

The Province of Quebec, being governed by the civil code, has a few ideas of its own on the subject of real estate. "Hypothec", for example. This is real right upon an immovable made liable for the fulfilment of an obligation. There is only one really immovable, by its nature, and that is land. But the civil code recognizes as immovables: land and buildings, windmills and waterwheels, uncut crops, unpicked fruits, and standing timber.

A hypothec gives the creditor two rights: (1) on failure of the debtor to fulfil his obligation, the right to compel the holder of the immovable hypothecated to surrender it, so that it may be sold, and (2) the right to be paid by preference out of the proceeds of the sale.

Originally, when the debtor was in default, the holder was compelled to surrender the hypothecated immovable to satisfy the obligation. He could not avoid the surrender: not even by offering to pay the debt. This rule was relaxed, and the holder was allowed, as he is now, to avoid surrender and to stop it by the payment of the debt.

A mortgage is a hypothec in Quebec — hypothecs rank in order of their registration. The deed creating a hypothec is registered with the registrar in the same manner as any other deed. Three conditions are necessary:

(a) The deed must contain a description of the land according to the number it bears on the official plan and book of reference, or on the subdivision plan.

(b) The grantor's title to the hypothecated land must be registered, for, until it is, the registration of any hypothec granted by him is without effect.

(c) The grantor must still be the registered owner of the land hypothecated at the time of registration of the hypothec.

The registrar is not the judge of the validity or regularity of documents, but must transcribe them as they are, provided they are in registrable form.

All lands in Quebec, generally speaking, are held under free tenures. The owner of land holds it as absolutely as it is possible for anybody to hold it, and can dispose of it freely.

The owner may be an individual, or a group of individuals owning in equal or unequal shares, or a legal entity such as a corporation.

Two or more persons cannot at the same moment be the owners each for the whole of the same thing; the right of one is exclusive of that of the others. But the right of ownership may be split, as in usufruct, where one person, called the usufructuary, has the enjoyment of the property as the proprietor (owner) himself.

In all of Canada, with the exception of the Province of Quebec, your real estate purchase and sale will be handled for you by a lawyer.

In the Province of Quebec, it will be handled by a legal practitioner known as a Notary, whose chief duty is to draw up and execute deeds and contracts. No one in Quebec, other than a practising notary may, on behalf of another person, draw up deeds under private signature affecting immovables (land and buildings, etc.) and requiring registration or the cancellation of any registration.

The late Will Rogers was fond of saying "Buy land — they're not making any more of it". He was so right.

Remember the good old days when properties were priced at about half of today's market value? If one thinks today's selling prices are high, they *could* look reasonable in retrospect tomorrow.

Get involved. Buy some real estate. If you already own some, buy more. Beneath everything is the land — it will always be there.

3

Land Titles

Land registration systems are very ancient, and probably go back to Babylonian days. They were common in medieval Europe, but before the middle of the last century there was no system of land registration anywhere in the world which included all the desirable features of the "Torrens" or Land Titles system of registration.

If property is registered under the Land Titles system the title is guaranteed by the provincial government, and in Canada, what better guarantee could there be?

All property ownership in Alberta and Saskatchewan is registered under Land Titles, and in most of British Columbia and Manitoba. In Ontario, Land Titles were made available as far back as 1885 in the County of York, and later all the northern districts and many other counties were added. The remainder of our provinces do not use the system.

Compared with registry office systems, Land Titles transfers have no complicated covenants as in deeds. The whole title, and everything to which it is subject, is contained in a single page. Long descriptions are not required. The system saves a great deal of time in "searching title," because everything is on one page, and the search can be done in a few minutes.

There can be no adverse possession (squatter's rights) under Land Titles, which does happen in the registry system.

The Land Titles system originated with Sir Robert Richard Torrens, former Premier of South Australia, Collector of Customs, and Registrar-General of Deeds.

One of the most controversial figures in South Australian history, Torrens was both vilified and eulogised by the Adelaide press, politicians, and legal fraternity.

When South Australia was granted responsible Government in 1856, Torrens was elected as one of the members for Adelaide, and became Treasurer. In 1857 he formed a Cabinet himself, but was Premier for only a month.

So much property was passing so quickly to so many new settlers in the early days of South Australia that the old English conveyancing laws could not cope with the situation. Bitter agitation among the settlers led to the formation of an active committee, in an endeavor to evolve a more simple, secure, and less costly method of obtaining title to property.

Torrens conceived the idea of applying the simple method of registration of shipping to the registration of land, and thereby setting up a simple straightforward method of procedure in dealing with land. He was the author of the "Real Property Act", an act to simplify the laws relating to the transfer and encumbrance of freehold and other interest in land. It was assented to on January 27, 1858, and took effect on July 1st the same year.

Torrens became the first Registrar-General under the Act, and was promptly vilified by the press and legal profession who opposed the measure. The lawyers adopted every device possible to render the Act ineffective and advised their clients not to deal in any land which was under the act.

Lawyers objected to the Act because it was too simple — and apparently would cost them dearly in lost legal fees.

Even the Bench showed a very critical attitude towards the Act years after Torrens had won the battle. In 1874 Mr. Justice Gwynne said of certain sections: "I would countenance this simple system (if anything so crude, so illconceived, clumsily executed, and unscientific can be called a system) and accept it with all its sins against the science of jurisprudence, contenting ourselves with the reflection that it is cheap and simple and sufficient for the general purpose of the colonists . . . In my opinion the Real Property Act as it stands at present is a scandal on the legislation of the Colony."

Despite the objections of the legal fraternity, within 16 years the principles of the South Australian Act were being used by all the Australian States and New Zealand. Later, it spread to many parts of the world (about 60 countries) and to many States in the U.S. The "Torrens" system has been described as South Australia's greatest export.

The system removes all risk from defective deeds by stipulating that the ownership of the person whose name shows in the register book shall be paramount. Registration makes his ownership conclusive. It cannot be forfeited. A person deprived of land through the operation of the system does not suffer loss, and if he is the victim of fraud he can recover possession of his land.

If an innocent third party has become registered as proprietor, the victim can proceed against the wrongdoer, not for the land, but for pecuniary damages, as the third party's title will be indefeasible. It that action fails, the victim can recover compensation from the provincial government.

The original act was extensive, containing no less than 50 pages, and because of a man named Torrens, millions of people the world over sleep just a little more soundly.

Before Torrens departed for England in 1862, he was given an address signed by 10,000 citizens of Adelaide, and in 1864 petitions were made to both Houses of Parliament, signed by 14,000 people, praying that his services be recognized.

He was elected to the House of Commons for Cambridge in 1865, and received the KCMG in 1872. He was advanced to the GCMG in 1884, the year of his death.

II. Mortgages

4

Defining a Mortgage

On March 20, 1795, Walter B. Sheehan of the Township of Newark in the Home District of the Province of Upper Canada held and firmly bound himself to Francis Crooks in the sum of 215 pounds, 14 shillings, 7¼ pence, by way of a real property mortgage deed.

This mortgage, at 11 a.m. on April 13, 1796, became the first mortgage deed registered in Canada.

Our pioneers had great faith in the future of their country, as evidenced by Sheehan's mortgage. It was secured by way of a lease on his property for one thousand years!

Repayment of the debt, of course, cancelled the lease.

Just what is a mortgage deed?

A deed is a document containing a contract or agreement that is signed, sealed and contains proof of its delivery. It is effective only on the date of delivery.

The deed contains the mortgage, which is many things to many people.

In Quebec's civil code, it is a "deed of loan with hypothec".

A hypothec is a lien on an immovable.

An immovable is land and buildings, waterwheels, windmills, uncut grain, standing timber and unpicked fruit.

In the rest of Canada, under English common law, a mortgage of first priority is a conveyance of the property to secure the debt, if it is registered in a registry office.

If registered in a land titles office, it is a charge on a property. Secondary mortgages are called "equitable" mortgages (equity in property), and so are third, fourth, fifth.

The noun mortgage is derived from two French words, mort (dead) and gage (pledge). The real estate pledged becomes dead, or lost, due to failure to pay.

A popular definition of a mortgage is that it is a conveyance of real estate to a lender as security for the repayment of a debt, on the condition that if the debt is paid according to contract, the grant shall become void and the property reconveyed to the borrower.

Applying this definition to all mortgages is a misconception, because the majority of mortgages in Canada do not constitute a conveyance of property.

To understand this, one must clearly understand the two systems of real property (and mortgage) registration in Canada; the registry system and the land titles system.

As previously mentioned, Canadian land registry offices were established by authority of Upper Canada, Statute 35, George III, Chapter 5, on August 10, 1795.

It was originally an alphabetical system, registering the property owner's or mortgagee's name, which was found to be unwieldy. Today, the documents are registered against lots and plans, although the old "name" system can still be found in parts of the Maritimes.

It is only under this registry system that a conveyance of real estate is made in a mortgage deed, and only in the case of a mortgage of first priority, or first mortgage. Mortgage seniority is established by the time and date of its registration.

(The exception to this is Quebec's registry system, where a mortgage creates a "charge" on a property, and does not convey title for security.)

The mortgage deed is registered with the registrar, and English common law states that "the legal mortgagee is entitled to the title deed". No two mortgagees could be entitled to the same title deed, so we now come to our first definition, that of a legal mortgage.

All mortgages properly executed are of course legal, but there is only one mortgage that can properly be referred to as a legal mortgage, and it is the one in which the legal mortgagee is entitled to the title deed.

To ease any confusion, when one conveys property by way of a first mortgage in a registry office, he is left with what is known as an "equity of redemption".

If one wishes to borrow additional funds, he cannot legally convey his property twice, but he can mortgage his equity of redemption, and the loan will be secured by a mortgage that is known as an "equitable" mortgage. This would be commonly called a second mortgage, but it can also go right on down the line in seniority, as a third or fourth mortgage.

If the first mortgage is paid off and discharged before any junior mortgages, the junior mortgages move up the line in seniority, and the "second" mortgage would automatically become the first, or legal mortgage, in the registry office.

The land titles system is a registry system whereby all title documents accepted for registration are guaranteed by the provincial government from the moment of registration.

The land titles system was first made available to Canada in

Ontario in 1885, in York County. It is also used extensively in British Columbia, Alberta, Saskatchewan and Manitoba.

Mortgaging property under land titles never conveys title to a lender. The loan creates a charge against the property. Additional loans create further, but junior charges. A mortgage under land titles is known as an equitable mortgage.

Although the land titles system is not used in Quebec, the Quebec registry office system is similar in that mortgaging creates a lien on the property, and never a conveyance to a lender.

A mortgage, simply defined, is a lien, or charge, on some real estate.

5

Understanding Amortization

Amortize means to deaden.

To amortize a loan is to extinguish it by means of a sinking fund; in other words, an allowance of payments over a period of time will be made to reduce the debt to zero.

The most common method of amortizing a mortgage is to have the repayment schedule computerized to ensure that all monthly payments are identical, with each payment containing the amortized principal amount, plus interest on the outstanding balance of the loan.

To illustrate this, the following is the first year's repayment schedule of a 20-year, $20,000 loan, at 10%, compounded semi-annually, each line representing one month's payment, and each payment being exactly $190.34.

Payment Number	Interest Payment	Principal Payment	Balance of Loan
1	163.30	27.04	19972.96
2	163.08	27.26	19945.70
3	162.85	27.49	19918.21
4	162.63	27.71	19890.50
5	162.40	27.94	19862.56
6	162.17	28.17	19834.39
7	161.94	28.40	19805.99
8	161.71	28.63	19777.36
9	161.48	28.86	19748.50
10	161.24	29.10	19719.40
11	161.01	29.33	19690.07
12	160.77	29.57	19660.50

In the beginning, each payment is practically all interest. As the loan progresses, each payment contains less interest, and more principal. Each monthly payment still remains the same, with a minor adjustment on the last payment (to take care of the fractions).

Note the allowances for principal payments during the final year of this loan:

229	17.66	172.68	1989.91
230	16.25	174.09	1815.82
231	14.83	175.51	1640.31
232	13.39	176.95	1463.36
233	11.95	178.39	1284.97
234	10.49	179.85	1105.12
235	9.02	181.32	923.80
236	7.54	182.80	741.00
237	6.05	184.29	556.71
238	4.55	185.79	370.92
239	3.03	187.31	183.61
240	1.50	183.61	.00

One thing to be quite clear about is that regardless of the differences of principal and interest in each payment, the borrower only pays interest on the outstanding principal balance of the loan at the time of each payment.

As the loan progresses the borrower is making larger principal payments, because there is less principal on which to pay interest.

If this loan were amortized with equal principal payments, plus interest, this is how the monthly payments would vary:

1st month: $ 83.33 principal plus
             $163.29 interest ($246.62)
120th month: $ 83.33 principal plus
             $ 81.64 interest ($164.97)
240th month: $ 83.33 principal plus
             $ .68 interest ($84.01)

The obvious disadvantage with this method is that the highest payments are in the beginning, when the home owner probably needs all the available money to support his family.

With rising interest rates, the only possible way to keep monthly mortgage payments down is to lengthen the amortization of the loan.

Unfortunately, this financial rubber band can be stretched just so far.

To illustrate, note what happened when National Housing Act loans were extended to a maximum amortization of 40 years:

Take a 40-year N.H.A. loan of $25,000. When one becomes a mortgagor in such a deed, a 1% insurance fee (in favour of the lender) must be added to the loan.

This produces an N.H.A. mortgage of $25,250.

Using an interest rate of 10%, compounded semi-annually, the monthly payment is 210.41.

If this loan were amortized at the previous maximum level of 35 years, the monthly payment would be $213.17.

A difference of *two dollars and seventy-six cents.*

By taking advantage of this $2.76 monthly saving, the borrower will bind himself not only to a further five years in the loan, but to an additional debt of more than *eleven thousand dollars!*

And N.H.A. regulations, by allowing the interest to be adjusted every five years, could mean an even bigger difference if interest rates increase.

At this point some mathematical genius will undoubtedly point out that if the borrower invested the $2.76 each month, compounded at 10% for 40 years, he would end up with about $11,000.

However, such an investment would be highly unlikely.

The following illustrates the repayment of 30, 35 and 40-year amortized N.H.A. mortgages of $25,250, 10%, compounded semi-annually. The total amount of interest to be paid will stagger you.

	40 year loan	35 year loan	30 year loan
Monthly payment:	$ 210.41	$ 213.17	$ 217.83
Yearly cost:	2,524.92	2,558.04	2,613.96
Total cost:	100,996.80	89,531.40	78,418.80
Total interest paid:	75,746.80	64,281.40	53,168.80
Principal amount owning at end of:			
5 years	$24,922.78	$24,710.25	$24,351.32
10 years	24,389.79	23,831.09	22,887,47
15 years	23,521.65	22,399.00	20,502.96
20 years	22,107.55	20,066.25	16,618.85
25 years	19,804.10	16,266.45	10,292.07
30 years	16,052.00	10,077.01	
35 years	9,940.24		
40 years			

Do not confuse the *amortization* of a loan with its *term.* If one is told that a mortgage is amortized for 20 years, it must *not* be assumed that it has a 20-year term. The following chapter will explain.

6

The Mortgage Term

The term of a mortgage is the period of time a borrower has before the lender can demand the pricipal balance owing on the loan, subject to mortgage default by the borrower.

It is very important to understand it clearly.

Until recently, it was a common practice of lenders to make loans for long periods of time, such as 25 years, at a fixed rate of interest.

With the shrinking value of our dollar, this did not make economical sense.

Furthermore, the demand for mortgage funds kept pushing the rate of interest up, and in one six year period it jumped from 7% to 11%!! Lenders bound to a 25-year 7% loan must have shuddered when they looked at the 11% and realized that they had another 19 years to go at 7%.

Canada's Central Mortgage and Housing Corporation, being fully aware of a shortage of mortgage funds for housing, considered that if it amended the long term fixed-interest regulation to one that would allow an adjustment of interest at five year periods, it would attract more mortgage money.

The amendment was made, and what happened?

Other lenders naturally sighed with relief, and fell in line.

With the exception of banks doing business with their valued customers, and some private lending, a mortgage today with a term of more than five years is uncommon.

There are other reasons for the five year term.

Trust and mortgage loan companies are offering a prime rate of interest to the public for investing in 5-year certificates and debentures.

The trust and mortgage loan firms use the money for mortgage investments at about 2% increase to the mortgagor. The term of such loans must obviously match the term of the certificates — 5 years.

The following is a prime example to illustrate how repeated five year terms in a mortgage could conceivably take more than 100 years to pay off the loan. It may seem a little extreme, but don't panic — you will be shown in this chapter how to avoid it.

If you were the borrower with a repayment schedule amortizing a loan over a period of 20 years, and the mortgage had a five year term, it would mean that despite the 20 year amortization, you would have to repay the outstanding principal balance of the loan at the end of five years.

This can be dynamite to your pocketbook.

Take a look at the following table in a $20,000 loan, 9½%, compounded semi-annually, amortized over 20 years:

Principal balance owing at end of:

Year	1	$19,640	Year	11	$13,420
Year	2	19,240	Year	12	12,420
Year	3	18,820	Year	13	11,320
Year	4	18,340	Year	14	10,120
Year	5	17,820	Year	15	8,800
Year	6	17,240	Year	16	7,360
Year	7	16,620	Year	17	5,760
Year	8	15,920	Year	18	4,020
Year	9	15,160	Year	19	2,100
Year	10	14,340	Year	20	0

You will notice that in 20 years the loan will be extinguished, but here is where the five year term will grab you.

At the end of the five years, the lender wants his money, namely $17,820. To repay the loan, you probably will have to commit yourself to another mortgage, and borrow the rounded balance of $17,800. If you commit yourself for a further five-year period (same amortization and rate) this is what your outstanding balance will be over the next five years in round figures:

Year 1	$17,479
Year 2	17,123
Year 3	16,749
Year 4	16,322
Year 5	15,859

At the end of this five year period, when you have to repay the loan, you may repeat the process. We'll do this just twice more, to take us to the end of four five-year terms.

Third five years: ($15,800 loan)		Fourth five years ($14,000 loan)	
Year 1	$15,515	Year 1	$13,748
Year 2	15,199	Year 2	13,468
Year 3	14,867	Year 3	13,174
Year 4	14,488	Year 4	12,838
Year 5	14,077	Year 5	12,474

Each new five year term will result in smaller monthly payments because the principal amount of each succeeding term will be less.

If one keeps up the pattern of the five year terms by starting each new term with the outstanding principal balance of the previous one, and amortizing the loan over 20 years, it will take more than 100 years to reduce the loan to zero.

Whereas if the term of the mortgage had been 20 years, it would have been reduced to zero in that time, although the monthly payments would have remained constant (and larger) than under each renewed five year term.

If the 20 year mortgage is to be retired, or paid in full in 20 years, then each time the mortgage is renewed, the principal balance owning must be amortized for no longer a period than the remaining number of years in the original amortization.

Examine the chart and remember it.

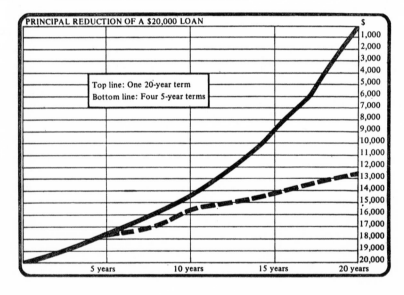

PRINCIPAL REDUCTION OF A $20,000 LOAN

Top line: One 20-year term
Bottom line: Four 5-year terms

7

Knowledge of Interest

Many years ago loans were regarded as forms of help that one owed his neighbour in distress. To profit from his distress was considered to be evil and unjust.

The noun *usury* is from the latin *usura,* meaning the "use" of anything — borrowed capital for example.

About the year 300, usury was defined as "where more is asked than is given", and was prohibited for hundreds of years by the Church and State. Usury was considered to be a form of robbery; it still is, but in a different sense.

Pope Eugene III decreed that "mortgages, in which the lender enjoyed the fruits of a pledge without counting them towards the principal, were usurious", and Pope Alexander III declared that credit sales at a price above the cash price were usurious (12th century).

However, it was gradually accepted that a loss could occur through lending — the latin verb *intereo* means "to be lost" — interest was not profit but loss — and interest came to be considered the compensation due to a creditor because of a loss incurred through lending.

This concept derived from Roman law, where it was considered the difference between the lender's present position and that in which he would have stood if he had not loaned.

The term "interesse" became standard early in the 13th century.

In early cases, loans were interest-free, but incurred the penalty of interest if not repaid promptly. Lenders then adopted the practice of charging interest from the beginning of a loan.

For many years, our federal government has condoned the practice of extracting exorbitant interest on money loaned.

A prime example of this is the Small Loans Act, which allows a lender to charge "two per cent per month on the unpaid balance" for the first $300 of the loan. When one desperately needs $100, the cost of paying $2 for its use for a month may not sound unreasonable, but look at it from the lender's side.

Two per cent per month on the unpaid balance is 24% per annum. Compounding the interest monthly produces a still higher annual yield to the lender.

The consumer's attitude toward borrowing money usually is unrealistic. His first question is: "How much a month will it cost?" The rate of interest is often ignored.

The one in the most vulnerable position is the one who needs the money most urgently and can least afford to pay the 24% — the borrower of $300 or less. This is the one who gets it in the neck with the ferocious rate of interest.

Fortunately, even at today's inflated rates, the interest charged on mortgage lending is lower than other forms of financing — lower, for example, than financing an automobile, or financing through the services provided by large department stores, finance companies, or the increasingly popular charging system of the chartered bank.

In Nova Scotia, a Royal Commission on the cost of borrowing money found that one well known finance company charged more than 56% interest on small loans.

In personal loans, the closest one can come to mortgage rates of interest is in loans secured at chartered banks, where the rates charged will fluctuate with the covenant and security of the borrower.

To properly understand financing, and especially mortgaging, one must have a full understanding of what interest is all about. In many mortgage loans, the borrower pays too much interest on the loan by not understanding how the effective use of interest rates can help.

This financing error is not restricted to the "man on the street". Many lawyers and real estate agents, for example, are unfamiliar with the use of interest rates.

There are two types of interest: (a) simple (or fixed) interest, and (b) compound interest.

If one borrows money and agrees to repay it plus 10% interest when the loan is repaid, the principal amount of the loan would be repaid plus the 10%, regardless of the repayment date. This is simple or fixed interest — interest on principal (the amount borrowed).

However, if one agreed to repay the loan at 10% interest *per annum*, a loan is immediately created with compound interest, because if the loan is not repaid at the end of the year, the 10% will be added to the indebtedness, and when the loan is repaid at a later date, interest will be paid on the new outstanding balance of the loan, which requires interest to be paid on interest.

If the interest were compounded "semi-annually" for example, here is how it would look on $1,000 at 10%.

— Interest for first six months: $\frac{10\%}{2}$ of $1,000, totalling $50.

— Interest for second six months: $\frac{10\%}{2}$ of $1,050, totalling $52.50.

— Interest charge at end of year totals $102.50.

It must be remembered that *the more frequent the com-*

pounding, the greater the yield to the lender. If this interest is compounded quarter-yearly, it will produce $103.81 interest at the end of the year, monthly compounding would yield $104.71.

However, these figures only apply if the loan interest is paid once a year. Not many loans are payable once a year, so to compensate for this, an interest factor (rate) is used to compute the interest to be paid on the loan balance on each payment date.

Interest is not payable in advance, and to illustrate this, assume that this loan interest is compounded semi-annually, with *interest only* paid once a month.

The interest rate in this case would be .816485%. In other words, $8.16 would be paid each month.

Multiplying $8.16 by 12 months produces $97.92, which is what the borrower would actually pay in interest over the 12 months on the 10% loan.

Despite the fact that the borrower paid $97.92 over a year, the loan produces an effective annual yield of 10.25% to the lender.

It is called an "effective" yield, because if it were to be an actual yield, there are only two ways it could be accomplished:

(a) If the loan interest were paid once a year.

(b) If the lender immediately re-invested the monthly interest payment to exactly match the loan on which it was paid.

If the lender, receiving the interest monthly, did not re-invest it, he would have just 9.79% to show for his 10% loan at the end of the year.

So what the lender actually receives for his investment depends on what he does with his monthly interest payment.

If the monthly interest payments were taken out of an old shoe box, the borrower would pay 9.79% for the 10% loan, because money in a shoe box draws no interest.

Interest rates are very easy to establish, providing the payments are to be made *with the same frequency.* To establish the interest rate on a loan in which the interest is compounded monthly, simply divide the annual rate of interest by 12. If the interest were compounded quarter-yearly (every three months), divide the annual rate of interest by four, and so on.

However, if one wishes to compound interest, quarter yearly, for example, and pay the interest monthly, what then?

Unless one is a mathematician, a table of interest rates will be needed. Such a table is provided in this book.

Here is an example of how to save money using the interest rates provided:

If a loan, for example, stipulates interest at 10% per annum, and no mention is made as to how the interest is compounded, pay it on a basis of annual compounding.

Many borrowers make the mistake of dividing the annual rate of interest by 12 to estimate the interest to be paid for the month. This is wrong, unless the interest is compounded monthly. If the loan agreement does not stipulate monthly compounding of interest, don't pay it that way.

Study the tables of interest rates — don't be surprised if you save some money. If you have been paying too much in the past on your loan, the excess can probably be recaptured; business is business.

Calculate:	from the latin *calculus* which means pebble
↑	or stone used in counting. *Calculus* from the
(synonymous)	*latin calx*, which means small pebble. *Calculate* means *compute*.
↓	
Compute:	from the latin *com* which means together, and latin *puto* which means reckon.
Reckon:	from Old English, Swedish, Danish, etc., which means *count*.
Compound:	from *compounen* (to put together). Composed of two or more parts; not simple. *Synonymous* with Amalgamation, combination, mixture.
Simple Interest:	That interest which arises from the principal sum only.
Compound Interest:	That interest which arises from the principal with the interest added at stated times, as yearly, twice-yearly, etc. *Interest on interest*.

Central Mortgage and Housing Corporation (and many other lenders) could take a lesson from Kinross Mortgage Corporation in the administration of mortgage applications.

Kinross TELLS the applicant that the interest will be compounded "semi-annually not in advance". N.H.A. applications make no mention of a frequency of compounding interest, although it is found in the fine print of the mortgage deed.

KINROSS	N.H.A.
Interest Rate (Compounded Semi-Annually not in advance) % per Annum	INT. RATE: .... %
THE RIGHT WAY	**THE WRONG WAY**

Truth in lending should start with the application. It should not be "sneaked" into the deed.

8

How NOT to Figure a Mortgage Payment

The following is a common error made by many mortgagors (borrowers) when figuring their monthly mortgage payments.

Dividing By Twelve!!

In mortgages other than conventional loans made by banks, trust companies, etc., the two most common repayment requirements are, for example:

(A) Payment to be $150 monthly, to include principal and interest.

(B) Payment to be $50 monthly off principal, plus interest.

Assume that we are concerned with a $12,000 mortgage loan, at 10%, compounded semi-annually.

Here is how many borrowers will estimate the first two month's payments under (A):

$$10\% \text{ of } \$12,000 = \frac{1200}{12} = \$100 \text{ interest}$$

Therefore, the payment of $150 will be made up of $100 interest and $50 principal.

At the second month, $50 will be deducted from the loan of $12,000 leaving $11,950 outstanding.

The payment for the second month will be:

$$10\% \text{ of } \$11,950 = \frac{1195}{12} = \$99.58 \text{ interest}$$

Therefore, the payment of $150 will be made up of $99.58 interest, and $50.42 principal.

This system will be repeated throughout the loan.

Under (B) the same system will be used to estimate the monthly interest, but the payments will be constantly smaller because exactly $50 principal will be added to each month's interest payment.

In the second payment, for example, the $99.58 interest will be added to $50 principal producing a payment of $149.58 for the month.

It will come as a surprise to many borrowers *and* lenders to discover that this is entirely *wrong*, and by doing so, the borrower is paying *too much!!*

Whenever there is an allowance of principal in a mortgage payment, the federal Interest Act requires the mortgage to contain a statement showing the annual rate of interest in the mortgage, "calculated half-yearly, or yearly, not in advance".

Assuming that the mortgage in the example complied with the Act, here is why this system of estimating mortgage payments is wrong:

The borrower, by dividing by twelve, is compounding the interest *monthly*, which costs more.

In compounding the 10% interest semi-annually, here is what the first two payments should be:

1. $12,000 × the monthly interest factor .816485 = $97.97 interest.

Therefore, the payment of $150 will be made up of $97.97 interest and $52.03 principal.

2. At the second month, $52.03 will be deducted from the loan of $12,000 leaving $11,947.97 outstanding.

The payment will be:

$$11,947.97 \times .816485 = \$97.54 \text{ interest}$$

Therefore, the payment of $150 will be made up of $97.54 interest and $52.46 principal.

By doing it correctly, the borrower, in the first two payments alone, has saved $4.07. Over the term of the mortgage, a consistently greater monthly saving is made by doing it correctly.

Where does the .816485 come from?

From the tables of interest rates. Use them, study them, and save yourself some money.

9

You Might Have an Interest-Free Mortgage

One puzzling aspect of mortgage lending that has never been satisfactorily explained is the common practice of extracting more money out of the borrower's pocket than is necessary by a frequency of compounding the loan interest.

When one applies to conventional lenders, such as banks, trust companies, life insurance companies and even Central Mortgage and Housing Corporation for a mortgage loan, the application states that the interest rate will be, for example, 10%.

The applicant naturally thinks he will be paying 10% per annum, but what he does not realize is the practice of these lenders of compounding the interest semi-annually, which costs the borrower more money than he would be paying if the interest were compounded on an annual basis.

For example, an N.H.A. 40-year mortgage loan of $25,250.00, 10%, compounded annually, would cost the borrower $205.90 per month. However, by the time the borrower has signed the mortgage deed, this payment jumps to $210.41 because of semi-annual compounding. This represents an additional cost to the borrower of $4.51 each month.

During the entire period when the N.H.A. interest rate was expressed legislatively, or by order-in-council as a ceiling rate, it was compounded (or computed) semi-annually. The executive director of Ceneral Mortgage and Housing Corporation has stated that "the reason for this is not entirely clear, but seems to have been largely the result of general market practice".

This practice is not illegal. There is no government legislation that controls the frequency of compounding mortgage interest, but it is a practice that definitely leads a borrower "down the garden path".

The more frequent the compounding, the greater the yield to the lender. This is not understood by the majority of borrowers. Many mortgage applications make no mention of any frequency of compounding the interest. It simply states what the annual rate of interest will be.

When one goes through the procedure of applying for a mortgage loan, he is told what the monthly payment will be. It is natural for the borrower to assume that this figure is correct and based on a true annual rate of interest.

Then comes the time to sign the mortgage deed. How many borrowers read it? In the body of the deed, it will state that the interest will be "calculated half-yearly". These are three words that are expensive to the borrower.

The answer to this appears to be found in the federal Interest Act, which imposes a drastic penalty on a mortgage lender not complying with the Act.

Whenever the terms of a mortgage require it to be paid on a sinking fund plan, or on any plan under which the payments of principal money and interest are blended, or on any plan that involves an allowance of interest on stipulated repayments, the mortgage deed *must* contain a statement showing the amount of such principal money and the rate of interest chargeable, "calculated yearly, or half-yearly, not in advance".

The lender then provides the statement, showing the annual rate calculated half-yearly, which costs the borrower more.

In Ontario (and some other provinces), a lender (mortgagee) is not required to sign the mortgage deed, just the borrower. How then is a private investor lending money to know that his mortgage will contain this statement?

One can be sure that conventional first mortgages will contain the statement. But what about other mortgages?

If you are a borrower (mortgagor) in a second or third mortgage deed, examine the mortgage carefully and see if it does contain the required statement.

Why?

If a mortgage does not contain the statement, the borrower will have to pay absolutely *No Interest* on his loan. Furthermore, in such cases, any interest that has been paid in the past can be deducted from the principal amount owing on the mortgage.

Says who? Says the federal government!!

Note: In practice, the law does not designate any one department as having a responsibility for enforcing the Federal Interest Act. This has come to be recognized as a defect and the Department of Consumer and Corporate Affairs has been asked to assume responsibility for a review of the characteristics of the present Act, and the jurisprudence stemming from it, with the end in view of proposing amendments that would serve to modernize and otherwise improve the Act.

If you have any opinions (or research) in this area, the Consumer Research Branch of the Department of Consumer and Corporate Affairs would be pleased to hear from you. . . .

10

When Can a Mortgage Be Paid Off?

The answer to this question is not clear to many borrowers. There are four types of repayment privileges in mortgage deeds — your mortgage will conform to one of them:

Corporate Borrowers

The Interest Act precludes any prepayment privileges in a mortgage where the borrower is a joint stock company or other corporation, and in any debenture issued by any such company or corporation.

If the mortgage is one with a 20-year term, the mortgagor is bound to its deed for 20 years.

However, if the lender wishes to allow the borrower to repay the loan before its maturity, it is his priviledge to do so. This can be written into the deed, or otherwise negotiated.

If the prevailing interest rates at the time of a request to discharge such a mortgage are much higher than the rate in the mortgage, this would probably create no problem. The lender would obviously be glad to have his money returned in order to re-invest it at a higher rate of interest.

Conventional Loans

Here I refer to loans made by such corporations as insurance and trust companies, banks, and other large lenders in loans other than N.H.A. mortgages.

Again the Interest Act applies. Whenever any mortgage is not payable until a time of more than five years after the date of a mortgage (a mortgage with a term of more than 5 years) the borrower is entitled to repay the principal balance owing at any time after the first 5 years.

With this prepayment, an additional interest charge equal to 3 months interest of the mortgage balance is to be made.

The Interest Act states that the balance may be paid in such circumstances "together with three month's further interest *in lieu of notice*".

One might assume that if a borrower gave the lender 3 month's notice of his intention to repay the loan, no additional interest would be required. But with no guarantee that the borrower will in fact repay the mortgage in three months, such notice is not acceptable by lenders, and the additional interest must be paid.

National Housing Act Loans

There are two basic types of N.H.A. loans. The "direct" loans made by Central Mortgage and Housing Corporation, and loans made by approved lenders of C.M.H.C.

If the mortgage money comes directly from C.M.H.C., the prepayment privileges are very generous. At any time after the date of the mortgage, the borrower may repay any or all of the principal balance owing at any time without paying any interest penalty.

If the mortgage money comes from an approved lender of C.M.H.C. and the loan is not in default (i.e., payments have been kept up to date), the borrower has the privilege of paying an additional amount of principal, not in excess of 10% of the original amount of the mortgage, on the first anniversary of the date for adjustment of interest (when the mortgage is one year old).

A similar amount of principal may be paid on the second anniversary date. In each case, three months' interest must be paid on the amount of any such additional payment— these two repayment privileges are not cumulative.

When the mortgage is three years old, and on any monthly installment date thereafter, the borrower may repay the whole amount owing, or any part of it, together with three months' additional interest on any such additional payment.

"Open" Mortgages

It is quite common for a property owner to accept a mortgage as part of the purchase price of the property he is selling.

The majority of the "purchase mortgages" will contain a clause allowing the mortgagor to pay any part (or all) of the mortgage at any time, or on any payment date, without requiring the borrower to pay any interest penalty.

The obvious reason is that the lender would be delighted to get his money.

In addition to the above, of course, conventional and private lenders can (and often do) insert additional repayment clauses in deeds.

11

The Advantage of Mortgage Acceleration

Mortgage payment accel   'ion is one of the greatest means available today to force oneself t   ...e money.

The example used is a repayment schedule of the first 12 months of a 40-year National Housing Act 10% mortgage loan of $25,000 (plus 1% insurance fee which must be added to the loan), with each payment being $210.41.

Payment No.	Interest	Principal	Balance Owing
1	$206.16	$4.25	$25,245.75
2	206.13	4.28	25,241.47
3	206.09	4.32	25,237.15
4	206.06	4.35	25,232.80
5	206.02	4.39	25,228.41
6	205.99	4.42	25,223.99
7	205.95	4.46	25,219.53
8	205.91	4.50	25,215.03
9	205.88	4.53	25,210.50
10	205.84	4.57	25,205.93
11	205.80	4.61	25,201.32
12	205.76	4.65	25,196.67

When a mortgagor reaches the 12th payment of this loan he has the privilege of paying an additional amount of principal, not in excess of 10% of the original amount of the mortgage.

The additional payment made under this privilege is not made in a round figure such as exactly $100. It is a payment that will reach a future balance of the loan. For example, the principal balance owing at payment No. 32 is $25,095.36.

The difference between the balance owing at the 12th payment and the balance owing at the 32nd payment is $101.31. By paying the lender this amount, 20 payments of $210.41 each are eliminated. This amounts to $4,208.20.

The chart illustrates the savings that can be effected by making various additional mortgage principal payments at the end of the first year. Further principal payments can be made as outlined in the previous chapter.

Additional Payment	No. of Payments Eliminated	Payment Dollars Eliminated	Balance Owing	Time Left on Mortgage
$101.31	20	$ 4,208.20	$25,095.36	37 yrs., 4 mos.
201.38	37	7,785.17	24,995.29	35 yrs., 11 mos.
301.91	52	10,941.32	24,894.76	34 yrs., 8 mos.
407.48	66	13,887.06	24,789.19	33 yrs., 6 mos.
508.04	78	16,411.98	24,688.63	32 yrs., 6 mos.

12

When Selling, Get Rid of Mortgage

There is one especially important step that a homeowner should take (or the owner of any real estate for that matter) when selling.

If there is a mortgage registered against the property, and if the vendor is under covenant in the mortgage as the original mortgagor — *remember this*:

When accepting an offer to purchase the property in which the purchaser agrees to assume the existing mortgage, the vendor would be well advised to introduce the purchaser to the mortgagee, and ask that the purchaser be accepted as covenant to be solely responsible for the debt, at the same time obtaining a release of the vendor's obligations under the mortgage.

For example, under the Ontario Limitations Act, such a vendor could be liable for the debt, and such other things as property taxes, for a minimum period of ten years after selling the property. If the mortgage has a very long term, this could conceivably hold the original mortgagor (vendor) liable, under certain circumstances, for many, many years.

The reason for this is that the Act allows the mortgagee to commence action upon a mortgage covenant within ten years after the cause of the action arose *or* within ten years after the date upon which the person liable on the covenant conveyed or transferred his interest in the mortgaged land, *whichever is later in point of time*.

The person buying the property is also liable, but this does not release the original mortgagor unless he has been released by the mortgagee.

For example, if the mortgagee found that the property taxes had not been paid, the mortgagee could pay them to protect his interest in the property, and add the amount to the mortgage debt.

It would be a stiff jolt for somebody selling his property to be sued for taxes many years after vacating the property, but it could happen.

When selling — ensure that you are free of the property *and* your mortgage debt.

13

Importance of the Postponement Clause

This short chapter can save many headaches.

Remember, mortgage seniority is established by the time and date of registration in a land registry office or land titles offices.

If one becomes a borrower in a second mortgage, and the term of his second mortgage has a longer period of time to run than the existing first mortgage on the property — what happens when the first mortgage becomes due?

When such a situation occurs, the first mortgage cannot be renewed or replaced without the express permission of the one holding the second mortgage.

This could mean trouble.

If there are two mortgages on a property, it is unlikely that the mortgagor would have the funds to pay off the larger first mortgage and allow the second to take its place.

There is only one solution.

The second mortgage must contain a postponement clause, which would automatically allow the mortgagor to renew, or replace the first mortgage when it becomes due.

This does not mean that a $10,000 first mortgage can be increased to $15,000 with the borrower putting the $5,000 in his pocket.

Any increase in the principal amount of a first mortgage being renewed or replaced under these circumstances would be paid to the second mortgagee to reduce his mortgage.

Know the mortgage expiration date, and remember the postponement clause.

14

Costs of Arranging a Mortgage

Many real estate buyers receive their indoctrination into the realm of financial shock upon receiving the final bill for charges and services rendered. A review of letters I have received from coast to coast strongly indicates that "caveat emptor" (let the buyer beware) truly prevails, and the chief complaint appears to be that "nobody told us".

There are financial charges in obtaining a mortgage loan, which are paid by the borrower. These charges amount to hundreds of dollars which the unsuspecting borrower knows nothing about until he gets the bill. This is written to reveal how you can avoid many, or even *all* of them.

The two most misunderstood charges to a real estate buyer are the legal fees in obtaining a mortgage loan, and the insurance fee added to many mortgages.

A lawyer is entitled to reasonable compensation for his services, and considering the work involved in acting for a purchaser, the generally accepted tariff appears to be fair.

In acting for a purchaser, there is one necessary aspect of the lawyer's work that surely must drive some of them "up the wall". That is when a property is registered in a Registry Office.

In a Land Titles Office (not used east of Ontario) all title documents registered are guaranteed by the Provincial Government, but not so in the Registry Office. Hours and hours of patient sifting through abstract books can be required, going from page to page and book to book, the lawyer all the time being acutely aware that there just might be something wrong in the chain of title that will interfere with the client's enjoyment of the property at a later date.

The legal fees in acting for a purchaser can amount to about 1¼ % of the cost of the average home. This is for the lawyer's services, and in addition to this, there will be adjustments to the date of closing made on such things as the municipal property taxes, hydro and water charges, insurance, and if oil heated, the cost for a full tank.

Then there will be a charge for a land transfer tax, which the Provincial Government gets.

There will be a charge made by the registry offices for every document registered. If the property covers parts of more than one lot, it costs more.

Some mortgage lenders will deduct a portion of future municipal taxes from the mortgage principal, which can be annoying to one's pocketbook, resulting in more cash to be coughed up by the buyer. Also, many mortgage lenders require an up to date survey, and if one is not available, this can cost a hundred dollars or more.

Then there will be a final check made with the Sheriff's office to see if any last minute liens or charges have been made against the property, for which there will be a nominal charge.

The average buyer, after paying for much of the foregoing, can be forgiven if he finds himself in a state of shock upon being presented with an additional bill for third party mortgage charges. The following are the three basic areas of financial escalation in mortgaging costs for the borrower, and will clearly indicate just how you can save money in mortgaging.

A common method of mortgaging in buying real estate is for the purchaser to "assume" an existing mortgage, one already registered against the property. The one assuming the mortgage is agreeing to basically maintain the payments and be jointly responsible for the debt with the one who originally signed the mortgage deed.

Assuming a mortgage when buying real estate normally incurs no extra financial charges to the buyer — it is already there.

Another method is for the seller to agree to "take back" a mortgage from the purchaser for part of the mortgage price. This is another cheap way to get a mortgage.

Such a mortgage has several advantages. It requires no credit check of the borrower, no appraisal fees to be paid by the borrower, smaller legal fees than other mortgaging, instant knowledge that the "mortgage application" has been approved, and in many cases can be secured at a lower rate than third party mortgages, with longer terms. Furthermore, they usually have "open" repayment privileges.

The most expensive method of mortgaging is for a purchaser to arrange a mortgage from a third party, such as a bank, insurance or trust company.

Charging an inspection fee of about $40 does not seem unreasonable, but the big financial crunch comes when a lawyer presents his bill for legal fees and disbursements. In a typical, recent $18,400 mortgage, the borrowers were charged $28.50 for disbursements, and $235 for legal fees, for a total of $263.50!

Legal tariffs in mortgaging can be just as much proportionately as they are for services in closing the purchase. The reason for this is that many of the services performed in mortgaging are identical to services in closing. For the lender's protection, the title must be searched in the same manner, right down to a last minute visit to the sheriff's office.

Lending institutions usually prefer to retain the services of their own approved lawyers, which is understandable. This results in a complete job being done in the title search, etc., in addition to the one done by the purchaser's lawyer for closing purposes. Result — the additional fee.

If a purchaser is fortunate enough to have his own lawyer do the legal work in the third party mortgage, the combined fee for mortgaging and closing will undoubtedly be much less than the separate fees of two lawyers. It therefore follows that it can be advisable for a purchaser to determine what lawyer will be acting for the mortgage lender, and retain him to also close the purchase.

Or better still, have one's own lawyer arrange for the funds through a lender who will allow him to act in the mortgage.

One thing to keep in mind is that the mortgagee (lender) pays for absolutely nothing, with the exception of a small charge for registering the mortgage. The borrower pays all costs, the simple reason being that if the lender paid for any part of it, his investment would be "watered down". When a lender advances money at 10 percent he wants 10 percent, and he *gets* 10 percent.

The second puzzling charge confronting a borrower is the mortgage insurance fee. This charge is found in two types of mortgages, National Housing Act loans and loans insured by the Mortgage Insurance Company of Canada.

When a mortgage is obtained that amounts to no more than 75 percent of the value of the property, it is generally accepted that there is sufficient equity in the property to require no monetary insurance.

But when the loan amounts to as much as 95 percent of the purchase price, it is understandable for the lender to consider that the borrower, having a 5 percent equity in the property. is a risk that requires additional assurance that the loan will be secure. This assurance is realized by having the loan completely insured, and the borrower pays the premium.

The insurance premium is not normally paid for directly out of the borrower's pocket. It is added to the principal amount of the loan and the total will be the registered principal sum in the mortgage deed, although M.I.C.C. will accept a direct payment. The lender then sends a cheque matching the premium to the insurer, Central Mortgage and Housing Corporation, or the Mortgage Insurance Company of Canada.

If the loan is repaid before the mortgage term expires there is no provision for any rebate of the insurance premium.

Regardless of the source of mortgage funds, the lender will require the borrower to have the security adequately covered by property insurance. It is mandatory, written into the mortgage deed, and paid for by the borrower.

Consider very carefully how mortgaging is going to affect your pocketbook. The young couple who were the borrowers in the $18,400 mortgage deed were hit with mortgage charges totalling $569.50, which they did not expect or understand. Nobody told them.

Caveat emptor.

Summary . . . Consider the following:

(a) Property where there is a mortgage already registered at current rates or lower. If you can't come up with cash to the mortgage, see if the vendor will hold a second at a reasonable rate of interest.

(b) Property where the vendor will take back a mortgage for a large part of the purchase price.

(c) If you must go to a third party for a mortgage, retain the mortgagee's lawyer to close your purchase, or have your lawyer act for the mortgagee (lender) if possible.

(d) Be wary of short term mortgages that have to be replaced. It can be expensive.

If you must get a new mortgage, whether it is to help in the purchase of real property or to refinance your own property, your best source for mortgage money is your local Realtor.

When you approach one lender directly, you have no choice. A Realtor is fully aware of current mortgage markets, is constantly in touch with the lenders, and knows where and how to get you the best deal for your particular situation.

Not all lenders like investing mortgage money in the same types of property — the Realtor can save you a lot of time.

15

National Housing Act Mortgages

Canada's federal government has been involved in housing development since the depths of the depression.

In 1935, the Dominion Housing Act was passed, principally as a means of providing jobs, but also to help improve the quality of Canadian housing and to establish building standards.

Under the Dominion Housing Act, the federal government provided one-quarter of the money for high-ratio mortgages with private lenders providing the balance. The objective was to make it easier for people to build and buy houses by supplying bigger mortgages — and make possible smaller down payments than would be available from private lenders.

Between 1935 and 1938, about 5,000 new houses were put up with the financing provided in part under the Dominion Housing Act.

Then, in 1938, the first Act was replaced with the new National Housing Act which provided more mortgage money and which, for the first time, offered loan assistance for the construction of housing for low-income families.

But the federal government really didn't come into its own in the housing field until the Second World War. Housing starts fell off during the war, so when hostilities ended there was an enormous backlog of demand. To help meet this demand, a new National Housing Act was passed in 1945.

Central Mortgage and Housing Corporation, a Crown Corporation, put up 17,000 new houses for veterans and took over ownership of all other wartime housing so that, by 1949, the government agency owned 41,000 houses. Most of these wartime houses have since been sold to former tenants.

Under the 1945 National Housing Act, postwar housing construction entered a real boom period. In the early years, lots of private money also was available for mortgage financing. Canada's output rose from 64,400 new houses in 1946 to 92,350 in 1950, when almost half of the year's total production was financed under N.H.A.

By the early fifties, however, private mortgage money sources began to dry up — the boom had been so explosive that most "conventional" money was fully committed.

So in 1954 the National Housing Act was again overhauled, this time establishing a system of insurance of N.H.A. mortgages so that these mortgages became an attractive alternative to bonds as long-term investments. Under this system, the full amount of the mortgage was provided by a private lender and the government guaranteed, first 98%, and finally the full loan amount (the borrower paid the insurance fee that provided this guarantee). In this way the government for a while stopped actually lending money, except as a last resort, for housing and simply made it 100% safe for private lenders to provide the funds.

At around the same time, the Bank Act was changed so that, for the first time, the chartered banks were allowed to make long-term mortgage loans. This provided tremendous new funds for home building.

By 1958 the number of housing starts in Canada had risen to the unprecedented total of 164,000.

Since then things have become more difficult for builders and buyers alike. Land costs, wages and materials have all risen, driving the price of new houses up, to say nothing of rising interest rates.

Because the banks were limited by law to charging 6% interest, they virtually stopped putting money into N.H.A. mortgages in 1959 when rates started rising. The other lenders, life insurance and trust and loan companies, still had money to put into mortgages, but they put more and more into higher-paying private mortgages, less into the low-paying N.H.A. variety.

So, although housing starts reached an all-time record of 166,565 in 1965, the supply of private money for mortgages began to dwindle away.

To keep the industry going and to put roofs over Canadians' heads, the Government changed the Bank Act again to allow the banks to lend mortgage money at interest rates higher than 6%. Even more significantly, the government has pumped vast amounts of public money directly into housing as private funds started staying away. By 1967, the federal government was holding, through C.M.H.C., about three *billion* dollars worth of mortgages.

Under other federal government programs, grants and loans are provided through the provinces to municipalities for such purposes as urban renewal, public housing, sewage treatment systems and so forth. Federal money also goes into student housing at universities and colleges across Canada.

In 1969, and 1972, the National Housing Act was again amended. Here is a summary of the regulations:

Loans for New Homes: For home owner and condominium type units in single-detached, semi-detached and row housing form, the maximum loan is $30,000. For condominium type units in apartment form, the maximum loan is $23,000. The loan ratio is 95% of value.

Loans for Existing Housing: For home owner and condominium type units in single-detached, semi-detached and row housing form, the maximum loan is $23,000. The loan ratio is 95% of value.

Co-operative Housing Loans: In single-detached, semi-detached and row housing form, the maximum loan is $30,000. In apartment form the maximum loan is $23,000. These loans are available for new construction only.

Insured Loans for Rental Housing: For single-detached, and row houses, the maximum loan is $30,000. For apartments, the maximum loan is $20,000 per unit. Up to 15% of the maxima may be permitted as an additional loan for added amenities and facilities that go beyond strictly residential use.

Loans for Low Rental Housing: For single-detached, semi-detached and row houses, the maximum loan is $30,000. In apartment units, the maximum loan is $20,000 per unit. In hostel and dormitory accommodation the maximum loan is $10,000 per bed. Up to 15% of the maxima may be permitted as an additional loan for added amenities and facilities that go beyond strictly residential use.

Public Housing Assistance: For single-detached, semi-detached and row houses, the maximum loan is $30,000. In apartment units, the maximum loan is $20,000 per unit. In hostel and dormitory accommodation, the maximum loan is $10,000 per bed. Up to 15% of the maxima may be permitted as an additional loan for added amenities and facilities that go beyond strictly residential use.

Loans for Student Housing: The maximum loan is $8,000 per student bed.

— There is no government ceiling on mortgage interest rates for mortgage funds provided by approved lenders. On direct loans provided by C.M.H.C., it sets the rates, which are slightly lower.

— Mortgage terms may be extended to 40 years. For existing housing, the term cannot exceed the estimated remaining life of the building. However, the interest on the loan may be adjusted every five years.

— Mortgage insurance fees are 1% of the face value of the mortgage for home-ownership, and 1¼% for rental housing.

N.H.A. loans are financially guaranteed by requiring the borrower to pay the fee. This insurance is the *lender's* protection against loss, despite the fact that the fee is paid by the *borrower*.

The fee is not, and cannot, be paid in one lump sum. It is added to the amount of the loan, and repaid with the monthly payments during the life of the mortgage. If the mortgage is paid off before maturity, there is no insurance refund to anybody.

Canada's National Housing Act stipulates that a 30% "gross debt service ratio" must not be exceeded in the administration and approval of N.H.A. mortgage loans, whether the loans are made by Central Mortgage and Housing Corporation, or through its approved lenders.

What this means is that a borrower must be able to meet the interest and principal payments on the mortgage, and the municipal taxes on the real property, with a sum of money that cannot exceed 30% of his gross income.

In establishing gross income, from 20% to 50% of a wife's income may be added to that of the husband. However, N.H.A. regulations state that an approved lender MAY include in the gross annual income of a home owner or home purchaser such portion of investment income and such portion of 50% of the gross earnings of the wife as the approved lender considers appropriate.

In the case of loans made directly by C.M.H.C., the following are the considerations regarding the wife's income:

(a) The duration that the added income may be required.

(b) The source and duration of the wife's income.

(c) How much or what percentage of the wife's income is required to reduce the gross debt service ratio to 30%.

(d) Other obligations which have a demand on the wife's income.

The following chart illustrates the income required to qualify for a maximum N.H.A. mortgage loan of $30,000. (plus the 1% insurance fee), with different amortizations, using $500 as a municipal tax figure.

INCOME REQUIREMENTS TO QUALIFY FOR NATIONAL HOUSING ACT LOANS
$30,300. — 9% — compounded twice-yearly

Loan Amortization (in years)	Monthly Mortgage Payment	Yearly Mortgage Cost	Taxes	Total	Gross Income Required
25	$250.88	$3,010.56	$500	$3,510.56	$11,700.00
30	240.23	2,882.76	500	3,382.76	11,275.00
35	233.84	2,806.08	500	3,306.08	11,020.00
40	229.90	2,758.80	500	3,258.80	10,862.00

16

The High-Ratio Mortgage

Prior to 1964, a Canadian buying a house under conventional mortgaging had either to come up with one third of the value of house and lot in cash, or put down less cash and assume, or obtain, a second mortgage. This second mortgage usually carried a fairly high rate of interest.

Consequently, many were unable to realize their dreams of owning their own home. In 1964, high-ratio mortgages became available and the picture changed dramatically. For six years, until 1970, variations and refinements made the high-ratio mortgage an important part of the housing scene.

In March of 1970, amendments to the Canadian and British Insurance Companies Act, the Foreign Insurance Companies Act, the Trust Companies Act, and the Loan Companies Act were passed by the Parliament of Canada. Lending institutions operating under this legislation, as well as the chartered banks, are now authorized to make mortgage loans over 75% of value, provided the excess is insured by a policy of mortgage insurance, issued by an insurance company registered under the Canadian and British Insurance Companies Act. The Mortgage Insurance Company of Canada (M.I.C.C.) leads the field in providing such a service.

Since 1964, more than *fifty thousand* Canadian families have bought their own home, using the M.I.C.C. insured high-ratio mortgage plan. Under this plan, the mortgage lender is insured against loss in the event of default by the purchaser.

Using a M.I.C.C. high-ratio mortgage, a house may be purchased with as little as 5% down to one 95% mortgage. The loan amount obtainable is based on a formula as follows:

> 95% of first $40,000 of value
> 75% of next $20,000 of value
> 50% of value over $60,000

A mortgage insurance premium is payable by the borrower. It does not have to be paid in cash, but may be added to the mortgage. On loans up to $18,000 the premium is 1% of the loan amount. Loans in excess of $18,000 carry a premium of 1¼%.

The following examples illustrate loan amounts, down payments and mortgage insurance premiums:

House Value:		$30,000		$18,950
95% of Value:		28,500		18,000
Premium:	(1¼%)	356	(1%)	180
Total Mortgage:		$28,856		$18,180
Down Payment:		$ 1,500		$ 950

M.I.C.C. high ratio mortgages are available to finance the purchase of a new or existing home, to finance the construction of a new home for sale or occupancy, and to refinance an existing mortgage to obtain cash, consolidate debts, or carry out home improvements.

The interest rate on such a mortgage today, all across Canada, is generally the going market rate of interest on conventional loans. There is a complete lack of red tape, and no special procedures are involved.

The low down payments make buying easier. The larger mortgage amount also makes selling easier, should the homeowner decide to move.

The advent of the insured high ratio mortgage has opened up the housing market to a large number of Canadians who could not save the large down payment required, or who were unwilling or unable to pay the high interest rates demanded on many second mortgages. Thousands of homeowners would undoubtedly be still paying rent, unable to enjoy the pride of ownership of their homes if it were not for this service.

Most mortgage lenders follow the general rule that a borrower should not commit himself to pay more than 27% to 30% of his gross salary for his mortgage payments and taxes.

Example: Gross monthly income: $800
                                27%   216
                                30%   240

Therefore, a man with an income of $800. a month (before deductions) should normally not pay more than $216 to $240 per month on his mortgage, including taxes. The lender also looks at the borrower's other debts, credit rating, etc. when reviewing a mortgage application. A portion or all of wife's income can be used, depending on wife's age, and quality of income.

When the affordable monthly payment has been worked out, the affordable mortgage can be determined. Assume that the monthly payment is $240 and taxes are $40 per month. Then the amount available for mortgage principal and interest is $200. a month.

What amount of mortgage will payments of $200. a month repay?

At an interest rate of 9%, an amount of $8.28 per month would repay $1,000. in 25 years. Assuming that you can obtain a mortgage at 9% on a 25 year repayment plan, then $200 per month would handle a mortgage of:

$$\frac{\$200 \times \$1,000}{8.28} = \$24,154$$

Application for a high ratio mortgage loan is made in the normal way to any M.I.C.C. approved lender, such as The Bank of Montreal, The Toronto-Dominion Bank or the Bank of Nova Scotia.

For a complete list of approved lenders, and detailed information of this service to homebuyers, write to:

The Mortgage Insurance Company of Canada,
Suite 1212, Simpson Tower,
401 Bay Street, Toronto, Ontario

17

How to Buy a Mortgage

The most common mortgages bought and sold are the "second" mortgages. There is no mystery about them and they are, if properly purchased, a sound and profitable investment.

Before buying one, however, there are a few guidelines to follow to help one arrive at not only a sensible decision about which one to buy, but also to ensure that the price is right!

The four prime areas that require scrutiny are (1) the real estate used as security, (2) the equity in the property, (3) the covenant, or the ability of the mortgagor (borrower) to repay the loan and (4) the details of the mortgage terms.

Whenever a mortgagee (lender) is asked to loan money, the property involved will be inspected and appraised to ensure that there is sufficient tangible security for the loan. The mortgagor pays for the inspection.

In considering the purchase of second mortgages one cannot very well have an appraisal done on all the real estate involved. This would require a fee to be paid for each mortgage considered.

The alternative is for the mortgage purchaser to inspect the property himself. In this inspection, it is wise to carefully check not only the condition of the building, but also to note how the title holder (owner) is maintaining it.

Regardless of any documents produced to show evidence of what the current market value of the property is, the mortgage purchaser should, if possible, make comparisons and inspect properties that are offered for sale in the same area that are of a similar plan and size to the one secured by the mortgage.

Also, check with the hydro authority, municipal buildings department and registry office to see if there are any outstanding work orders issued against the property. If there are, the work will have to be done, and the cost of repairs or renovations must be considered in the value.

Mortgage seniority is established by the time and date of registering the mortgage deed. A second mortgage ranks second, so that the mortgagee of first priority has first claim to the dollar value of the security.

Other, but junior mortages may be registered against the property, but the second mortgage will take precedence over these.

The equity in a property is its market value, less the total amount of all mortgages and other financial charges registered against the property. It is therefore important to know something about the mortgagor and his ability to repay the loan, because his only stake in the property is this equity.

If there is very little equity, it does not necessarily mean that the mortgagor will be any more lax in his payments than one with a larger equity, but regardless of the tangible security, a mortgagee likes to have some reasonable assurance that the debt is going to be paid, and paid according to contract.

The financial decision in purchasing a second mortgage must be based on two prime factors: (1) the rate of interest, and (2) the terms of the loan.

Second mortgages, having a secondary position, normally require a higher rate of return than first mortgages. If the current rate of interest, for example, is 14% on secondary financing, then the rate in the mortgage considered must be adjusted accordingly.

The hard-headed mortgage buyer will demand it, and his rule of thumb method of rapid calculation will be:

Assuming the rate of interest on an existing second mortgage is 9%, and one wishes to have it produce 14%, the 5% difference will be multiplied by the number of years remaining in the term of the mortgage, or to its maturity, when the principal balance is due and payable.

The result will be the discount at which he will purchase the mortgage. Some illustrations are shown in the chart.

By purchasing a mortgage in this manner, two obvious bonuses will be secured: (1) the additional interest extracted from the mortgage is obtained in advance and (2) this additional interest is based on the present outstanding principal balance of the mortgage, and not on a reducing balance which occurs as the loan payments progress.

Examples of One Method Mortgage Buyers Use in Discounting Second Mortgages

Mortgage Principal	Rate of Interest	Interest Required	Difference	Mortgage Term	Discount
$2,000.00	10%	14%	4%	3 years	12% ($ 240)
3,000.00	9%	15%	6%	4 years	24% ($ 720)
4,000.00	8%	13%	5%	5 years	25% ($1000)
5,000.00	10%	14%	4%	2 years	8% ($ 400)

To know the *exact* price one should pay for a mortgage to produce a specific yield, write to *Consumers Computer Limited,* Box 400, Willowdale, Ontario. A tailor-made analysis will be made for you for about five dollars.

18

Mortgage Repayment Schedules

There are more than *one million* new and refinanced mortgage transactions each year in Canada.

Conventional mortgagees such as banks, insurance and trust companies provide the borrower with a computerized repayment schedule showing the interest and principal parts of each payment, and the principal balance owing on each payment date. This ensures that the borrower and the lender each know exactly where they stand, right to the penny.

However, in many areas of mortgaging, and especially secondary financing, millions of dollars is undoubtedly being lost annually by borrowers simply because the mortgage repayment is not computerized.

The following is an example which illustrates why under normal circumstances, it is incorrect to compute an interest payment on a level balance over six months.

Calculated vs. Compounded

The statement of interest in most mortgages may read, for example, "6% per centum per annum calculated half-yearly not in advance".

Note: It is the *Interest Rate* which is calculated half-yearly *Not* the *Interest Payment.*

In most cases the interest payment is due monthly with the principal. The word "calculated" does not imply that the interest payments are computed on a level balance over six months. In fact, the following shows it is quite incorrect to compute interest payments in this way.

Interest Paid Monthly for Six Months
vs.
Interest Paid on a Level Balance Over Six Months

Suppose for example, a mortgage of $10,000.00 with interest at 6% per annum calculated half-yearly, is to be paid off in equal installments of $100.00 interest and principal included. The 6% per annum interest rate calculated semi-annually is equivalent to a monthly interest rate of 0.4938622%. The first six rows of schedule will read as follows:

Payment Number	Interest Portion	Principal Portion	Total Payment	Balance of Loan after Payment
1	49.39	50.61	100.00	9949.39
2	49.14	50.86	100.00	9898.53
3	48.88	51.12	100.00	9847.41
4	48.63	51.37	100.00	9796.04
5	48.38	51.62	100.00	9744.42
6	48.12	51.88	100.00	9692.54
TOTAL	292.54	307.46	600.00	

On examining the schedule you will note that the sum of the interest on the first six payments is $292.54 whereas the interest of $10,000.00 for half a year at 3% is $300.00. The difference arises because the principal is being reduced by a portion of the monthly installments as the amount of interest decreases within the six month period.

It would be improper under the Interest Act for the lender to compute the balance due after the sixth payment by simply adding $300.00 interest and subtracting $600.00 in total payments to obtain a balance of $9,700.00. In fact if $300.00 were actually collected the interest rate would not be 6% compounded semi-annually but approximately 6.22% compounded semi-annually. This would then contravene the mortgage agreement.

Simple vs. Compound Interest

Question: On a $10,000 loan at 7% compounded semi-annually and payable in monthly payments of $100.00, principal plus interest, I calculate the interest of the first payment to be $58.33. Your figure is $57.50. Please explain the difference.

Answer: When you calculated the interest payment you probably used a simple interest calculation. If you did this you are assuming, incorrectly, that interest is compounded monthly. The computation schedules are based on the assumption that interest is compounded as stated, that is, semi-annually. Examine the schedules below.

Loan $10,000.00   Rate 7%   Compounded Monthly
Payments $100.00   Payable Monthly
Simple Interest

Payment Number	Interest Payment	Principal Payment	Balance of Loan
1	$58.33	$41.67	$9958.33
2	58.09	41.91	9916.42
3	57.85	42.15	9874.27
4	57.60	42.40	9831.87

Loan $10,000.00   Rate 7%   Compounded Semi-Annually
Payment $100.00   Payable Monthly
Compound Interest

Payment Number	Interest Payment	Principal Payment	Balance of Loan
1	57.50	42.50	9957.50
2	57.26	42.74	9914.76
3	57.01	42.99	9871.77
4	56.76	43.24	9828.53

The Computerized Schedule
(*Courtesy CSC P.O. Box 400, Willowdale, Ont.*)

Examine your schedule carefully. It should correspond to the lender's figures. Make certain he has a copy of the schedule. (an example is shown on the following page).

Note that:

1. The basic amounts should correspond exactly to your mortgage terms.

2. Compounding should be identical to the statement of interest in your mortgage: e.g. 9% per annum calculated (compounded) *semi-annually* not in advance.

3. The first payment is recorded and made on the proper date.

4. If the compounding is semi-annual, the amount of interest on the first payment is *less than* one-twelfth of $25,000 times the annual interest rate. The lender and borrower should both be aware of this: $184.08 is less than $25,000 × 9% ÷ 12 = $187.50.

5. Each payment and exact current balance can be easily kept track of by checking off each date as the payment is made.

6. The interest portion plus the principal portion will add up to the total payment amount.

7. The interest on each subsequent payment is slightly less than the interest on the previous payment. Verify that this occurs not just once each half year but for every payment.

8. The interest accumulated over a calendar year is mandatory information for lenders who must declare interest as income. Send the schedule (copy) in with your income tax as a supporting document.

9. Verify that the mortgage pays out in 25 years.

Obtaining the Schedule
(*Courtesy CSC P.O. Box 400, Willowdale, Ont.*)

CSC **Computing Services ∮ Consumers'** Computer Limited

P.O. BOX 400, WILLOWDALE, ONTARIO

LOAN $ 25000.00 BLENDED PAYMENT $ **VARIABLE** PAYABLE **MONTHLY** GIVEN TERM

RATE % 9.000 COMPOUNDED SEMI-ANNLY INTEREST PAYMENT FACTOR **VARIABLE** GIVEN PERIOD

START STARTING DATE 04/01/73 FIRST FIRST DUE DATE 05/01/73

PAYMENT NUMBER	PAYMENT DATE	TOTAL PAYMENT	INTEREST PAYMENT	PRINCIPAL PAYMENT	BALANCE OF LOAN
1	MAY 1 1973 ✓	207.00	164.08	22.92	24977.08 ✓
2	JUNE 1 1973 ✓	207.00	183.91	23.09	24953.99 ✓
3	JULY 1 1973 ✓	207.00	183.74	23.26	24930.73 ✓
4	AUG 1 1973 ✓	207.00	183.57	23.43	24907.30 ✓
5	SEPT 1 1973 ✓	207.00	183.40	23.60	24883.70 ✓
6	OCT 1 1973 ✓	207.00	183.22	23.78	24859.92 ✓
7	NOV 1 1973 ✓	207.00	183.05	23.95	24835.97 ✓
8	DEC 1 1973 ✓	207.00	182.87	24.13	24811.84 ✓
9	JAN 1 1974 ✓	207.00	182.69	24.31	24787.53 ✓
10	FEB 1 1974 ✓	207.00	182.51	24.49	24763.04 ✓
11	MAR 1 1974 ✓	207.00	182.33	24.67	24738.37 ✓
12	APR 1 1974 ✓	207.00	182.15	24.85	24713.52 ✓
13	MAY 1 1974 ✓	207.00	181.97	25.03	24688.49 ✓
14	JUNE 1 1974 ✓	207.00	181.78	25.22	24663.27 ✓
15	JULY 1 1974 ✓	207.00	181.60	25.40	24637.87 ✓
16	AUG 1 1974	207.00	181.41	25.59	24612.28 ✓
17	SEPT 1 1974 ✓	207.00	181.22	25.78	24586.50 ✓
18	OCT 1 1974 ✓	207.00	181.03	25.97	24560.53 ✓
19	NOV 1 1974 ✓	207.00	180.84	26.16	24534.37 ✓
20	DEC 1 1974 ✓	207.00	180.65	26.35	24508.02 ✓
21	JAN 1 1975 ✓	207.00	180.46	26.54	24481.48 ✓
22	FEB 1 1975 ✓	207.00	180.26	26.74	24454.74 ✓
23	MAR 1 1975 ✓	207.00	180.06	26.94	24427.80 ✓
24	APR 1 1975	207.00	179.86	27.14	24400.66 ✓
25	MAY 1 1975	207.00	179.67	27.33	24373.33
26	JUNE 1 1975	207.00	179.46	27.54	24345.79
27	JULY 1 1975	207.00	179.26	27.74	24318.05
28	AUG 1 1975	207.00	179.06	27.94	24290.11
29	SEPT 1 1975	207.00	178.85	28.15	24261.96
30	OCT 1 1975	207.00	178.64	28.36	24233.60
31	NOV 1 1975	207.00	178.43	28.57	24205.03
32	DEC 1 1975	207.00	178.22	28.78	24176.25
33	JAN 1 1976	207.00	178.01	28.99	24147.26
34	FEB 1 1976	207.00	177.80	29.20	24118.06
35	MAR 1 1976	207.00	177.58	29.42	24088.64
36	APR 1 1976	207.00	177.37	29.63	24059.01
37	MAY 1 1976	207.00	177.15	29.85	24029.16
38	JUNE 1	207.00	176.93	30.07	23999.09
39	JULY 1	207.00	176.71	30.29	23968.80
40	NOV 1 1996	207.00	26.57	1.43	3290.
284	DEC 1 1996	207.00	24.23	182.77	3107.97
285	JAN 1 1997	207.00	22.88	184.12	2923.85
286	FEB 1 1997	207.00	21.53	185.47	2738.38
287	MAR 1 1997	207.00	20.16	186.84	2551.54
288	APR 1 1997	207.00	18.79	188.21	2363.33
289	MAY 1 1997	207.00	17.40	189.60	2173.73
290	JUNE 1 1997	207.00	16.01	190.99	1982.74
291	JULY 1 1997	207.00	14.60	192.40	1790.34
292	AUG 1 1997	207.00	13.18	193.82	1596.52
293	SEPT 1 1997	207.00	11.76	195.24	1401.28
294	OCT 1 1997	207.00	10.32	196.68	1204.60
295	NOV 1 1997	207.00	8.87	198.13	1006.47
296	DEC 1 1997	207.00	7.41	199.59	806.88
297	JAN 1 1998	207.00	5.94	201.06	605.82
298	FEB 1 1998	207.00	4.46	202.54	403.28
299	MAR 1 1998	207.00	2.97	204.03	199.25
300	APR 1 1998	200.72	1.47	199.25	0.00

$2,180.18

Here is a sample of how to fill in a schedule order form:

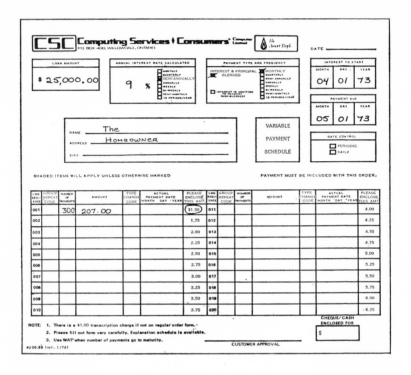

State the:

— Loan amount.

— Annual interest rate and compounding.

— Blended payments (interest and principal included in one payment) *or* fixed principal payments only, with interest in addition (non-blended).

— Date that interest is to be calculated from (usually the mortgage closing date).

— Date the first payment is due.

— Date control; *periodic* means that payments are made on a regular day each month.

— Number of payments until the mortgage is paid off.

— The amount of each payment.

Other Computerized Schedule Services

There are many variations of the mortgage repayment schedule. Some examples and their uses are:

1. *The Variable Payment Schedule* (above) can be used for many other situations. It will handle payments that change, extra lump sum payments, tax payments (as minus amounts), investment situations, missed payments, payments made on different dates and payments that are not large enough to cover the interest. The payment amount and payment date can be listed for each individual transaction.

2. *The Regular Mortgage Repayment Schedule* is similar to the above except that it does not include dates or any variations.

3. *The Level-Balance Schedule* calculates interest on a fixed balance over six months. The interest amount decreases only once every six months. It has the effect of not crediting the principal portion of each payment until six months have elapsed.

4. *The Blanket Mortgage Schedule* (Piggy Back) is used by a borrower to secure additional funds — the borrower gives a third party a mortgage blanketing an existing mortgage. The new lender covenants to be responsible to maintain the existing mortgage payments, lends the borrower the additional funds (secured by a mortgage) and the borrower then makes his mortgage payment to the new blanket mortgagee (lender).

5. *Yield Calculations*:   Lenders buy and sell mortgages between themselves just as goods are bought and sold. The purchaser will often want to discount the mortgage so as to yield a higher rate of interest.

6. *Interest Calculations*:   A series of sixteen special calculations are available. Want to find an effective interest rate? convert an *add-on-advance* rate to *not-in-advance?* calculate a present worth on a loan amount? or evaluate a fund accumulation?

7. *Table Services*: A number of tables are available for the finance business. Examples are: small loans consumer tables for installment financing and conversion tables for metric, mensuration, payroll and tax conversions.

The Computer Tells You

Some of the things that these schedules and calculations will show you are very interesting. For example, if you had arranged a $25,000 mortgage, 25 year, at 9% compounded twice yearly with a blended payment of $207.00 per month you could:

1. Increase your monthly payment:
 — $ 5.00 more to $212.00 saves $ 3,500.00 in interest.
 — $10.00 more to $217.00 saves $ 6,300.00 in interest.
 — $20.00 more to $227.00 saves $10,500.00 in interest.
 — $50.00 more to $257.00 saves $17,900.00 in interest.

2. Prepay with borrowed money: Make extra anniversary payments with borrowed money at a higher rate, say 10%. Pay this loan back over a year.

— $ 500.00 borrowed each year at 10% saves $15,300.00
— $1,000.00 borrowed each year at 10% saves $20,900.00

3. Pay fixed principal interest: Divide the $25,000 into equal principal amounts of $83.33 per month over 25 years. You pay more on the first payments and less thereafter. You save $9,300.

4. Avoid paying "simple interest". Dividing by twelve means total interest repaid is $40,444 rather than $37,093 (if the rate is compounded semi-annually). You save $3,300.

5. Avoid the "level-balance" technique: The borrower pays $41,649 rather than $37,093. You save $4,500.

6. Avoid extending the amortization period. A 1% interest rate raise to 10% after 5 years with the payment remaining at $207.00 per month means you pay $14,000 more than the original $37,093 in interest.

7. Did you know that $85.00 per month invested at 1% per month for 40 years makes you a millionaire?

All calculations above are illustrations only. Specific calculations are to be interpreted in accordance with the terms of the particular mortgage document. The calculations do not include adjustments for taxes, inflation and/or interest earned on alternative investments.

For further information on all the foregoing, and to obtain your tailor-made mortgage repayment schedules, write:

CSC Amortization Department,
P.O. Box 400, Willowdale, Ont.

19

Averaging the Interest Rate

If you wish to know what your annual rate of interest is on a combination of mortgages, here is how to do it:

Take the per cent of each mortgage to the total debt (of 100%) and multiply by its rate of interest. viz:

Example	*Principal Amount*
1st mortgage: 8%	$16,000
2nd mortgage: 14%	4,000
Total mortgage debt:	$20,000

$$\frac{16,000 \times 100}{20,000} \quad \frac{}{1} = 80\% \times \ 8\% = \quad 6.4\%$$

$$\frac{4,000 \times 100}{20,000} \quad \frac{}{1} = 20\% \times 14\% = \quad 2.8\%$$

Total: 100% (average)   9.2%

Example	*Principal Amount*
1st mortgage: 8.25%	$12,544
2nd mortgage: 10.50%	3,724
3rd mortgage: 13.00%	3,332
Total mortgage debt:	$19,600

$$\frac{12,544 \times 100}{19,600} \quad \frac{}{1} = \ 64\% \times \ 8.25\% = 5.280\%$$

$$\frac{3,724 \times 100}{19,600} \quad \frac{}{1} = \ 19\% \times 10.50\% = 1.995\%$$

$$\frac{3,332 \times 100}{19,600} \quad \frac{}{1} = \ 17\% \times 13.00\% = 2.210\%$$

Total: 100%   (average) 9.485%

(Sometimes you're not as bad off as you think you are . . .)

20

Foreclosure

Missed a couple of mortgage payments? The lender bugging you, putting on the pressure? You are short of cash and worried? Naturally.

A situation like this is bound to create anxiety, perhaps even cause one to wake up at 5 a.m. in a cold sweat, but the mortgagor, the borrower in a mortgage deed, can loom largely as a formidable opponent in an action by a mortgage lender.

The remedies and means available to a mortgagor to hang onto his property are quite fair. Unfortunately, not all the remedies are spelled out in a writ of foreclosure or a notice of sale delivered on behalf of the lender to the hapless borrower.

This is not written to be of any help to the lender, most of whom don't need any advice. The large lenders have a well-oiled legal machine at their disposal. It is written to help the borrower who is worried about maintaining a roof over his head.

For the thousands of homeowners worried about an unknown horror that might take place and possibly leave them on the street, here is some advice on what can be done. In this, there are two principals, the mortgagor-borrower-defendant, and the mortgagee-lender-plaintiff.

The following is the practice in Ontario, and outlined to illustrate at least one Provincial Government's rules of the game. It must not be construed or read as legal advice; it is based on practical observations by the author.

The two chief means employed to force a mortgagor to pay principal and interest arrears are (1) foreclosure, and (2) mortgagee's power of sale.

The *power of sale* is usually employed when the market value of the property is insufficient to cover the mortgage debt, or close to it. The reason is that when a property is sold by the mortgagee, the mortgagee has recourse to sue the borrower for any balance owing on the mortgage that was not realized from the proceeds of the sale.

If the mortgagee sells the property without notice to the mortgagor, it is worth noting that a *land titles office* will NOT accept its registration (which will probably surprise some wise-guy money sharks).

A *final order of foreclosure* cancels the mortgage debt completely. If the lender sold the property after foreclosure, and the proceeds of the sale did not erase the mortgage debt, the lender could not look to his former mortgagor to make up the difference.

However, the equity (difference between market value and mortgage debt) held by a mortgagor will be lost to him by foreclosure, but if the property were lost under power of sale, any surplus from the sale will be paid to the former owner-mortgagor.

If there appears to be sufficient equity in the property to adequately satisfy the mortgage debt, it is customary for a mortgagee to proceed by way of a writ of foreclosure.

Being served with such a writ can be a traumatic experience for one unaccustomed to the appearance of a sheriff's officer at the front door. After the initial shock, when one has settled his jangled nerves and mustered the courage to read the contents of the writ, it is quite normal at this stage to bite your nails and reach for a drink (and you might as well have a double), because the writ states quite clearly that the plaintiff is suing for not only the arrears, but the entire total amount of the mortgage principal.

The first indignant thought would be that if one fell behind in the payments, how could it be possible to pay the entire thing off?

But take heart. Help is at hand.

The help is the law. Section 20 of the Ontario Mortgages Act comes to the rescue of the harassed homeowner. The following outlines the recourse available to the defendant:

The interest and principal arrears may be paid within 15 days (assuming the debt is over $3,000) and the court shall dismiss the action.

For example, if one is four payments behind, hustle around and borrow the money, make the payments, plus a small amount of interest owing on the late payments, plus about $100 costs, and you are right back where you were before you were sued. But keep up the payments or the lender might get mad and do it again.

If the defendant cannot raise the money to pay the arrears within 15 days, there are two things that can be done within the 15 days.

Instruct a lawyer to prepare a "notice D.O.R." and a "notice D.O.S."

The D.O.R. is the mortgagor's request to have an opportunity to redeem the property. This notice is served on the solicitor for the plaintiff, which you can do yourself. If the solicitor refuses to accept service and acknowledge receipt of the notice, it can be left in his office with one of his employees.

Noting the name of the employee, the next step is to sign an affidavit of service, which is a sworn statement that the notice was left with the lawyer's employee.

Then go to the office of the Supreme Court of Ontario, pay a nominal fee (at the time of writing $2) and file the notice and the affidavit. It will be recorded.

Once this is done, the defendant can breathe a sigh of relief, because he has just been granted a six month's moratorium during which time he doesn't have to pay anything to the plaintiff.

However, the plaintiff's lawyer is not going to take this sitting down, so he will immediately act to protect his client by obtaining a judgment for the entire mortgage debt. The court, on the other hand, will stay proceedings in the judgment for a period of six months.

The six month's period does not start from the day a defendant files the D.O.R., it starts from the day the mortgagee obtains the judgment of foreclosure. If the mortgagee or his solicitor does not act promptly, the six months could stretch to eight or nine.

During or at the end of the six month's period, the defendant must pay all the interest and principal *arrears* owing on the mortgage. If this is not done, the plaintiff will obtain a *final* order of foreclosure, and game over.

When the arrears have been paid, the defendant-mortgagor may go on making his normal mortgage payments, but don't miss one! Remember, the plaintiff obtained a judgment, and the court stayed proceedings. If payments are missed, the court, upon application, may remove the stay, and that means foreclosure, out, you've had it.

At the time of filing the D.O.R., the defendant should seriously consider filing a "Notice D.O.S.", the opportunity to have the property sold in the event that it is impossible to pay the arrears owing on the mortgage during the six month's redemption period granted by the court.

Remember, a final order of foreclosure not only cancels the mortgage debt, it also conveys the equity in the property once owned by the defendant to the plaintiff. If one had a substantial interest in the property over and above the mortgage debt, this would be a serious loss.

The D.O.S. will prevent such a thing happening. This will mean that although the plaintiff will obtain a judgment of foreclosure and sale, it will stop the final order of foreclosure and force the plaintiff into a sale of the property at the end of the six-month period if the defendant has not been able to pay the arrears.

If the action ends in a sale of the property, here is the order of payment from the proceeds of the sale:
1. The costs incurred in selling the property.
2. The interest owing on the debt.
3. The principal owing.
4. Money owing subsequent encumbrancers.
5. Anything left goes to the one who lost the property.

In the hungry thirties, provincial governments passed mortgage moratorium acts, which allowed a borrower to make no principal payments on the mortgage debt. As long as interest payments on the loan were maintained, he was secure. With today's countless numbers buying homes with about a 10% (or even 5%) down payment, a rising tide of unemployment would certainly create problems for mortgagors, but such government help wouldn't really be much help because with a 90% mortgage debt most of the mortgage payments would be interest anyhow.

If you are served with a writ of foreclosure, or a notice of sale of your property, *call a lawyer immediately and have him spell out your legal rights for defence.*

III. Buying and Leasing

21

Caveat Emptor!
Let the buyer beware!

Most Canadian real estate is bought and sold through the efforts and/or assistance of real estate salesmen. They are employed by real estate brokers who, in effect, operate a clearing house for the salesman's business. Some brokers are tied to their sales staff; they would perish without it. They are excellent administrators but weak as salesmen. Other brokers are top drawer salesmen themselves, and if their sales staff deserted them they would not be unduly concerned; they would press on and make a remarkable living without it.

Do not assume that because a real estate salesman has been selling real estate for years he is an encyclopedia on the subject. Some are lazy and do not care to exert themselves to the point of learning anything about the business that does not touch their particular field. Others are just the opposite. The ideal salesman is one who, aside from his selling ability, is constantly confronted with questions and problems he can't immediately answer (as we all are) and who just as constantly finds the answers, and remembers them. He doesn't side-step a thing.

On the other hand, do not write off a salesman who has just started and is a new man at the game. He could have the property you would ideally like to own.

When you are in the market as a buyer, the salesman's initial job is to introduce you to the property. Before you get carried away with the idea of owning it, it is a good idea to have a check-list of points to remember before you even consider making an offer to purchase the property. Read the following carefully. It can help you.

Zoning: What is the approved and legal municipal zoning? On the property, on the street, in the neighbourhood? Look at a zoning map, then study the by-laws.

The fact that a house is being used as a rooming or boarding house does not necessarily mean that you could buy it and continue to use it as such. It could be used this way under legal non-conforming use, which means that it was used as a rooming or boarding house before the area zoning was reclassified. Zoning legislation does not necessarily mean retroactive legislation, and therefore the owner of the property could be quite within his legal rights in carrying on, despite the new restrictions prohibiting such an operation in the area. Once the ownership changes, the new owner could be forced to obey the law and abide by the new zoning. You may be told that this would not affect you providing you carried on, without interruption, the same use of the property as the present owner, but it is advisable to check this with the municipal authorities.

I can show you an abattoir and a trucking business that are being legally operated on residential streets by owners who had their business established there long before the zoning was upgraded, but if the properties were sold, I doubt very much that the new owners could obtain permission to carry on.

Municipal zoning laws could be very important to you. Some neighbourhoods allow multiple roomers in houses. Perhaps you don't want this, with the possibility of a lot of transients in your neighborhood. There are areas in cities that forbid a property owner to rent even one room. The properties must be occupied by the owner and his family and no one else.

A nice house could be on the fringe of industrial zoning, which isn't the best location. It could have a basement apartment in it leased to someone, and you might find to your dismay that the apartment was not legally there at all, with the result that you would be deprived of its use as a source of income.

Look carefully at all factors in zoning. Do not assume anything about what you see in the property. Be sure that it conforms with all municipal by-laws. If you don't, you could be one very sad buyer.

Condition of Property: Don't let a can of paint or a piece of wallpaper fool you. Check very carefully the condition of the structure itself, the heating plant and equipment, the plumbing, the wiring, and the roof. I am constantly amazed at the number of people who commit themselves to spending tens of thousands of dollars in buying a property after they have taken 20 minutes to inspect it. If you are unsure about something, get professional help and advice. It will be worth it.

Work Orders: Regardless of the type of property you are looking for, check to see that it will stand rigid inspection by the fire department, and that no part of the land or any building or other erection on the land has been confiscated, taken or expropriated by and Provincial, Municipal or other competent authority. Check that no alteration, repair, improvement, or other work has been ordered or directed to be done or performed to or in respect of the land or any building or erection thereon to any of the building, heating, water, drainage or electrical systems, fixtures or works of the same by any Municipal, Provincial or other competent authority. Read this again.

Sometimes a municipal department will have ordered the owner of a property to repair or replace parts of the building or equipment. If this is the case, the costs of such repairs of replacement must be taken into consideration.

Now that you have satisfied yourself as to these three important points. you come to the value of the property. You, as the potential buyer, will have a great bearing on this. Perhaps you have found the ideal property. Perhaps it is worth more to you than the listed price. Perhaps less. You are the one to decide this, remembering that the price of real estate is created quite often by the law of supply and demand. If you find *your* property, act quickly, but not hastily. If you have satisfied yourself on zoning, condition of the property and the work order points (which can all be done in a day) then sit down with the salesman and discuss the details of the offer. Here are a few points to help you.

Price: Remember, most real estate has been listed, within reason, realistically. Some people put their property on the market fishing for a dream price, but the average seller has a reason for selling, and that reason usually isn't a fishing trip looking for a sucker. If you want further confirmation, ask the salesman to show you comparison properties.

Unless it is very obviously a "hot buy", the average buyer will not offer the full listing price for the property. If it is a hot buy, you can be assured that some alert real estate broker or salesman will have snapped it up before you got to it. However, if you feel that property is just the last word as far as you are concerned, blanket the opposition by offering a couple of hundred dollars *more* for the property than the listing price. Two hundred dollars can be peanuts spread over the years if you have found just what you want.

If you are going to make an offer, there is a danger of making it too low. This could anger the seller to the point where he might sign it back at the full price, or reject it altogether. Do not make an insulting offer. Make one that can be considered to be respectable by any standard. Remember that whatever your offer may be, the salesman is under obligation to present it to the vendor.

Terms: If you intend to pay cash for the property you buy, the seller will have to consider discharging all financial encumbrances against it. If recent mortgaging has taken place, this could run into a sizeable sum getting the mortgagee to agree to discharge. This may have a bearing on the price.

If you agree to assume the existing mortgage, have your salesman call the mortgagee and get all the facts. There could be an open or prepayment privilege not noted on the listing. The term could be shorter than you realize, which may not be brought to your attention until your lawyer checks it.

If you are going to ask the seller to receive an equitable mortgage as part of the purchase price, always have an "open" clause inserted. You may be in a position and wish to discharge it at your pleasure. You might also include a clause here to the effect that if the mortgagee of this equitable mortgage wished to sell it (and if he does, it will be sold at a discount in all probability) you are to have first refusal rights to the offering. Perhaps you could be in a position to save money.

It is very important to have no misunderstanding about what chattels go with the purchase price. For instance, do not assume that the chandelier in the living room goes with the property because it is a fixture. A chandelier is not necessarily a normal fixture. List *everything* in your offer. I actually remember an argument between a buyer and seller over two nicely painted garbage pails! This is extreme, but illustrative. Ensure that the property boundaries are clearly outlined in your offer. Be specific.

You must be clear about any possible tenancy. Make it a part of your offer. The present tenant in that little flat on the third floor may look all right today, but is the seller going to tell you he gets drunk and noisy every Saturday night? He might even be the second mortgagee!

Don't expect to call for the production of any title deed, abstract, survey or other evidence of title except such as are in the possession of the vendor.

Allow yourself (your lawyer) as much time as possible to examine title. This will be at your expense. If within this time any valid objection to title is made in writing to the vendor, which the vendor is unable or unwilling to remove, and which you will not waive, the agreement will, notwithstanding any intermediate acts or negotiations in respect of such objections, be null and void and you will have your deposit returned without deductions.

Once you have made your offer, and once it has been accepted, all buildings and equipment on the property will remain at the risk of the vendor until closing.

Pending completion of the sale, the vendor will hold all insurance policies and the proceeds thereof in trust for the parties as their interest may appear, and in the event of damage to the premises, you may either have the proceeds of the insurance and complete the purchase, or alternatively, you may require the vendor to use the proceeds to repair the damage so that on closing you will be acquiring the property in its condition at the time of acceptance of your offer. It is possible that, under these circumstances, the premises may be so damaged that the contract of purchase may be voidable.

The deed or transfer is prepared at the expense of the vendor.

The mortgages are prepared at your expense.

If the vendor is a trustee, the deed or transfer will contain trustee covenants only.

In your estimates of purchase cost, you must not forget the costs that will incurred by the services of your lawyer, and the costs that may be incurred in the adjustments of insurance, rentals, mortgage, taxes, water, fuel and local improvements.

Do not commit yourself to something you cannot handle. Remember always that, in addition to the mortgage payments, you will have to heat the place, pay the light, insurance and taxes, and maintain it in good repair. If you let the taxes slide, your mortgagee will have something to say about that.

When you make out your deposit cheque to go with the offer, make it out in trust to the listing *broker* — not to the owner of the property. The broker holds your cheque in trust for the seller, but if something on the seller's part makes it impossible for him to convey title to you, it is sometimes difficult to have your money returned if the seller has it in his bank account. He may have left for a three months' holiday. Your broker is always there.

Why Buyer Needs a Lawyer

Closing a barn door after the horse has run away is apropos of contacting a lawyer after one has signed a legal document, and a legal document of large financial proportions is an agreement of purchase and sale of real estate.

One would be well advised to seek a lawyer's counsel before signing such an agreement.

This is when a lawyer's assistance may be the most useful, regardless of whether one is buying, selling, leasing or mortgaging. For example, here are some of the things a trained legal mind will think about on your behalf if you seek his advice before you sign an offer to purchase a property:

Is the description of the property clearly stated?

Is there a private drive or a mutual drive?

What are your rights and responsibilities over a mutual driveway?

Are there any easements to which your property will be subject?

Where do you stand financially when the mortgagees have to be paid off?

Are there any hidden charges?

Does the purchase involve the sale of your present property?

If it is a summer cottage:

(a) Is it leasehold, or freehold?

(b) Is there a right of way to a beach?

(c) Is there an assured legal right of way to the cottage from a public highway?

The time to be thoroughly advised is before you sign the contract. Your lawyer is the best one to advise you. He will perform the service of explaining and advising about the offer to purchase as part of the service of acting for you as a purchaser.

After your offer has been accepted by the vendor, your lawyer has a number of responsibilities:

To discuss with you the legal aspects as to how you will have the property registered:

(a) In your name.

(b) In your wife's name.

(c) To the two of you jointly, or as tenants in common. (Here there can be complications of inheritance, succession duty, dower, and division of the property if there may be marital problems).

To search title — are there any legal outstanding interests which will interfere with your full legal enjoyment of the property, or hold up a sale when that time comes? Title defects have a way of lying dormant for years only to come to light when you are selling the property.

To approve of the deed, affidavits, statutory declarations, and to prepare legal documents.

To attend to the proper registrations of the various legal documents when the purchase is closed.

To give an opinion as to your title and a complete report to you of the transaction.

A lawyer's training qualifies him to serve you by giving your legal affairs and problems patient study. He will advise on the laws of real estate and mortgages. He has the ability to explain fine print, knowledge of drafting legal documents, and above all can think and act for you in working out the terms and completion of an important legal contract.

It requires the professional judgement of a well-trained lawyer to advise and assist from the beginning to the final registration in purchasing real estate, and his help is no less important in selling or leasing.

If you wish to sign an agreement of purchase or sale, or an offer to lease, and cannot see your lawyer personally, at least read it to him over a telephone.

Do yourself a favour by letting him in on your plans from the beginning, before you sign.

Remember, sometimes it is too late for help after you sign!

How to Get Service from a Salesman

There is an old saying in real estate — "all buyers are liars." It is not meant literally, but many people who go looking for a home or other real estate really don't know what they want.

Two-storey buyers buy bungalows, new-house buyers buy

resales, detached-house buyers buy duplexes or doubles, downtown buyers buy in the suburbs, and so it goes.

The new salesman can't understand it. The buyer did say he wanted to be near the subway, and now he has bought in the country.

This can be disconcerting to a salesman who patiently has done his homework for days to find the "right" house, but it can be delightful for the salesman who suddenly made a quick sale. The latter got the buyer at the end of his search, when the buyer was fed up with house hunting and simply bought one, or suddenly found one he thought was ideal.

Everybody who is setting out to buy a house, for example, should accept the fact that probably he too, has the same peculiarities. It is possible that because of them he might buy a house that he really didn't want.

Here are some suggestions on how to work with a real estate salesman to get the best possible service from him — or her — so that in the end you wind up with the house you really want at the best price.

Once you have settled on an area in which you feel you would like to live, visit the offices of real estate brokers in the immediate vicinity, preferably one who is a member of a local real estate board, because he has access to all the properties listed for sale through a co-operative listing system. This system not only provides the details of each property, but also a photograph.

Do not restrict yourself to one broker. Visit as many as possible, because brokers will have their own exclusive listings, which other brokers probably do not know about, and one of these listings could mean the end of your search. However, do restrict yourself to one salesman in each broker's office. He has access to all the listings in his office, and if he feels that you are his "exclusive" client, he will work harder for you.

When you have half a dozen salesmen from various offices assisting you, you might lean toward one over all the others for any of several reasons, such as his knowledge of the market, enthusiasm, deportment, etc. Do not ignore the calls from the others, because they could have your house. But sticking to one can be helpful.

If you notice an advertisement in the newspaper, or a "for sale" sign on a house that looks good, regardless of the area or the broker's name call your No. 1 man. He can get all the information for you, and physically introduce you to the property.

Your No. 1 man knows what you are looking for, and this can relieve you of the pressure of a new man trying to make a sale. This saves confusion.

By co-operating with one salesman he will feel that he has a red hot client who is really sticking with him, and will knock himself out to get results that will please you.

Do not be annoyed if your enthusiastic salesman calls you away from your dinner table to tell you about a house. It could be just the one.

The Danger of the Private "For Sale" Sign

An approach to buying a home that could be very dangerous to you financially is to knock at the door behind a private "For Sale" sign.

Here's why — The obvious reason for a private sale of property is to obtain as much money as possible from the sale, usually excusing the effort by saying one wishes to avoid paying a real estate sales commission, and therefore saving the buyer some money.

This can be dynamite to an unsuspecting buyer's pocketbook, especially to one who is of the opinion that he too is being clever in avoiding a real estate agent.

There is certainly nothing illegal or wrong in selling one's own property privately, but if you are considering such a buy, ensure that it is done properly.

The most vulnerable buyer is one who is searching for a house in an unfamiliar area. Values are not consistent from province to province, and certainly not from city to town.

A standard six-room bungalow in an urban fringe-town with a market value of $28,000 could very well command as much as $10,000 more in the city, and not only that, the city property would probably be on a much smaller lot.

A buyer, after searching in the city and becoming discouraged with its inflated market, could reasonably look to the suburbs and surrounding towns. Coming across a private "for sale" sign in a town on a comparable $38,000 city property could be an expensive experience. If he found the vendor asking $33,500 for the property, it might seem like a bargain, when in reality the market price locally might dictate a value of $28,000.

I am not suggesting that a buyer should ignore a private sign, because the home might be very suitable for his particular needs. What I do strongly suggest, however, is that a true, and reasonable local value be determined.

This can be done by employing an established local real estate broker to do one of the following:

(a) Appraise the property. This will cost about $100.

(b) Act as a counsellor for the purchase for a prescribed fee.

A vendor who is not actively engaged in real estate is not really qualified to appraise his own home — the basic reason being that he has a built-in inflated idea of what his own home is worth.

As a matter of fact, a wise real estate broker will enlist the aid of other brokers in valuing his own home.

So an appraisal must be done to establish just what the value is.

If the private seller is doing a good job, he will have had an appraisal done to at least justify the selling price.

The potential purchaser in objecting to paying for an appraisal, is not being realistic, and if the seller objects to having one done, there may be a fly in the financial ointment.

The appraisal will only come into the picture when a purchaser has found a property he is genuinely interested in buying, and when one reaches this stage, it is better to be out $100, rather than $3,000 or $4,000, which could happen. If the appraisal should justify the private seller's price, then it would certainly be worth $100, to know that one at least did not pay more than the market value of the property.

Retaining a broker on a fee basis means that the broker would have to negotiate the purchase, and this would cost more than an appraisal. But the broker would know, through experience, what the market value of the property really is, and his advice in negotiating would be invaluable.

When you're the buyer get a little help to make sure the price is right.

If you wish to buy property owned by a non-Canadian resident, be careful, VERY CAREFUL.

The Department of National Revenue has a deep and abiding interest in such transactions, and woe to the buyer who doesn't know how to protect himself.

The income tax act requires that gains or losses on the disposition of real property owned by a non-resident be reported. If there is a gain (profit) a tax of 25% of such profit is to be paid to the Government.

If the vendor does not pay the tax, the PURCHASER will be liable to pay the Government an amount equal to 15% of the total purchase price of the property. Wow!

To ensure that you will not be stuck with a big fat bill to pay, contact the nearest office of the income tax department or write to the Department of National Revenue, Ottawa, Ontario, and tell it about your proposed purchase.

22

Buy or Rent?

For some families, ownership of a home is like a love affair. They find exactly the right place in the right location. Home ownership has always been their goal. It will make them independent and respected.

For others, ownership has an economic value. A house is an inflation-resistant investment and a tangible incentive to save.

Others are less enchanted by ownership. They have neither time nor inclination to manage the upkeep of a house. They may find available rental properties best suited to their needs. They fear hidden or unexpected expenses sometimes connected with ownership and shrinkage of capital if property values go down.

Others do not have and may never have the capital to buy a house. Renting makes adapting to changing family needs easier than owning. Because real estate transactions take so much time, the mobile family wants no house to lessen its bargaining power for a new position or to lose mobility for other than occupational reasons. This, of course, can sometimes be contingent upon the lease.

The decision to own or rent is related to stages in the life cycle that begins at marriage and extends some time after the dissolution of the family. A typical sequence of changes upgrades shelter with increases in assets, age, and family needs. Net worth is normally highest after 35. Home ownership is greatest after that, and does not begin extensively before age 25.

The residential cycle may begin in a small rented apartment, perhaps after a couple has lived for a time with the parents of one. The next step may be a larger apartment, or the purchase of a small new or used house with equity. The family may sell this after about age 35 in favour of a larger, newer house.

Later, demands of children call for expansion by remodelling or even buying another house. If finances permit, a custom-planned house may be built at this stage.

It may be the last house until old age and retirement indicate a smaller house, a co-operative or rental apartment. The spouse remaining after the death of one partner may remain awhile, but later may seek accommodation with children or other relatives, or in homes or projects for the aged.

Families move through the life cycle at varying rates, and with varying numbers of moves. When changed residential status is not caused by moving to a new position or upgrading accommodations, turning points usually come during the expanding and contracting phases. Changes in residence, rented or owned, entail changes, often abrupt and substantial, in allocation of family resources. Whether as rent, mortgage installments, taxes or repairs, the residence claim is regular, and it is inexorable.

Home ownership is most often achieved with the help of mortgages. The average time required to pay off a mortgage on a house is about 25 years, which is about the same time it takes to rear a child from infancy to maturity and slightly longer than the couple has together after the children have left. If a family moves several times during this period, the feat of owning a home free and clear of debt is accomplished by enlarging the equity in succeeding houses.

A young family buying its first home often has little money. The only choice may be a loan insured by our Central Mortgage and Housing Corporation, but lent by a conventional institution approved by C.M.H.C. Their houses must be new and built to C.M.H.C. standards, generally speaking, although C.M.H.C. now has other avenues of help for the home owner.

Other avenues are open to those with modest down payments by the agreement of a seller to receive an equitable mortgage for the difference between the principal balance of the first mortgage and the down payment. Secondary financing by other means is more costly.

Besides the down payment, buyers need closing costs — legal fees, mortgagee's service charges, and adjustments necessitated in balancing taxes and insurance to the date of closing. These are items not to be overlooked.

There are pros and cons for both buying and renting.

Some morning when you are shovelling snow in front of your house wondering whether it is worth the effort, and you see your cousin Joe come waltzing out of his apartment whistling cheerfully, you think he might have the answer. On the other hand, when Joe is feeling a bit cramped in July in his apartment, and he sees you entertaining friends with a nice outdoor barbecue in the garden, he begins to think that you might have the answer.

Let's examine this from both sides. What are the advantages of *owning* your home, and what are the advantages of *renting* your home. Then we shall get into a straight dollars and cents look at it.

Owning as Opposed to Renting

Pride of Ownership: This is ours. Our house. We can make a beautiful home out of it, or we can choose to live in abject surroundings. We can keep up, or down, with the Joneses. As long as we comply with

the by-laws of our municipality, we can live just the way we want to live.
Apartment: We are restricted. We have to watch the noise. No parties
or loud talking after midnight. Turn down the television. No smelly
cooking; it might offend the neighbours. Can't be ourselves. Somebody
always complaining.

Children: A really big reason. One or a dozen; no matter.
Pack them all in the house. Double bunks if necessary, but we'll get
them in.
Apartment: No children allowed in many places, or they restrict the
allowance to an age group, or make you live on children-only floors.

Roominess: Lots of room to stretch. Get out of each other's
hair. Workshop in basement for father, mother on main floor attending
to her work, the children upstairs watching T.V. or doing their homework. Barbecues outdoors and gardening.
Apartment: Cramped. Get on each other's nerves.

Pets: Just got a cute little pup that's going to be as big as a
baby horse in a year? So what? If I can afford to feed it, I'll keep it.
Apartment: What? If you are going to have a dog, lady, make it a
small one. Or none at all.

Credit: Property ownership definitely is an asset when you
want to put the touch on the local friendly loan company. If you paid
two thousand dollars down for your house, who is to say that your
equity now isn't worth four?
Apartment: Renting goes on debit side of credit application, unless
you have been in the building for a few years.

Stability: Real solid citizen. That's Mr. Smith, he owns 537
up the street.
Apartment: Oh, we live in an apartment.

Income Potential: Couple of extra rooms? Perhaps you can
rent them, if the by-laws allow it. They will pay the taxes. Two rooms
@ $10 a week amounts to $1,040 a year. Probably enough left over
to redecorate the house.
Apartment: Nothing extra here, unless you are renting an extra room
in the apartment, and if you do have an extra room, why?

Possible Appreciation: Property values do go up. Especially
in a good neighbourhood with well kept homes. For every dollar you
credit yourself in paying off the principal on your mortgage, you could
be adding another dollar in increased value.
Apartment: Nothing goes up except the rent.

Better Furnishings: When you have settled into a house, you
feel that this is it; and you can safely spend more money on furniture
and decoration because you feel you will be there long enough to get the
long range economic enjoyment out of it.
Apartment: Too many factors can cause you to move, so why spend a
bundle on decorating the temporary premises?

Buy or Rent?

Peace of Mind: Usually a responsible man living in a house will carry term insurance to cover the principal balance of his mortgage to ensure his family will be left with a debt-free roof over their head if the breadwinner is gone.

Apartment: What's going to happen to my family?

Permanence: It's nice to make friends out of compatible neighbours, people you know who have roots like your own. It is a nice feeling to open your front door and welcome friends into *your* home.

Apartment: Too many come and go.

Responsibility: A man needs it. Good citizens have it. A properly run household is like running your own small business. It takes planning, foresight, and decisive action.

Apartment: Something wrong? Phone the superintendent, if he isn't too busy.

Civic Mindedness: Everything your municipality discusses concerning your neighbourhood concerns you. Join a ratepayers association; they are stimulating and interesting.

Apartment: Couldn't care less. So what if they are going to rip down those houses up the street or build a parking garage next door.

Economy: You think about money when you own your home. You don't splash it around. Too many things you could use the money for on the house. Your principal payments on the mortgage force you to save, to gain equity.

Apartment: Let's have a party. I got a bonus today.

Renting as Opposed to Owning

Freedom: Ah, this is it. When I leave my apartment, I can just close the door and walk away knowing the superintendent is on the job. I can move into a new building as soon as my lease expires. Try something different with new surroundings.

House: Can't stay away too long. If I go on holidays, I have to notify all services and police that I shall be away for a while. Bit concerning. Stuck in same neighbourhood.

No Capital Tied Up: I can do what I want with my bank balance. It's flexible; there when I want it. I can invest it in anything I like, and readily.

House: Down payment tied up, and equity in house.

Debt Free: Chunky mortgage commitments don't worry me, or maintenance or other service bills. All I do is pay the monthly rent, hydro (sometimes not even that) and telephone.

House: Always concerned about major disaster. New furnace? stove? fridge? roof? Other necessary expenses. Always something.

Freedom Loving Neighbours: I live in a building with some gorgeous chicks and nice neighbours. We really enjoy that pool. Care-free types with happy outlook on life. Company readily available.

House: Sourpuss neighbour next door. On other side can't communicate. I like to mix a bit.

No Children: Haven't any of my own. Can't stand them as a steady diet. Always under your feet. Noisy. They are on children-only floors.

House: Well, they are my own little darlings, but some of those other kids they bring home from school. Phew!

Less Housekeeping: Small area to look after. Easy, once over lightly. Compact.

House: My wife is always complaining about all the work she has to do to make the house like a home.

No Pets: Boy, do I hate the sound of a yappy pekingese at 1 a.m. Especially when it's not mine! Not bothered with that! They're all on the pets-only floor.

House: The first thing the kids want when they can talk is a shaggy dog. I have to look after it and feed it, and pay the vet's bills. I can't tell them there is no room for it.

Save Money on Furnishings: I just have to provide modest furnishings. The owner supplied the stove and fridge, my living room was broadloomed when I moved in, and the drapes were in place.

House: At least five rooms plus stove and fridge. Wow!

Dollars and Cents

The examples I am going to use are not imaginary. They are actual figures taken from the household records of a man and his family who owned a house for 2 years, sold it, and moved into an apartment. The living area in each case was comparable, about 1,000 square feet, with 3 bedrooms. I am ignoring the possibility of any capital appreciation in the value of the house, and I am just using actual figures for the 2 years in each case. Here is the picture.

	House	Apartment
Rent:	$	$2,040
Insurance:	15	10
Water/Hydro:	85	120
Oil Heat:	180	
Maintenance:	150	
Gardening:	100	
Taxes:	392	
Interest on Mortgages:	1,287	
Interest on $3,000 cash down payment @ 6%	180	
	$2,389	$2,170

(a) This house was purchased with $3,000 cash as a down payment to two mortgages totalling $18,000. The down payment, regardless of it being tied up, is still worth a nominal 6% per year interest, and must be entered as a debit. Future principal payments on mortgages increase equity, or capital tied up, which would increase this figure.

(b) The first and second mortgages both were on a fully amortized basis, 25 years, 7½%, compounded yearly, not in advance. The second mortgage had a term of 5 years, but the owner just used the first two. The second owner has to worry about paying off the principal outstanding balance of this second mortgage in 3 years' time.

(c) The figure for gardening was a nominal one, and took into account the depreciation on the power mower.

(d) The insurance figure is lower for the apartment because it covers contents only; no building.

(e) The maintenance figure was a fair one. There is always something to fix in a house that you own. The figure included nominal allowances for redecorating when necessary.

(f) The one additional disbursement the home owner will certainly have here is the principal repayment of the mortgages, which will have to be added to the total shown. In this case the yearly figure would amount to $274.76. All entries and figures represent an average yearly figure for 2 years. This also includes mortgage figures, which represent the average yearly figure for the first two years' life of the mortgages.

From this you can draw your own conclusions. There are fringe benefits in both cases:

The apartment has a nice swimming pool and sauna. The freedom of movement is there. The cash is in the bank.

The house has a nice garden and barbecue area for entertaining. It provides forced savings, roominess and human roots. There is also the strong possibility of property appreciation, not considered in our example.

The decision is yours, but the costs either way must be fitted into the budget.

23

Buy AND Rent

If you are in the market for a house of your own, there is something you really should consider in your plans for aesthetic and financial security, and that is the advantage of buying something like a four-plex. There are excellent tax advantages connected with this, all approved and condoned by our government.

Pride of ownership and financial stability are two of the arguments in favour of owning a house, and there is plenty of both in owning a fine looking four-plex that someone else is helping you pay for! When you purchase a single family dwelling, you pay for it, 100% of it, right out of your own pocket, and the money you use to pay for it comes out of the little you have left after the income tax bite.

Let us assume you are one of the lucky ones who can afford to buy a nice cosy nest worth $30,000 with $10,000 cash as your down payment. The following is a fair estimate of your annual expenses (before mortgaging):

Taxes:	$ 500
Heating:	200
Insurance:	50
Maintenance:	150
Hydro & Water:	160
	$1,060

In addition to this, the $10,000 down payment you have tied up in the house is worth at least 6% to you, so that's another $600. If you obtain a mortgage loan at 7½% ($20,000) 25 year amortization, compounded yearly, it would carry for $144.60 per month, or $1,735 a year in round figures. Now let's see what the house costs you per year:

Running Expenses:	$1,060
Interest at 6% on $10,000	600
Mortgage:	1,735
	$3,395

Wow! And that's the bare minimum, before they install the telephone and hook up the T.V. Remember, this $3,395 comes right out of your take-home pay *after* taxes.

Your cousin also has $10,000 to invest in a property, but he has a few ideas of his own, and he found a very nice four-plex for $60,000.

The 4-plex has a mortgage of $40,000, 7½%, compounded yearly, 25 year amortization, carrying for $289.20 per month, or $3,470 yearly in round figures.

The vendor of the property agreed to receive from the purchaser, as part of the purchase price, an equitable mortgage of $10,000, 7½%, compounded yearly, same amortization, carrying for $72.30 per month, or $867.00 yearly in round figures. Here is where his money goes:

Taxes:	$1,300
Heating:	500
Insurance:	90
Maintenance:	300
Hydro and Water:	220
	$2,410

Interest @ 6% on $10,000:	600
First Mortgage:	3,470
Second Mortgage:	867
	$7,347

Your cousin occupies one suite with his wife. He rents the other three at $150 per month, to give him a total gross annual income of $5,400. Now see what it costs him:

Expenses:	$7,347
Income:	5,400
	$1,947

The situation is improving, but we are only beginning. Your cousin is allowed to deduct from his income tax return the operating expenses of the building, including the interest paid on the mortgages. He will not, of course, be able to use the accommodation he uses with his wife as a deductible item, which chops ¼ off his deductions. Here is the picture for his first year's operations:

Gross Income:		$5,400
Expenses		
Operating	$2,410	
Interest on—		
Ist Mortgage:	2,882	
2nd Mortgage:	720	
	$6,012	
Less ¼ Personal:	1,503	4,509
		$ 891

The picture is getting rosier for your cousin every minute. He would like to get rid of that $891 net income figure so he can show a nil return on the operation on his income tax.

That's easy. He knows he can claim his capital cost allowance (depreciation) on the building, which is valued at $40,000, apart from the land, *less* the portion he occupies himself, so his depreciation would effectively be taken on a valuation of $30,000. He can take up to 5% each year on a reducing balance, but 5% of $30,000 is $1,500, which is too much, so he just takes what he needs to eliminate the net return. Now he shows —

Net Income:	$891
Depreciation:	891
Net return for income tax purposes:	NIL

What has it actually cost him *out of his pocket?* Why, the original figure of $1,947, which represented his expenses less income.

You are paying $3,395 a year. This figure represents your total cash outlay, including the mortgage principal and interest payments.

Your cousin's yearly outlay will be $1,947 for the first 7 years. Under his illustration, by the time he submits his statement for the 8th year, he will have used the depreciation credits he had built up and must now take no more than the maximum allowable. The return on operation keeps getting larger because the interest payments on the reducing mortgage keep getting smaller, allowing him less each year to show as a tax deductible item. The 8th year return will show a taxable balance after depreciation of about $130. By the 10th year, it will show $375. This isn't too bad, but his taxable return on the operation will become progressively larger, and at this stage he will sit down with his accountant and decide whether it would be more advantageous to keep the property or to sell it.

If he keeps it, his depreciation allowance will be progressively reduced. If he sells it, he will have the problem of paying income tax on the depreciation he had claimed over the years.

Let's examine the first 10 years' of ownership for you and your cousin, ignoring the fact that your cousin had to pay income tax on about $750 over the last 3 years of this period.

	You	Cousin
Net cost out of pocket:	$33,950	$19,470
Less Principal Paid on mortgages:	8,326	10,407
Net Cost:	$25,624	$ 9,063

It will cost you $16,561 *more* to carry a property worth *half* the value of your cousin's.

These examples were taken from two good properties in a

large Canadian city. Property values, income and expenses will naturally vary in different locations. The figures will not remain constant, because property values change and costs go up (incomes, too, of course) but I used the projection to give you a comparable example. You can use this chapter as a guide in making your own comparisons in your community when considering the advantages and disadvantages of the situation.

The disadvantages of the four-plex are that it requires you to live in one of the 2-bedroom suites, which will limit your movement, and will force you to put up with the tenants. You would probably have difficulty in getting a vendor to receive an equitable mortgage for a term in excess of 10 years, and if you retained the property you would have to juggle this secondary financing around. By that time you could probably increase your first mortgage by an amount that would allow you to pay off, or discharge, the secondary financing.

The end result and clear advantage of the 4-plex is a monetary one.

The detached home will give you more room and privacy. It will cost much more.

There is one more item of expense that is applicable in both cases. Every time you reduce the principal balance owing on the mortgage, you are effectively burying money that is not producing any interest to you, and you should add this interest as an expense to the interest on the down payments that I have already charged you with.

In considering something like this remember that it can be estimated on anything from a duplex up. You can overcome the cramped feeling of the four-plex by selecting a large triplex, or other multiple dwelling with larger suites. The constant tax requirement is that you cannot make any deductions on the proportionate share of the operation that will benefit you as accommodation.

24

Condominiums and Co-operatives

Condominium is the division of buildings into separately owned units.

All provinces except Newfoundland and Prince Edward Island have special condominium legislation.

Let's see how it works in Alberta:

When a condominium plan is registered, the certificate of title to the parcel described in the plan, except mineral rights, will be cancelled and a separate certificate of title for each unit described in the plan will be issued. For example, if an apartment building were registered as condominium, each apartment in the building would have its own certificate of title, the person purchasing the individual apartment would have his own title deed to the apartment, and would be free to do his own mortgaging, or sell his unit, just as he would in owning a house.

When a certificate of title for a unit is issued, the owner's share in the common property is shown, and such common property is held by the owners of all the units as tenants in common in shares proportional to the unit factors for their respective units. The owner will hold his unit and his share in the common property subject to any interests affecting the unit or the common property notified on the condominium plan.

What is this "common property"? It is defined as so much of the land comprised in a condominium plan as is not comprised in any unit shown in a condominium plan. In other words, the grounds, driveways, lobby, elevators, etc.

The driveway between two houses quite often is a mutual drive. Each homeowner has his right of easement over the other to use the driveway. So it is with condominium. There is an easement for and against every unit owner covering the roof, walls, passage and provision of water, sewerage, drainage, gas, electricity, garbage, artificially heated or cooled air and other services (including telephone, radio and television services) through or by means of any pipes, wires, cables or ducts for the time being existing in the parcel to the extent to which those pipes, wires, cables or ducts are capable of being used in connection with the enjoyment of the unit.

The owners of the units are members of a corporation, but it does not come under the provisions of the Companies Act. The voting rights of the owner of a unit are determined by the unit factor for his unit. If a unit is subject to a registered mortgage, and the mortgagee has given written notice of his mortgage to the corporation, then the owner does not have any vote — it is exercisable by the mortgagee of first priority.

The building is regulated by by-laws made by the corporation which provides for the control, management, administration, use and enjoyment of the units and of the common property. The corporation has an elected board of managers to administer the by-laws.

A fund is established for administrative expenses sufficient for the discharge of obligations of the corporation in maintaining the property. In adding to the fund, the amounts required are raised by levying contributions on the owners in proportion to the unit factors for their respective units.

Where a building is insured to its replacement value, the owner of a unit may affect a policy of insurance in respect of any damage to his unit in a sum equal to the amount secured, at the date of any loss referred to in the policy, by mortgage upon his unit, and payment shall be made to the mortgagees by the insurer in order of their priorities. If the building is uninsured, or has been insured for less than its replacement value, an owner may effect a policy of insurance in a sum equal to the replacement value of his unit less a sum representing the amount to which his unit is insured under any policy of insurance effected on the building.

The condominium status of a building may be terminated by a unanimous resolution, and may also transfer or lease the common property, or any part of it.

The duties of the owner are:

(a) To permit the agents of the corporation, at reasonable time on notice, to enter his unit for the purpose of inspection.

(b) Forthwith carry out all work that may be ordered by any public authority in respect of his unit.

(c) Repair and maintain his unit in a state of good repair.

(d) Use and enjoy the common property in such a manner as to not interfere with other owners or their visitors.

(e) Not use his unit or permit it to be used in any manner or for any purpose that will cause a nuisance or hazard.

(f) Notify the corporation immediately of any change of ownership or of any mortgage or other dealing in connection with his unit.

The duties of the corporation are:

(a) To control, manage and administer the common property for the benefit of all owners.

(b) Keep in a state of good and serviceable repair and properly maintain the fixtures and fittings used in connection with the common property.

(c) Where practicable, establish and maintain suitable lawns and gardens on the common property.

(d) On the written request of an owner or registered mortgagee of a unit, produce the policies of insurance and premium receipts.

The corporation may: purchase, hire or otherwise acquire personal property for use by owners in connection with their enjoyment of common property; borrow money required for the performance of its duties or the exercise of its powers; secure the repayment of money borrowed by it; invest as it may determine any money in the fund for administrative expenses; and do all things reasonably necessary for the enforcement of the by-laws and the control, management and administration of the common property.

At meetings of the board all matters shall be determined by simple majority vote. A general meeting of owners shall be held within three months after registration of the condominium plan, and subsequently once a year.

Co-operative ownership is shared ownership.

If you owned an apartment in a co-operative building, you would not have a separate title deed to your apartment. You would own a share of the entire building, and any mortgaging of the building would involve all the shareholders under one mortgage, with each being charged, and paying, a proportionate share according to the size of his holding.

It is customary for the building to be owned by a corporation under a provincial charter, established for the benefit of the shareholders, who would be the occupants of the building.

An annual meeting is held by the shareholders, at which time a board of directors is elected for the ensuing year.

Co-operative ownership is under a shareholder's agreement, which outlines the responsibilities of the shareholders, the shared costs pro rata they would undertake for the operation of the building, maintenance and repair, and such other regulations as their position if they wish to sell their shares and vacate etc.

Condominiums and co-operatives are likely to become more popular as more Canadians move to big cities and urban land costs rise. Systems like these have been common for a long time in crowded European countries.

You may not think condominium or a co-operative apartment is the answer to your housing needs now, but your ideas may change in a few years. So it makes sense to include these forms of ownership in your mental list of housing options.

25

Selecting Your House

The Choice is Yours: Most of us have a number of houses in a lifetime. We increase our incomes; we move. We are transferred by our company; we move. We enlarge the family; we move. We decrease the family; we move. Count the number of moving vans the next time you are on the highway, and when are *you* going to move?

Let the choice be a good one or at least a thoughtful one, for even if you stay in a place only a short time it can influence you and your family's well-being, sometimes even involvement and identity, and happiness. A mistake, if you make one, can be corrected, but a mistake almost always leaves some kind of mark.

The Community: Before you make your choice, compare the costs of commuting in money, time and fatigue with the advantages and disadvantages of space, privacy, and quiet for yourself and your family.

Do not overlook differences in public amenities and municipal services, and in taxes and the cost of insurance and utilities. Choose, if you can, to live within the jurisdiction of a municipal government that has a master plan of zoning and development, and legislation to support it. During this period of increases in population and fast-growing cities, it is hard to forsee the future of a community or to influence its development. Without a plan, growth is chaotic and unpredictable.

Many families have built houses in the country only to find the city at their doorsteps sooner than they had expected. Many others have built or rented in city neighbourhoods whose residential character becomes eroded by conversion to incompatible uses. Do not buy or build a house on land that has a potential for industrial, commercial, or multiple-housing development except as a calculated investment. Seek a site protected by zoning.

You will find other advantages in legislation for planning. Visual quality — beauty and order — depends on the good will and sensibility of each property owner and the competence of the architect, but laws can control some of the influences that have contributed to the deterioration of the landscape — signs, billboards and utility structures. Some communities limit the location of billboards, the size of signs, and require that wires and pipes of utilities be put underground. Choose a community like this and one that is alert to the possibilities of such improvements.

Local government and pulic education are financed largely by taxes on real property. Tax rates and assessment practices vary among communities, but do not assume that communities with low taxes are necessarily more efficient. They quite often provide fewer or inferior services. The property tax has inevitable shortcomings, because it penalizes quality by rewarding shoddy property with low assessments.

Nothing is more important than good schools. They are not easy to develop. They are built by the efforts of dedicated people over long periods. Your children of school age get no benefit from long range improvements. They need good schools now. Good schools are expensive. Usually they co-exist with higher real property taxes, but differences in tax rates in communities with good schools and those with poor schools are seldom great enough to influence one's choice and are never worth the savings.

Communities with good schools usually are stimulating in other ways. So when you are looking for a place to live, look into opportunities for intellectual activity: libraries, museums, theatres, concerts, or perhaps even an amateur symphony or little-theatre groups. Mutual interests foster friendships more than geography does.

Look also for a beautiful place, or at least one that is not ugly. Visual quality, like a good school system, is not achieved quickly. It depends on long traditions of pride and long-continued programs of responsible public works. Street trees take years to mature. Established visual elegance in a residential community is literally priceless.

Consider also convenience to work, shopping, and schools in terms of distance and methods of transportation, for a house for most families today is a centre from which to commute to work. Children travel to school; parents to shops. Anticipate travelling costs in your estimate of housing costs.

The place you live often determines whether you need one or two automobiles or none. Sometimes it will be found to be cheaper to hire cabs while travelling within the community and renting cars on week-ends when you want to get away, rather than tying your cash up in the cost of owning an automobile or two.

The European lives in his city at large. Public and neighbourhood gathering places — piazzas, parks, sidewalk cafes, coffee-houses — serve as extensions of his house into which some social parts of life are projected. We have fences along our property lines, but we are experiencing a revival of interest in public amenities; especially in cities. Consider then the relationship between the kind of urban situation in which you live and the kind of housing facilities you may need or that are available.

Sometimes a neighbourhood is so attractive that it determines one's choice of community, but usually the community is selected first. Transportation may influence the second decision as well as the first. So, inevitably, will the housing situation. If you are interested in a particular kind of house or lot, or one at a certain price, you may find it only in a limited number of places. But, assuming there are alternatives, how to proceed?

Sometimes, when moving into a community, there is an advantage in renting for a while. Many qualities, especially the intangibles that have to do with sociability, common interests and even climate, cannot be understood without experience. Renting in an unfamiliar community will give you a clearer idea of the kind of house you want and the neighbourhood in which you would like to live.

Look for visual character. It is even more important in the neighbourhood than in the community, because the neighbourhood is closer to home.

Established neighbourhoods have at least two advantages. You can examine the houses and the landscape has had time to mature. Some of our best houses are very old, but middle-aged houses and neighbourhoods tend to deteriorate.

Judge the viability of an established neighbourhood before placing a new house there. If you don't trust your own evaluation, seek professional advice. New developments still under construction are harder to visualize, but plans can give some indication of their eventual completed appearance.

Houses for sale or rent and remaining lots in stable residential neighbourhoods command higher prices. So does property in thoughtfully planned and sensitively designed new residential areas that can reasonably be expected to develop admirably.

Your choice is difficult. Whether to accept an area that it not attractive and probably will not be developed attractively, or place a larger percentage of your investment in land and improvements to take advantage of a superior location, remembering that you will be able to do little to change the aspect of the neighbourhood.

Look for a location where you can walk to stores and shops, schools and a park. That may be difficult because much zoning legislation has produced antiseptic neighbourhoods, which by being unvaried are also lacking in services. Communities vary a great deal in the availability of facilities and programs for recreation. Do not overlook the importance of these for children.

Select a location that is free from unpleasant sources of noise, fumes and dirt and not near a main traffic artery, railroad, airport or objectional industry. Noise travels surprising distances on quiet nights. So do fumes and dust on breezy days.

Consider the views. If the terrain is hilly, the views are more extensive, but construction costs will probably be higher.

What does the street look like? Purely local streets have advantages of relative quiet and safety. Subtly curved streets usually are more attractive than straight ones, but excessively curved patterns are puzzling to strangers and casual visitors.

What do the neighbourhood houses look like? Fencing? Landscaping? What is the orientation of the lot? Can you take advantage of winter sunshine, yet keep out excessive summer sun? What is the direction of the prevailing winds? Are cooling summer breezes accessible? Is the lot readily drained? What is the charater of the soil? Is it subject to movement, settling, slides?

Check the zoning regulations. Find out what you can and cannot do there, the restrictions on the house itself and the kinds of room rental regulations in the area. Can you practice a part time profession or occupation, or build a swimming pool?

Ask whether there has been a recent flood in the neighbourhood. If not, and if it has survived a severe rainy season, its drainage facilities are adequate unless subsequently overloaded by new developments.

Inquire about provisions for collecting trash and garbage.

Is there a periodic water shortage, or is the supply adequate for house and garden?

Locations near an attractive and compatible development, such as a new college campus, golf course or public park exert stabilizing influences on nearby residential properties. If you follow these criteria and acquire a well designed and soundly constructed house, property values probably will be sustained. A house that is no more expensive than the average in the neighbourhood, and perhaps a little less so, is a conservative investment.

The House: When we acquire a house, we are inclined to think of the enterprise as an investment. A house can be ostentatiously out of place in its neighbourhood or too expensive for a given market to support, especially in small communities without diversified demands.

Experience does not support common assumptions about the effects of ethnic homogeneity. When a minority group moves into a neighbourhood, property values do not automatically decline. Sometimes they increase.

Of course, all the economic factors involved in the venture should be considered. The relative advantages of renting and owning; indirect costs, such as transportation; and the direct costs — the land and improvements, building, landscaping, furnishing, and operation (maintenance, taxes, insurance and what about the mortgage?).

Land costs are lowest in the country and highest in the central city, and vary with the desirability of the location and the extent of its improvement.

Do not overlook the costs of site improvements. As a prospective property owner, determine your liability to the municipality for current or future work. All things considered, it is better to live in a community that requires first-class utilities, drainage, street construction and lighting.

At the other end of the process, think of landscaping and furnishing costs. Families often find themselves with inadequate funds for these items simply because they follow site and structure in the sequence of acquisition.

Insurance costs vary with the quality and proximity of fire and police protection, but differences in premiums do not measure the advantages of adequate protection.

The building itself represents the largest single expenditure. Many varaibles influence its cost. For families with reduced incomes, cost will be critical and the alternatives severely limited, but for many others, several choices will be available at similar prices.

At this point, turn to considerations other than price to find measures of value. Who else can understand precisely how important to you are an escape to an unspoiled stretch of wilderness or the sound of music or the company of friends?

Existing houses, new or old, can be examined before the purchase. Building a new house, on the other hand, presents the opportunity to achieve a uniquely personal environment, given competent professional design — at least an architect, and preferably also a landscape architect.

Many houses could have been put up more economically had an architect designed them, but good professional service entails costs and so does custom building. Select your architect carefully on the basis of his work — one who is interested and experienced in house design. Select the builder carefully too. Most people assume that competitive bidding is the only way to solicit a reasonable price. Sometimes it is, but limit the bidders to good contractors. The best procedure, if you can manage it, and if your community is fortunate enough to have such men, is to select the best builder just as you selected the best architect. A man who takes a professional interest in his work usually quotes the same price whether he is bidding competitively or simply invited to bid.

If your house is being designed for you, its form has limitless possibilities. Take advantage of the opportunities to make it truly original, but avoid exotic excesses, which disrupt visual harmony in the neighbourhood and can make it difficult to sell in some unforseen future.

In the final analysis, the value of a house, regardless of its location, can be judged only in terms of its success as a personal environment for each member of the family in an emotional as well as a functional sense.

A Well Built House: How can you tell whether a house you are thinking of buying is well built?

First, get a copy of the plans and specifications. Compare what you can see of the house with what is shown on the plan. Sometimes plans are revised during construction, for better or for worse, unless the builder has registered his plans for mortgaging.

Some general features are not structural but still may be important to you. Among them are: Which way does the house face? Is the arrangement and size of rooms good? How about natural light and cross ventilation? Do the rooms provide enough wallspace or storage space? Does the plan permit some flexibility of living arrangements? These are partly matters of personal taste. Do they satisfy your family's needs or preferences?

From this we go to the structural parts of the house — the foundation, walls, floors, ceilings and roof. Start from the outside. Walk around the house.

Look at the foundation walls, which should extend well above the finish ground level. Watch for vertical cracks, which may indicate the structure has settled. Hairline cracks in the concrete are due to volume changes and have no great significance.

If the concrete is uneven or honeycombed, or has broken corners, it probably did not have enough cement or was carelessly placed in the forms — a sign of poor workmanship.

In block or stone walls observe the character of the joints. Use a pocketknife to pick at the mortar and see if it crumbles easily. If it does, it is a sign that too much sand or a poor quality cement was used. A nail driven into the joint will indicate if the mortar is skimpy there. If you wish to check the wall thickness, measure through a basement window.

The slope from the foundation at the grade line should be enough for rain to run off.

Basement windows wells must drain readily. Water from the roof should be carried away by adequate eaves troughs and downspouts of non-corrosive material. If downspouts are not connected to a storm sewer or other suitable outlet, splash blocks at the outlet will divert the water.

Check basement window jambs and trim to see if they fit snugly against masonry wall. The sills of all windows should have sufficient pitch to drain water outward. Here is a place where decay may have occurred — probing with a small screwdriver will soon tell you.

After a final look at the foundation walls to make sure the corners are even and walls are vertical, we can inspect the framed sidewalls. They may be covered with wood or composition siding, shingles, brick, stucco, stone, or other types of enclosing materials. All are good if used properly.

If the siding has been painted, examine the condition of the paint. See if the paint film is dense and opaque, or if the wood is showing through. Check for any gloss on the surface. Painted surfaces that are dull and chalky indicate that repainting is necessary.

The horizontal lap siding should be laid evenly, with correct overlap and tight butt joints. At the corners, the siding may be mitered or fitted snugly against vertical corner boards. An end of the siding board should not be exposed to the weather because it will soak up moisture.

Make sure the nails are of the non-corrosive type and that the space between the nailhead and the face of the siding has been filled in before painting. Simply scratch to find out.

Windows and doors should have a protective flashing of non-corrosive metal above them. They should be checked for weather-stripping. Check the sills for sufficient pitch for good drainage. A drip groove under the sill will permit the water to drop clear of the siding.

You have now had an opportunity to form an opinion on the quality of workmanship that has gone into the outside walls. Neat foundation walls, good metal eaves troughs and downspouts, snug-fitting woodwork, and provision for surface drainage all indicate the builder has made a conscientious effort to erect a house that will endure.

Signs that the builder has skimped are chipped or honey-combed concrete, loose mortar in the brickwork, large cracks between the ends of the siding and window or other trim, rust stains from an inferior grade of outside hardware, and thin or flaked-off paint in a nearly new house.

Now go inside the house. In the basement look more carefully at the foundation walls, post, and girders, and at the floor joists if they are not concealed by the ceiling material. The basement floor should be dry.

The basement floor should slope to the floor drain to permit quick runoff. A concrete floor should have a hard smooth surface without spalling, cracking or dusting.

The joists that support the floor above rest on the foundation walls and are supported by wood or steel girders. These girders in turn are supported by posts or division walls. If wood posts are used, they should be set on a concrete base block above the finish floor level.

When wood girders are built up by nailing several members side by side, make sure the members are well nailed together and that joints are over a post or a division wall.

Check to see that the ends of wood joists are not embedded in masonry or the concrete wall, as this practice may invite rot unless there is an air space at the sides and end of the beam.

The wood joists should be spaced evenly. Examine them for sagging, warping, or cross-breaks. Look carefully at any joists that have been cut for heating ducts or piping. Notches or holes on the bottom edge or near midspan have the greatest weakening effect.

Check the area between the foundation wall and sill. Any opening should be filled with a cement mixture of a calking compound. The filling will lower the heat loss and prevent the entry of insects or mice into the basement.

Most construction in the living area will be hidden by various wall and ceiling finishes, but you can check the interior finish and such items as flooring, window, door and other trim. Examine the trim for any open joints, hammer marks, warped pieces or rough nailing.

Over the door where the side casings meet the horizontal, the joint is often mitered. If this joint is tight, as all joints should be, you have a pretty good sign of careful workmanship.

Note, too, if the baseboard fits snugly against the flooring and wall at all points.

Interior finishes are commonly of plaster or of such drywall construction as wood or composition materials. You seldom see plaster cracks in a newly built home, because they develop slowly. In a house a year or more old, the absence of cracks indicates a well-built house. Of course, cracks can be concealed temporarily by wallpaper or a coat of paint. Cracks extending diagonally from the corners of windows or doors may be signs of poor framing or that the house has settled.

As you walk over the floors, notice if they squeak or seem too springy. If the floor joists are big enough and the sub-floor has been laid correctly, neither fault should occur. If you wish to check to see if the floors are level, stretch a string across them.

If the flooring is exposed, hardwood flooring or the harder species of softwood are usually preferred. If carpeting is used wall to wall, the underlay may be of any material that presents a smooth and firm surface.

Look carefully for signs of nailing. Flooring of a standard thickness is tongued and grooved and is blind nailed along the tongue so that the nailing does not show. Small nailheads on the face or top of the flooring means that a very thin flooring has been used. Wood strip flooring normally becomes dry and cracks open between the strips in winter. These cracks, if they are not too wide, will close up in warmer weather.

Do not condemn floors in an old house simply because they are scratched and marred. Perhaps all they need is refinishing. If so, take this extra cost into account.

Perhaps the kitchen and the bathroom have tilework on the floor, on the wall, or wainscot. The tile floor should be smooth, without raised tile or depressed areas. Wall tiles should fit snugly around all windows, door trim and around the fixtures. Joists should be caulked tightly to keep water out.

Check the doors to see if they swing freely and close tightly without sticking. Is there a threshold under the exterior doors to keep out snow and cold winds? Some of these doors may have metal weatherstripping. Are the interior doors hung so as to clear your rugs? Do they interfere with other doors? Do they latch readily and stay latched? Check all doors to see that they are not excessively warped.

Windows usually are of the double-hung type; the lower sash slides up and the upper one slides down. Open and shut all windows to be sure they work properly and there is not too much play in the sash. The weatherstripping should not interfere with the ease of operation. Don't forget to raise the window shades to assure yourself there are no cracked windowpanes.

Check window woodwork and plaster for water stains and signs of decay. Note the kind of glass in the window. Is it clear and flawless, or does it create distortion? Also see that the putty that holds the glass in is in good condition and is painted.

It is well to check the attic for the thickness of insulation between the ceiling joists and to see if there is a moisture barrier on the room side of the insulation. Check the attic ventilators. They should be open summer and winter. In summer, ventilation helps to lower the attic temperature. In winter, ventilation removes moisture that may work through the ceiling and condense in the attic space.

Frost on the ends of nails in winter indicates insufficient ventilation and excess moisture.

Check the roof rafters or trusses to see that they are unbroken and that framing joints are right. Can you see any daylight under the eaves. Waterstaining on the rafters or roof sheathing is a sign of a roof leak.

Questions that are more complex or that cannot be answered by comparison with standards may require the services of an architect. Find a man who has a good reputation and is well qualified; the cost of his services may be small compared to the troubles that can arise from a serious defect.

26

Buying and Leasing Crown Land

In the first two editions of this book, details were provided concerning Provincial rules about Crown land acquisition. However, there is now so much flack about non-residents buying government owned land that by the time current rules are printed they would probably be out of date.

There is still *plenty* of Crown land available in Canada, but to be right up to date it is advisable to write Provincial authorities and get it first hand. Here are the addresses:

Director of Lands,
Department of Lands and Forests,
Legislative Building,
Edmonton, Alberta.

Director of Lands,
Department of Lands, Forests, and Water Resources,
Parliament Buildings,
Victoria, British Columbia.

Director of Lands, and Forests,
Department of Mines and Natural Resources,
Legislative Building,
Winnipeg, Manitoba.

Director, Lands Branch,
Department of Natural Resources,
Legislative Buildings,
Fredericton, New Brunswick.

Director,
Crown Lands and Surveys,
Department of Mines, Agriculture and Resources,
Confederation Building,
Saint John's, Newfoundland.

Registrar of Crown Lands,
Department of Lands and Forests,
Province House,
Halifax, Nova Scotia.

The Director,
Lands and Water Branch,
Ministry of Natural Resources,
Parliament Buildings,
Toronto, Ontario.

Commissioner of Public Lands,
Department of the Attorney General,
Province House,
Charlottetown, Prince Edward Island.

Chief, Lands Service Section,
Territorial Domain Branch,
Quebec Department of Lands and Forests,
Parliament Buildings,
Quebec City, Quebec.

Director, Lands,
Department of Agriculture,
Legislative Building,
Regina, Saskatchewan.

Yukon Territory —
Supervisor of Lands,
Northern Economic Development Branch,
Department of Indian Affairs and Northern Development,
P.O. Box 1767,
Whitehorse, Yukon.

Northwest Territories —
Supervisor of Lands,
Northern Economic Development Branch,
Department of Indian Affairs and Northern Development,
P.O. Box 1500,
Yellowknife, Northwest Territories.

27

Buying Investment Property

To the sophisticated investor, the contents of this chapter would be old hat, but not too many of us are sophisticated investors, so I am going to assume that you have very little knowledge or experience on the subject, and sail right through it from scratch.

I have found, through advertising investment properties for sale, that there are an amazing number of people with $50,000 or so, who are just itching to turn the money loose in a safe and secure piece of real estate that will do the following:

(1) Require the tenants of the property to pay all the expenses, including the interest and principal repayments on the mortgages.

(2) Provide a return of about 10% on the original investment.

(3) Provide a profit on the property in the event of sale.

I sold a 17 suite apartment building for $150,000. The purchaser got it for $40,000 cash. He borrowed $110,000 secured by a mortgage on the property, fully amortized over 20 years. The mortgage, interest and principal, is being repaid from the income the owner receives from the tenants. Not only that, the income he receives pays all the operating expenses and taxes on the property and it provides him with an extra $4,000 or so, which of course is a net return of 10% on his invested cash.

In twenty years the mortgage will be paid off, and he will have a nice, clean, clear title to a building that cost him $150,000 on paper, but with just $40,000. Furthermore, if real property keeps up the spiralling record it has set during the past 30 years God alone knows what the building will be really worth.

This situation is being created every day across Canada, but only by people who are not afraid to get their financial feet wet, and possibly take a calculated risk. If it required little or no effort, with 100% guaranteed security, everybody would be doing it. They would not necessarily have the $50,000 but they would insist on getting involved through some sort of share basis. After all, 10% is much better than 5% at the bank, especially with the fringe benefits.

All these people who turned up with $50,000 didn't have it all in their own bank account. Many of them had partners; one, two, three, or in one case I found, twenty. They all had one common goal. Get involved.

Every building in Canada is owned by someone. Some people undoubtedly wish they had never become involved in owning investment real estate, for personal reasons, or a bad buy, but the majority of owners are whistling all the way to the bank. How did they get started? What makes one man a wealthy property owner, and another, who had the same opportunities, just another average Joe?

Some got their start in the building trades. They started out as labourers on a house construction job, kept their eyes and ears open, saved their money and, when the opportunity arose to purchase a couple of building lots, they took the plunge, either alone or with a partner. The demand for houses was constant, they worked hard and stuck to business, and eventually ended up being one of the big ones, or at least moderately successful.

Others did it through education. Becoming a lawyer, for example, is one of the surest ways to financial success. It not only gives one a great education into legal aspects of how other people make money, but it puts one close to these people and great opportunities to get involved.

Some people simply inherit estates. Others are talked into buying by salesmen; stumble onto a good thing; lend a man money and foreclose; marry property; obtain it by accepting real estate to settle a debt; or find themselves sitting on a gold mine due to re-zoning, and, realizing the potential, go right out and buy more. But the majority of investment properties are owned by people who went head on into it after a lot of thought, and plunged the bankroll into the financial whirlpool that is the greatest money maker of all time — real estate.

If you have worked hard for years, watched the pennies and saved diligently, it is not always an easy thing to bring yourself to write out a cheque that will seemingly wipe out your life savings. You watched that bank book balance grow over the years, and sometimes it is a bit of a shock to look at it after all these years and find it so depleted, regardless of the knowledge that it left the bank and ended up as bricks and mortar.

If you have felt the urge to get involved, and have a timid heart, or nagging doubts about going it alone, don't. Get a partner. Someone you have known for some time. Someone you feel is a very solid type, with a good clear head on his shoulders, but especially one who has the kind of money you are considering as your investment. You can always be a minor or major shareholder, but don't set the scales too far off balance. If your allowance for this venture is modest, get two or three partners. After you do buy the property, you can always sell your share to your partners under your agreement if it doesn't work out.

Before you consider buying *any* property, you naturally have to know something about it, and you should know as much about it as possible.

Have the investment listing form shown on the following page copied. It will enable you to have a clear picture and record of every property you inspect. It is basically intended for listing apartment buildings, but can effectively be used for any type of investment property.

Five points: location; condition of building; income; expenses and proper financing.

The ideal location for an apartment building, for example, is always close to main traffic arteries. Not right on them; close to them. Traffic creates noise, and regardless of what you have heard about "getting used to it", it can still create problems with tenants, who didn't realize what they were getting into. Being near the main artery provides your tenants with transportation. It is nice to take a 4-block walk to the bus on a sunny spring day, but in the winter? Proper location will provide you with a better chance of keeping the building fully occupied.

If you have had no experience with the ins-and-outs of building construction, and you find a property that seriously interests you to the point of submitting a respectable offer, get some expert advice. Buildings that have been mortgaged through an approved lender of Central Mortgage and Housing Corporation are built to its standards, so you won't have to be very concerned about the quality of construction. Sloppy maintenance and appearance of the property can be blamed on poor management, a careless superintendent or inconsiderate tenants. This can be corrected. A badly constructed building is another matter.

Don't be dazzled by an income figure that seems great. It may be too high. You should check rental figures in the immediate area for comparable accommodation. If the figures are too high in your comparison, you could be in trouble at a later date. Work on the averages.

Despite the "audited statement" of expenses you may see, you should again speak to someone familiar with the expenses of operating comparable buildings. The average figures will give you an indication of what you may expect after ownership, regardless of what the owner tells you. Of course, there are many ways to cut down the expenses, and you should look critically at each item. Heat control is a good example. Some superintendents just blast away with the heat to forestall any possible telephone calls from a tenant with a complaint. The lack of storm windows is another thing to watch for in the heating bills. Is the hot water heated off the furnace or does it have its own unit? Are the garage doors properly controlled to remain closed? There isn't much point in having your financing well considered if the expenses are going to knock you right into a nil balance or debit.

When you have satisfied yourself as to the gross income and operating expenses (including taxes, which are easy to check), you have two other items to consider, which will come under operating expenses.

Bldg. Name _____

& Address _____

PRICE $ _____

CASH $ _____

1st Mortgagee _____

Amount $ _____ At _____ % Due _____

Payable $ _____

2nd Mortgagee _____

Amount $ _____ At _____ % Due _____

Payable $ _____

GROSS ANNUAL INCOME _____

OPERATING EXPENSES

Taxes _____

Insurance _____

Heating _____

Light _____

Water _____

Maintenance _____

Supplies _____

Elevator _____

Superintendent _____

Misc. & Audit _____

Management _____

Vacancy Allce _____

_____

_____

_____

_____

Income Before Debt Charges $ _____

MORTGAGE PAYMENTS

1st mortgage _____

2nd mortgage _____   _____

Net Cash Surplus (%) $ _____

PRINCIPAL PAYMENTS

(Average _____ years)

On 1st mortgage _____

On 2nd mortgage _____   _____

GROSS RETURN (%) $ _____

Estimated Capital Cost
Allowance 1st Year $ _____

SUITES ( )	MONTHLY	ANNUALLY
_____ Bachelor	_____	_____
_____ 1 Bedroom	_____	_____
_____ 2 Bedroom	_____	_____
_____ 3 Bedroom	_____	_____
_____ 4 Bedroom	_____	_____
_____ Garages	_____	_____
_____ Spaces	_____	_____
_____ Laundry	_____	_____
Sundry Income:	_____	_____

GROSS ANNUAL INCOME _____

Assessment Land: _____
         Building: _____
Construction _____

Fireproof _____	Age _____
Lot _____	Laundry _____
No. Storeys _____	Refrig. _____
Brick _____	Stoves _____
Incinerator _____	Inter-Com. _____
Heating _____	Lobby _____
Floor Suite _____	Rec. Pl. G. _____
Floor Hall _____	Air-Cond. _____
Elevator _____	Balconies _____

REMARKS

Vacancy allowance: It was customary a few years ago to charge a minimum of 5% of the gross income as an allowance for vacancies. Recently, this figure has been reduced because of low vacancy factors. You must decide what this figure should be in view of present and foreseeable expectancy in vacancies. An argument you will undoubtedly receive today from vendors is that why should there be *any* vacancy allowance when the building is filled and with possibly a waiting list of tenants?

Management: Larger buildings will usually be managed by contract at anything from a flat fee to 3%–5% of the gross income. Some owners spend their own time actively managing their own properties, and the owners of small buildings invariably manage their own. No matter who manages the building, the time is worth money, and this should not be forgotten in the debit side of the ledger.

Now, deducting all these expenses and allowances from the gross income, you arrive at the net income before financing. This is where the importance in mortgaging enters the picture. The more you save, or the less your outlay in mortgage payments, the more money you will have in your pocket as your net cash flow. As I have pointed out, your expense will include the principal payment as well as the interest.

There are just three ways to stretch the mortgage and make this item of expense thinner; lower interest rate, lengthy amortization, and smaller or no principal payments.

If you are going to assume an existing mortgage, there is nothing you can do about the rate of interest. If you are going to arrange a conventional mortgage, there is little you can do to lower the going, or current rate of interest. The only possible saving you might have is in the event of equitable financing on the part of the vendor. If the vendor will agree to accept a mortgage from you as part of your purchase price, you might be able to get a lower than conventional rate of interest from him. However, sometimes the only inducement for this as far as the vendor is concerned is a higher top price. So don't count on the possibility of saving money on the mortgage rate of interest.

The longer the period of mortgage amortization, the smaller the payments. The smaller the payments, the more cash in your pocket. The following will illustrate this; carrying charges per thousand dollars, per month:

9% mortgage, interest compounded twice-yearly

Years		Years		Years	
9	$13.46	18	$9.26	27	$8.12
10	12.58	19	9.07	28	8.05
11	11.87	20	8.89	29	7.98
12	11.29	21	8.74	30	7.93
13	10.80	22	8.60	31	7.88
14	10.39	23	8.48	32	7.83
15	10.06	24	8.38	33	7.79
16	9.75	25	8.28	34	7.75
17	9.49	26	8.19	35	7.72

Of course, the longer the amortization, the longer it will take to reduce the debt to zero. Some people aren't too concerned about long term debt for two reasons; it produces a higher cash flow and gives the borrower a higher tax deduction due to the interest charges.

Another reason is that future payments are made with cheaper dollars.

The difference between a 20 and a 30 year amortization plan in the above example amounts to $11.52 per year per thousand dollars. This means a plus or minus in your net cash surplus of $11.52 per year for every thousand dollars you have mortgaged. For example, on a $50,000 mortgage this amounts to a difference up or down of $576 per year to you in your hand.

The more money you owe, the more interest you pay, and the more interest you pay, the higher the figure you will show on your income tax return as a deductible item.

One thing you must remember to watch for very carefully is the *term* of the mortgage, or the length of time you have to reduce the debt using somebody else's money.

If your mortgage is *amortized* for 30 years, with a *term* of 5 years, what happens in 5 years? The balance of the debt is due forthwith. If the mortgagee doesn't feel inclined to renew the mortgage, you have to arrange to borrow funds somewhere else. This can be costly. It involves discharging one mortgage and paying the tariff for the new one. Get the longest term you can, or at least an agreement to renew the loan at the end of the 5 years.

The third means of reducing the mortgage payment expense, and thereby leaving you with more cash in your hand, is by having small, or no payments to make on the principal sum. This, of course, will mean that some day you will have a day of reckoning when the principal sum becomes due at the end of the term, but in the meantime it will provide you with more cash.

Financing is the big thing. You want to obtain a reasonable return on your investment, so you will naturally want to be clear on the four steps of investments.

1. The money you have left after deducting the operating expenses and vacancy allowance from the gross income is the *net return before financing,* or *income before debt charges.*

2. The money you have left after deducting the mortgage interest and principal payments from this figure is the *net return, or cash flow, or net cash surplus.*

3. The figure shown after you *add* the mortgage principal payment to the net return, is the *gross return.*

4. From this figure you deduct your capital cost allowance (depreciation) if it is necessary, or desirable to take it, and the figure you have left is what you will show on your income tax return as taxable income.

We have already gone through the stage of arriving at the net return before financing, and we have discussed the mortgaging. Therefore, all the operating expenses of the building *and* the total yearly mortgage payments (interest and principal) deducted from the gross income will take us to the end of the second step, and leave a figure that represents the net return, or cash in your hand.

When the mortgage payments were made they included the principal payment, and, insofar as your net cash flow is concerned, they represent an item of expense. However, the government doesn't take the same attitude, and as far as Ottawa is concerned, the only expense you have in connection with a mortgage, for income tax purposes, is the interest you have paid. So now you have reached the end of the year with about 10% cash return on your investment, and the government says you made more than that as far as they are concerned, so you have to add the mortgage principal payments you made to the 10%, or net cash flow you have, to arrive at your *gross* return on your investment for income tax purposes.

The only way you can reduce this figure is by taking as much capital cost allowance, or depreciation yearly as the law allows, and deducting it from your gross, or income tax return, figure. This final figure will be what you will use as your taxable figure on the operation for income tax purposes.

The Capital Cost Allowance

A Building is a term of wide range covering any structure with walls and a roof affording protection and shelter. The courts have held that the word structure includes anything of substantial size which is built up from component parts and intended to remain permanently on a permanent foundation. Portable shelters such as housing, office and other service units are also regarded as buildings if they are installed and intended to remain in a particular location.

The *Capital Cost of Property* means the full cost to the buyer and in addition to the cost of the real property includes such things as legal, accounting, engineering or other fees where they are incurred in order to acquire the property.

When purchasing an investment property, the capital cost of the building is separated from the capital cost of the land. The reason for this is very simple — land cannot be depreciated for income tax purposes — just the building.

One popular method of doing this has been to take the ratio of municipal assessment for the property and apply it as a guide. However, the income tax department will not always accept this, so it would be advisable to obtain expert advice in placing the value on the building. Also, some Provinces are now using a "market value" assessment, which unfortunately does not show the separated value of land and building.

Assuming you purchased a building and land for a total of $100,000, with a fair separated value of (1) land, $20,000 and (2) building, $80,000 the $80,000 would be your capital cost for income tax purposes, in determining your capital cost allowance, or "depreciation".

Depreciation allowances are not all the same. Some are greater than others. The most common is a "class 3" building, which is brick, blocks, etc. and has a 5% rate. Frame buildings have a 10% rate.

In each taxable year, you are allowed, for example, in "class 3" to take an income tax deduction of a maximum of 5% of the undepreciated balance of the capital cost of the building.

The first year's allowable depreciation on the $80,000 would be $4,000. The second year, 5% of the undepreciated balance of $80,000 minus $4,000 ($76,000) and so on.

If, for example, the first year showed a net return to you of $3,000 on the operation of a building, you would not take the $4,000 because you would not need it. This would leave an undepreciated balance for the second year of $77,000.

You and the Government keep track of all the depreciation you have taken and on which you have not paid any income tax, because when you sell the building your day of reckoning arrives and you pay tax on it.

The tax is payable at your choice of either (1) all at once in the tax year of selling, or (2) adjusting your past returns over five years.

Depreciation cannot be taken to reduce other areas of income, as it was in the past, and it cannot be transferred to another acquired building to avoid the tax bite.

A depreciation table is in this book to illustrate it for you.

Selling the Building

The "sale price of property" means the *net* sale price after deductions of all fees and commissions paid in connection with the sale.

When you sell a depreciable property and subsequently part or all of an amount owing to you in respect of the asset is reduced pursuant to a negotiated adjustment of the sale price, or pursuant to a legal obligation under a guarantee, warranty, etc., in the agreement of sale, such reduction should be taken into account in the year of sale for the purpose of calculating the amount to be included in income or for the purpose of calculating the undepreciated capital cost of the property.

When you sell depreciable property and the proceeds of disposition include an agreement for sale, or a mortgage on land which agreement or mortgage is subsequently sold by you at a discount from its principal amount, the amount of the discount will, if the sale of the agreement or mortgage takes place in the year of disposition of the depreciable property, reduce the proceeds of disposition.

If the sale of the agreement, or mortgage, takes place subsequent to the year of disposition of the property, the discount will be deductible in computing your income for that year to the extent that the amount of the discount exceeds any capital gain (excess of proceeds over capital cost) calculated at the time of disposition.

Remember the three areas of income tax in selling an investment property:

(1) The profit on the operation of the investment for all or that part of your taxable year in which you own the property.

(2) The "recaptured" tax on the capital cost allowance (depreciation) taken during your ownership.

(3) The capital gain tax now in effect. Review the chapter "Capital Gain Tax Appraisal".

When you have a situation where the land is worth more than the present use of the property as land and buildings, and it is your intention to abandon the buildings (or demolish them) in order to avoid paying a recaptured tax on depreciation, *think twice about it.*

The Supreme Court of Canada has ruled on this point in favour of the income tax department, and this financial gravy train appears to be grinding to a halt.

The Purchase Agreement

When you instruct an agent to prepare an agreement of purchase and sale, the following are points in your offer that should not be over-looked.

The initial part of the offer will cover the financing; deposit with offer, mortgage details, cash on closing (subject to adjustments), and any other financial consideration. Then you get into the property itself, and should note the importance of the following:

"The purchase price shall include all plant, machinery, attachments, fixtures and installations and equipment of every nature and kind, now on the subject property and which are not the exclusive property of the existing tenants, and, without limiting the generality of the foregoing, shall also include the master television antenna and all electrical and other appliances, fixtures and chattels.

The vendor warrants and represents that the apartment building on the subject property comprises (   ) apartment suites and that there are no outstanding orders issued by the Fire, Police, or Health Department of the City of (   ) and/or the Municipality of (   ) requiring change in or addition or alterations to the subject property.

The vendor warrants and represents that it has complied and will continue to comply with all building, zoning and other by-laws of the City of (   ) up to and including the date of closing hereinafter referred to, and that it has not committed or created a nuisance on the subject property.

The vendor warrants and represents that now and at closing,

all mechanical equipment including heating, plumbing, drainage and electrical wiring systems, and elevator equipment and facilities in the subject property, will be in good working order and condition, and that the roofs of all buildings, structures and appurtenances are water-tight and that the basement is dry.

The vendor warrants and represents that Schedule "A" attached hereto sets out all pertinent information for all the tenancies in effect in respect of the subject property, and covenants and agrees that on closing, it will deliver to the purchaser the following: a proper assignment of all leases herein, all copies of all leases herein and directions to each of the tenants herein authorizing payment of rentals thereafter to the purchaser as he may direct.

The vendor covenants and agrees that on closing it will deliver to the purchaser a Statutory Declaration made by one of its officers which will contain the following and other reasonable clauses that may be required by the purchaser:

(1) That the leases referred to in Schedule "A" to the agreement of purchase and sale herein dated (   ) are valid, binding and enforceable in accordance with the terms thereof:

(2) That there are no disputes between the vendor, as landlord, and the said tenants with respect to any matter arising out of the tenancies:

3. That all rent has been paid to the (   ) day of (   ) and that there are no prepayments or rent beyond the current monthly rental: (Note: if there are, this will be settled in the adjustments on closing and credited to the purchaser).

(4) That none of the said leases have been assigned nor have any of the tenants sublet the premises leased to them:

(5) That the leases have not been amended, changed or varied in any way whatsoever, and

(6) That there are no other tenancy arrangements affecting the subject property other than those set out in the said Schedule "A" to the Agreement of Purchase and Sale dated (   ).

The vendor shall within fifteen (15) days after acceptance, supply to the purchaser all plans, specifications, sketches, drawings and up-to-date surveys of the subject property.

On closing, the vendor shall assign to the purchaser all contracts and the benefit thereof, made by it in respect of the subject property, and the vendor shall further deliver all licenses, agreements, books, records and accounts and, without limiting the generality of the foregoing, all other documents, information and papers in the possession of the vendor relating to the subject property.

The vendor warrants and represents that the gross income received by it for the fiscal year ending (   ) was (   ).

The within offer and the obligation of the purchaser to complete the within transaction is entirely conditional upon verification by the vendor to the purchaser of the fulfillment of all conditions, warranties and representations herein set out.

Provided the title is good and free from all encumbrances except as aforesaid: The purchaser is not to call for the production of any title deed, abstract or other evidence of title except as are in the possession of the vendor. The purchaser is to be allowed until closing to investigate the title at his own expense. If with that time any valid objection to title is made in writing to the vendor which the vendor shall be unable or unwilling to remove and which the purchaser will not waive, this agreement shall, notwithstanding any intermediate acts or negotiations in respect of such objections, be null and void and the deposit shall be returned to the purchaser without interest or deductions. Save as to any valid objection so made within such time, the purchaser shall be conclusively deemed to have accepted the title of the vendor to the subject property.

The sale of the subject property shall be made in accordance with the Bulk Sales Act (Province) and the Retail Sales Act (Province) and the vendor hereby, covenants, undertakes and agrees to comply with all the provisions thereof and to pay all taxes and costs in connection therewith.

This offer is to be accepted by (   ) otherwise void: and sale is to be completed on or before the (   ) on which date possession is to be given to the purchaser subject to the tenancies herein set out, and the purchaser to be entitled to the receipt of the rents and profits thereafter.

This offer, when accepted, shall constitute a binding contract of purchase and sale and time in all respects shall be the essence of this agreement.

Until completion of sale, all buildings and equipment on the subject property shall be and remain at the risk of the vendor until closing and the vendor will hold all policies of insurance affected on the subject property and the proceeds thereof in trust for the parties hereto, as their interests may appear. In the event of damage to the subject buildings and equipment before the completion of this transaction, the purchaser shall have the right to elect to take such proceeds and complete the purchase, or cancel this agreement whereupon the purchaser shall be entitled to the return without interest of all monies theretofore paid on account of this purchase without deductions.

Unearned fire insurance premiums, mortgage interest, rentals, taxes, fuel, water rates and heating to be apportioned and allowed to date of completion of sale.

Deed or transfer and assignment of leases to be prepared at the expense of the vendor, and mortgage at the expense of the purchaser.

Any tender of documents or money hereunder may be made

upon the vendor at (address) and upon the purchaser at (address) or any party acting for him or it and money may be tendered by negotiable cheque certified by a chartered bank or trust company in the City of (   ).

This offer and its acceptance are to be read with all changes of gender or number required by the context.

Dated at (   ) this (   ).

Witness:

....
Purchaser

Good luck!

28

Buying a Farm

Getting away from it all by moving into the country and becoming a farmer, gentleman or otherwise, is not something to do on the spur of the moment. One's first winter away from urban amenity will take care of the city slicker.

Fortunately, Federal and Provincial Governments are anxious to keep the man on the land. Farm attrition, coupled with Canada's ever increasing population, results in the Governments' full cooperation in assisting one to get the plow moving and the cows milked as quickly as possible.

In searching, the best sources of information about farms that are for sale or rent are *farm* real estate agents, advertisements in *farm* magazines, *farm* newspapers, and rural newspapers.

The logical farm real estate agents will be ones in rural communities and towns. The local boys. Drive around the country, pick your location, and visit nearby agents. Also, pick up a copy of the area's weekly newspaper.

If you become seriously interested in an area, or a particular farm, talk to neighbouring farmers about the land. Contact the local Provincial Government agricultural agent, and talk to him about the land. You must know about the land, unless of course you are just loking for a 100 acre building lot in the country.

Take advantage of the many services provided by Provincial and Federal Agricultural departments.

The Department of Agriculture of the Federal Government carries on research into the physical and economic problems of agriculture. Experimental farms and research laboratories are located in various parts of the country. The results of this work are made available to farmers by means of bulletins, posters, articles in newspapers and farm magazines, and radio and television programs. Information on markets and prices for agriculture products is distributed in daily and weekly reports on radio and television, in farm magazines, and some newspapers.

Each province has an agricultural extension service with a rrepresentative located in each county or district. These agents interpret research data for farmers, provide assistance and advice in resolving problems, distribute extension bulletins, and give short courses on various aspects of farm management and other subjects. In addition, the extension services usually have a staff of consultants in specialized fields who may be asked for advice. Some of the extension services have home economists on staff who provide extension education services for the ladies.

Many agricultural marketing and supply firms have staff to advise farmers. For example, feed companies give advice on rations for livestock and poultry; building supply firms on building construction; chemical companies on the use of pesticides and herbicides; fertilizer companies on fertilizers and cultural practices; grain marketing companies on grain varieties and markets.

Also, many colleges and vocational schools have special short courses designed for farmers.

Financial Aspects of the Farm

The amount of capital needed to start farming on a full-time basis depends on the type of farm, the productivity of the soil, the proximity of the farm to markets, and whether the farmer buys or rents.

A farmer specializing in the production of hogs or poultry requires a small acreage of land compared with a wheat farmer but has a large investment in buildings and livestock. A cattle rancher, in common with the wheat producer, needs a large acreage of land but ranchland usually costs much less per acre than cropland. Lands near large urban centers naturally cost more than lands farther away.

The capital requirements of a beginning farm operator can be lessened if he rents land and equipment. However, competition from established operators greatly reduces the opportunities for him to obtain enough land for an efficient operation by renting. Purchasing used machinery, and hiring, borrowing or exchanging large machines are other means of reducing the initial investment, but starting with less machinery and equipment than is necessary for an efficient operation makes it difficult for a beginning farmer to compete with his established neighbours.

Volume of business is one of the chief things to consider when starting to farm. Reducing capital requirements by obtaining a smaller acreage of land or fewer livestock than is necessary for an efficient farm unit results in a small business. Unfortunately, the operator of a small farm usually finds it difficult to increase the size of his operation.

Financing the Purchase

The one selling the farm sometimes accepts a mortgage for a substantial part of the purchase price, which simplifies the financing. If this cannot be done, go after the Government.

Several government agencies lend money to farmers to finance the purchase. The Farm Credit Corporation of the federal government is the main source of this type of credit, and some provinces have agencies for lending provincial government funds for buying farms.

To be eligible for a loan a borrower must be a bona fide farmer, and under provincial government schemes a borrower must be a resident of the province.

An objective of all government farm credit agencies is to help a farmer establish his farm as a sound economic farm unit. The maximum loan allowed to a farmer is set by legislation and varies from province to province. Legislation of the federal government and some provincial governments provides for more credit and easier collateral to young farmers, but the farm operations are subject to supervision by the lending agency until the loan is reduced to a certain level.

Financing the Operation

Farmers may obtain short and intermediate term credit for production, farm improvement and development from several sources.

The federal government: A syndicate of three or more farmers may borrow money from the Farm Credit Corporation for joint purchase of farm machinery. Loans are secured by a promissory note signed by all membes of the syndicate.

Farm owners whose main income is derived from farming may obtain a loan for construction of a new house, or the remodelling of an existing house, under the terms of the National Housing Act. The Central Mortgage and Housing Corporation, administering the Act, insures loans made by approved lenders — life insurance companies, trust and loan companies, and banks, and may make loans when insured loans are not available from approved lenders.

Provincial governments: Most provincial governments provide credit to individual farmers for purchases of farm machinery, livestock, land clearing and drainage.

Commercial banks: Loans may be obtained from the commercial banks for operating capital and other transactions requiring short-term credit. In addition, an intermediate and short-term type of credit is available under the Farm Improvement Loans Act of the federal government. Under a government guarantee for repayment, the banks make loans to buy land, farm machinery and livestock, and to improve or develop a farm.

Credit Unions: Members of a credit union usually may obtain short and intermediate term credit for almost any purpose. Terms under which loans are available depend on the policies of the particular credit union.

Merchants, dealers and finance companies: Credit may be obtained directly or indirectly from dealers wishing to sell their products, and also through loan companies set up specifically to make money loans. This form of credit is usually easier to obtain than others, especially for borrowers with low equity, but interest rates are usually higher than those of other credit sources.

Processing and supply firms: May extend credit as part of what is termed "contract farming". There are various types of contracts, ranging from simple credit deals to profit-sharing arrangements. Company supervision of farm operations is sometimes involved.

With all the smog, noise, dirt, pollution and hurried atmosphere of urban areas, it is understandable why so many are interested in the country. Unfortunately, we must work where the money is, and financial roots are hard to pull.

If you are one of the lucky ones who can make a move to the country, contact the Farm Credit Corporation to enquire about a low-interest loan to help with the farm purchase. Here are the addresses:

British Columbia: P.O. Box 249, 1615 Ellis Street, Kelowna, B.C.
Alberta: 400 Chancery Hall, ♯3 Sir Winston Churchill Sq., Edmonton. P.Z. 15, Alberta.
Saskatchewan: 701 Midtown Tower, 11th Ave. & Hamilton St., Regina, Sask.
Manitoba: P.O. Box 767, 267 Edmonton Street, Winnipeg, Man.
Ontario: 2323 Yonge Street, Toronto 12, Ont.
Quebec: 2700 Laurier Blvd., Ste-Foy, Quebec 10, P.Q.
Atlantic area: P.O. Box 849, 567 St. George Blvd., Moncton, N.B.

29

Some Fringe Benefits of
Country Living

With so much interest in buying farm land and moving to the country, this letter received from Mr. V. C. Fox is published because of its sincerity, and the helpful insight it provides . . .

"Last May I decided that a widower's life was too lonely, and for the birds, and was smiled on from above by being blessed again by getting married to another wonderful girl.

This little lady was born and raised on a farm in the Listowel, Ont., area 45 years ago, and is the oldest of 11 brothers and sisters. Her love and desire to live on the farm was enough to awaken my own long desire to also live that kind of life. So off we went and looked and looked and looked, week-end after week-end, township by township, county by county in South Western Ontario from London north to Owen Sound, west to Lake Huron and east to Guelph.

We found our Shangri-La just north of Clinton (60 miles north of London) 50 acres of gentle rolling land with an ever running spring creek that cuts across the 25 acre pasture for a distance of about 800 feet. Adjacent to the pasture is 22 acres of excellent arable land that has apparently accommodated a corn crop for the past 15-20 years, all tiled for excellent drainage.

The house, equipment shed, large 85′ steel barn, two silos and large garden occupy the remaining 3 acres. Water is supplied to the house, barn and implement shed by a 140 foot drilled well which produces enough water to meet all of our requirements.

I purchased all of this for the total price of $25,750 through the director of the Veterans Land Act, (which is a good deal for veterans). My monthly payment on the V.L.A. loan plus interest is $89.23 plus taxes of approximately $300 per year.

The farm was originally 150 acres and set up for a dairy operation later converted to beef. Prior to my purchase 100 acres were sold off leaving the buildings and 50 acres.

At the time of the purchase I hadn't a clue as to what I should do with the farm except the desire to live there. It wasn't long before our good neighbours gave the "new honeymooners" a rousing welcome and hinted diplomatically what they thought we should do.

We followed their suggestions by first renting the pasture and secondly sowing some corn. From four of my neighbours I contracted their help and equipment to do the job, as follows:

1.	Cultivating 22 acres @ $3.00	$ 66.00
2.	Double discing 22 acres @ $2.25	55.00
3.	Purchase of seed corn and harrowing:	136.00
4.	Sowing the seed corn, 22 acres @ $2.25	49.50
5.	Purchasing and spreading fertilizer:	585.00
6.	Purchasing and spreading weed spray:	135.00
		$1,026.50

In October I contacted another adjacent neighbour who just a year ago installed a large commercial dryer and two large storage bins. He also possessed a 4-row combine and offered to combine my corn, haul it to the dryer, dry it and store it until I wished to sell it. This all sounded good to me, as I was getting somewhat concerned.

In November, one Sunday morning my neighbour arrived with his combine dragging two corn hoppers and his hired hand driving a box truck. They combined and hauled the corn all day (16 hours). He informed me that the yield looked excellent and that it was the best looking corn he had combined all year, particularly since this year was a bad year for corn, mainly caused by the "killer frost" in June that devastated so many crops and caused so many farmers to re-plant which in some instances never correctly matured as it would have in a normal season's growth. My loss to the frost was very minimal, in that there were only two short rows affected which were approximately 150 feet long next to my implement shed.

We took off 1980 bushels of corn which has been dried and stored. At this date the published price is $1.51–$1.53 per bushel, with indications that the demand would raise this figure by February and March. Even at $1.53 per bushel my sale of 1980 bushels should realize approximately $3,000.

Now deducting the total cost of planting which was $1,000 more or less, the cost of combining and storage which is somewhere near $700, my overall profit for the past corn growing season is:

Sale of crop:	$3,000
Planting and combining:	1,700
Profit:	$1,300

I also rented my 25 acre pasture for a sum of $600 for the period from May to October (6 months).

Therefore, without even getting physically involved, such as doing any of the work myself, I am to realize a net profit of $1,900 for the season which when added to all the other benefits of country living, isn't bad. At least I feel I have been fortunate in having a good start in this new venture.

We are presently remodelling my old farm house, and getting a lot of happiness in doing it.

Now that we are experiencing peace and tranquility at last, and away from the "rat race of city life", my only regret is that I didn't do all of this when I was much younger . . ."

Thank You, Mr. Fox!

30

Buying a Motel

Operating a motel, even a small one, in today's competitive market is not a job for retired persons or even for the semi-retired.

It is a full-time job which frequently demands considerable physical stamina. It demands poise in the face of pressure. It requires an aggressive, business-like approach to profitmaking. To be sure, there is a reasonably good future ahead for the motel business, and for many of those in other branches of the time-honoured calling of innkeeper. But the right starting time is not the year in which one quits work and retires.

The motel industry offers considerable opportunities to persons who are willing to invest adequate sums of money, to discipline themselves, and to adhere faithfully to proved standards of business practice.

On the other hand, anyone entering this business must bear in mind that regardless of how hard and skillfully he works, it is possible to fail anyway, because of an oversupply of motel rooms in some areas (leading to price cutting) or because of business conditions, local or national. In other words, if in your particular area there are too many motel rooms for the number of travellers, whatever the cause, one or more of the motels is going to be forced out of business.

The Basics

Your primary business as a motel operator will be renting rooms to guests, but there are other allied sources of income you may also want to explore.

Motels which have a restaurant on the premises, or nearby, generally are more popular than those which do not. As a motel owner, you may build and operate a restaurant yourself; you may erect the restaurant and lease it to an experienced restauranteur; or you may have no investment whatever in the restaurant, but refer your guests to one that is close by.

Some motels make money on gift shops, or on service stations. Vending machines can add to income. So can auto or boat rentals. And there are other possible profit-producing services. Any extra income, however, is usually peanuts compared with the take from the primary source — room sales. Unless room occupancy keeps above the break-even level, the motel itself will decline, regardless of minor secondary sources of on-premises income.

The motel industry has grown dramatically, and in many areas the competition is fierce. And yet there are other areas begging, through chambers of commerce and other development agencies, for operators to come in and build sorely-needed motels.

Pitfalls

A rude awakening for many novice motel operators occurs when they realize that they have taken on a 24-hour job with no days off.

As a host, you must see to the comfort and happiness of your guests, and as a businessman you must show a profit. These two responsibilities will keep you on the job for long hours and the work is often hard.

You not only must be a good and hospitable desk clerk, you also must be a fair plumber, electrician, advertising man, mechanic, accountant, and interior decorator. Of course, only a very few exceptionally gifted persons can be good at all these jobs, but as a motel manager you must hire personnel competent to perform these tasks, or you frequently will find you must do the best you can in situations for which you may not have been trained.

Physical stamina is essential, which makes motel management a poor choice as a retirement job. This does not mean that some middle-aged couples have not taken up motel owner-managership successfully. But it does mean that retirement is not found in the motel business.

As the operator of a small motel, you may be on your feet all morning as you go about supervising and assisting in the cleaning of rooms, repairing equipment and fixtures, and tending to highway signs. During the afternoon, you may have to get the bookkeeping up to date, purchase supplies, and prepare direct-mail advertising. Meanwhile, you will have to keep smiling, and in the afternoon and evening, greet guests and see that each party is made comfortable. During the night, there may be late arrivals or complaints from persons already roomed that the air conditioning has failed, that plumbing has broken down, or that guests in the next room are too noisy.

If you own and manage your motel, you may find yourself tied to it with seldom a chance for a day off. Rooms must be rented every night, and finding a person who is competent enough to manage the motel, and willing to work only on the occasions when you would like a holiday could be difficult.

Your family must be able to adjust to the confining routine. As a matter of fact, in the owner-managed motel the entire family usually works at various motel chores, and the temperament and training of each member must be considered.

There will be other pitfalls over which you may have little or no control. You may have an excellent location and do a good business — but others are aware of it and may build a bigger, better motel near yours. You may think the future looks cozy, but your Provincial highway department may decide it is necessary to by-pass your community or build a super-highway which will take away your direct access to traffic lanes.

Hazards

In fires, storms, and other natural disasters, you may find your insurance doesn't fully cover you, particularly if you count the business you lose, due to the disaster. Also, the death of a guest on your premises could result in a lawsuit which could hurtle you into bankruptcy, if your negligence is proved, and your insurance is inadequate. Or a dishonest employee may slowly rob you into insolvency through the almost invisible techniques of embezzlement.

Your biggest danger is also your greatest asset; *You*. It is your managerial abilities which will make or break your motel. It is your ability to act as a good host and a good salesman, day in and dy out. It is your success in building and maintaining a high room occupancy rate at adequate price levels which will determine whether your motel will make money or lose it.

Your attitude toward your business, your dealings with your guests, with your fellow motel operators, with your suppliers, and with all other persons with whom you come in contact in the course of your business will have a direct bearing on your success or failure.

Qualities you need

Ask yourself how well you are prepared for these essentials of motel management:

1. Ability to work long, hard hours.

2. Willingness to accept the confinement to the job (the smaller the motel, the less freedom for the operator).

3. Ability to deal tactfully with people, many of whom may have been travelling under difficult conditions all day and are not in the friendliest mood.

4. Knack of being a good host, making guests feel wanted, and anticipating their needs.

5. Constant awareness and practice of public relations.

6. Willingness to cope with all kinds of problems, which may range from a coin jammed in a soft drink machine to a guest who suffers a heart attack at 3 a.m.

7. Some knowledge of business management, personnel handling, accounting, and sales promotion, plus being a general handyman for do-it-yourself repairs and maintenance.

8. An appreciation of how important it is for you to take an active role in affairs affecting the entire motel industry, acting through joint efforts with others like yourself in local, Provincial and national motel trade associations.

9. Ambition to improve your own standards as a motel manager by studying books and journals on the subject; attending short schools, seminars and expositions; keeping abreast of current industry developments; and otherwise training yourself and your helpers.

10. Executive ability at least to the extent that you can and will be able to delegate authority.

Judging a Motel Location

Actually, only the record of a motel's profitability over a long period can be the final test of whether its location is good. The fact that you are beside a busy highway isn't enough, for a thousand passing automobiles are not worth the single car that stops and discharges guests who rent rooms.

In searching for a good motel location, keep these fundamental principles in mind:

1. The trading area must have an adequate potential. Look beyond the motel industry itself. If retail business generally is declining, if the region is losing population and otherwise slipping downward, a motel also may face a struggle for existence.

Of course, on the other hand, the area you are considering may show no immediate evidence of current progress, but still have some good potential for the near future. Perhaps you will find out that a sizeable new factory is being started, or that other industries will be expanded. Possibly you will learn that two super-highways will be completed with an intersection at a nearby point. Or perhaps your survey will disclose the fact that the proposed location is in a good spot between two growing urban areas and that highway changes between the two centers could conceivably generate business for the motel.

2. Guests should be able to get to the motel easily, and with a minimum of confusion.

If access to your place is difficult and if the directional signs are bewildering, strangers may give up after one try at finding you and will go on and stop somewhere else.

3. You should pick your location with a view to whether it is a convenient stopping place for travellers. Locations which are an average day's drive from major centers are likely to be good. Even a motel in an inconspicuous location can succeed if it is just about the right distance from a big city. Usually, however, more business can be intercepted at well-travelled highway interchange points, and of course near airports.

4. A group of motels often can help each other. In fact, each

one seems to do better when several of them are not far apart. This is partly because many travellers like to shop around before they reach a decision and sign the register. Travellers who know there are several motels at a given location will drive to that point.

Additional business develops also when there are large meetings that cannot be handled by a single motel. The delegates will occupy several in the same area.

5. Compatibility with other nearby businesses is desirable. Some types of enterprises help to build motel volume, while others drive potential guests away. Restaurants, drug stores, service stations, and similar businesses serving needs of the travelling public are assets to a location. Junk yards, railroad yards, slums and noisy or dirty neighbourhoods do not invite the traveller.

6. Although, as noted, competing motels can sometimes work together to mutual advantage, the prospective operator nevertheless should try to find out whether there will be too much competition for the business available. He should find out how many rooms there are in motels and other tourist accommodations in the area, and what percentage of them are occupied on an average night.

7. The prospective owner-manager should learn as much as he can about other possible hazards. For example, will the zoning bylaws of the municipality permit a livestock yard to be built next door? (A little extreme but you get the point.) Are there any plans for highway relocation which would result in the motel being by-passed by the bulk of the traffic?

The location will be a key factor in determining the type of motel you eventually build or buy. It will determine whether you will have a small one or a large one, whether you will offer nothing but room rentals, and whether you will need a swimming pool, restaurant, gift shop, barber shop, bellman, rooms with kitchenettes and a lot of other extra services. It will determine whether your customers will be mostly vacationers, or parents visiting children in college, or salesmen.

Remember the three most vital factors: (1) location (2) location (3) location.

The Established Motel

There are certain advantages in buying an established motel. New motels require from 6 to 18 months to go through a shake-down period during which daily operations are smoothed out and a regular clientele is developed. However, a successful existing motel will have already been through this shake-down. Personnel will be trained and on the job. The advertising and public relations programs will have attained some momentum. The motel perhaps will have acquired a solid reputation.

You also should be aware of the disadvantages of buying an established motel:

1. What changes would you expect to make in the property and in its established ways of doing business?

2. How much extra money would be required to correct deficiencies and shortcomings in the motel's construction and methods of doing business?

3. Is the motel in danger of losing its recommendation by an Association or referral agency? Why?

4. Has the motel acquired an unwholesome local reputation which may take years to overcome?

5. Are the established rates in line with others in the area? Does the motel enjoy favourable comparison with others in the area?

The Purchase Price

In evaluating the price, keep in mind these helpful points:

1. Appearance is perhaps the most important single factor in attracting business to a motel, but it might be a secondary matter in buying one. This is because external appearance can be changed, if you're willing to spend the money to do it. However, before you buy, you must get the facts about the structural quality of the buildings themselves. Are the foundations adequate? Roofing enduring? Rooms soundproof? Wiring adequate? Notice whether the builder cut corners to save costs.

2. Don't be misled by gracious living quarters for the owner or by spacious and attractive lawns, a big lobby or by wide curving sidewalks. These are nice, but they won't directly produce revenue for you. They mean the present owner has put a lot of money into these extras, and that the price he will try to get you to pay will include the cost of these things.

3. Inspect the books. Pay no heed to claims of unrecorded income or to estimates of income. If the books are not made available to you, just forget that particular deal. Once you have the full financial records, you'll want to divide the gross annual revenue by the number of rooms to get the actual "per room per year" figure, one of the most accurate measurements of motel achievement. Let your accountant see the books too!

4. Consider factors not related to the books. The current owner may have had to operate under conditions you will not have to face (for example, a long period of severe weather or of highway reconstruction). Also, consider whether you'll have to spend additional money for expansion or upgrading. Place a realistic value on the motel's earned reputation, for good or ill.

5. You are accepting the new burden, so buy for yourself, not the seller. Try to find out and take into account his reasons for selling.

If the price looks too low, the proposed deal should be scrutinized carefully. Remember that successful operations do not have to be sold at salvage prices. Pay for fair value. Also, be sure to obtain a satisfactory agreement that will prevent the seller from re-entering the motel business in the same area, thus becoming your competitor.

Firms which sell products may miss a sale today but sell it tomorrow for the same profit. Revenue from a motel room not rented tonight, however, never can be regained — it is lost forever. Fixed expenses continue, nevertheless.

In view of the size of the investment and the risk, one should give plenty of time and thought to reach a decision about going into this business. Do not be rushed.

31

Buying a Mobile Home

A misnomer perhaps?

They are called mobile homes because a set of wheels comes with each one, enabling it to be moved. However, today's mobile home is usually hauled from the factory to a lot in a subdivision, or private property, and permanently secured for years to come.

The permanence can be illustrated by the financial backing of the Royal Bank and Central Mortgage and Housing Corporation for 8¾% mortgage loans made on a large subdivision near Barrie, Ontario, called Sandycove Acres.

This large project covers 170 acres of land. It will provide homeowners with paved roads, curbs, sewers, landscaping and street lights; a private community beach and marina, two swimming pools and a centre for recreation, meetings, etc.

All homes are sold furnished, with prices starting at less than $12,000. This does not include the land, which is leased by the home-owner.

The implications are obvious. This type of housing is a logical answer for one of limited means who is unable to purchase a "conventional" home. Excluding camp trailers, there are more than 100,000 mobile homes now in Canada, 90% of which are used as year-round residences.

Despite the increasing popularity in this type of accommodation, the major drawback appears to be focused on municipal by-laws. Some municipalities are prone to look upon the proposal of a mobile home subdivision as another "trailer park" which would not enhance their image of a solid community. This view is supported by the severe restrictions on such developments now in force in many urban centers of Canada.

It therefore follows that if you are interested in buying a mobile home that is not a part of an approved subdivision or licensed park, the zoning by-laws of the municipality should be carefully checked to ensure that you can live in it once you buy it.

Today's mobile homes are truly something to see. They are usually 12 feet wide and 56 feet long (maximum dimensions for highway shipment in Canada) which provided about 670 sq. ft. of living space. Two units can be put together creating a 1,340 sq. ft. home.

The heating is mostly warm air, oil fired. Hot water tanks electric. Bedrooms are small and storage space limited. Walls thin but well insulated, prefinished panelling and aluminum siding — easy maintenance.

They are completely prefabricated, transported to the site and installed on a concrete slab, hooked up to services and ready for occupancy.

The author has received letters asking about the depreciation of the mobile home, and to answer this point it was tossed into the lap of C.M.H.C. which made some sensible observations, from which I quote:

"The mobile home has been considered and dealt with as a vehicle parked on a commercial parking lot rather than as a home in the traditional sense. Probably because of this and because of the marketing techniques that have been associated with the mobile home, i.e. dealership similar to the automobile industry, there has been in the past a high depreciation rate in the first few years of use. This fact is frequently overlooked by the purchasers of mobile homes who contemplate comparatively short tenures.

"Our research to date has indicated that the modern mobile very infrequently moves the second time. Because it is parked on a short term leasehold interest, the effect of market for a resale is considerably limited and frequently turns out to be the original selling dealer. There is nothing to suggest that the modern mobile home depreciates physically any more rapidly than conventionally built housing. There has been a decline of market or economic obsolescence that has come about because of the rapid improvement of the mobile home both in its physical nature and its dimensions over the past ten years. With the substantial use of the "double-wide" becoming the prevalent market we would expect this process to continue into the future at a much slower rate.

"We have been endeavouring to persuade the public that the mobile home is in fact another form of system building producing an acceptable small dimension single family house, a product that has not been extensively marketed in the last few years. As such, placed on a properly designed subdivision, rationalized properly into the community and adequately serviced, the mobile home can be the subject of long term financing and we have insured loans with an amortization period of as long as 20 years on such housing. As and if practices change along the lines suggested above we would anticipate depreciation, or more properly, decline in price on resale, will be considerably less than previous experience."

The author's research has indicated that the foregoing is essentially apropos to what the experience of mobile home owners in Florida has been for years. As long as the home remains in an attractive surrounding and properly cared-for condition, there is little likelihood of a noticeable drop in value.

However, it was pointed out, if one moves a home from its "home" to a less attractive location, *Look Out!*

If your pocketbook tells you to investigate the possibility of a mobile home, go and look at a few. If possible, inspect a mobile home subdivision.

Also, write to the Canadian Mobile Home & Travel Trailer Association, 55 York Street, Toronto 1, Ontario, for details. It can also make available for you a 13½ minute, colour-sound, motion picture illustrating the advantages of mobile home living in Canada.

32

You and the Landlord

An agreement for a lease, or an accepted offer to lease, is not a lease. The agreement provides for the execution of a document — the lease.

The agreement contains the basic terms of the lease, the lessor and the lessee, a description of the property to which exclusive possession is to be given, the stipulated rent, and when payable, the term, and commencement date. From these essentials, the lessor and lessee carry on with their particular terms and fine print for the lease.

There are basically three types of leases:

Net Lease: The *lessee's* responsibility embraces all the municipal charges and property operating expenses.

Gross Lease: The *lessor's* responsibility embraces all the municipal charges and property operating expenses, but this is quite often watered down in the lease by requiring the lessee to pay for one or more of the operating expenses, such as heating, janitor, cleaning, hydro, and hot water.

Percentage Lease: The lessor receives, as rent, an agreed upon percentage of the lessee's gross business sales.

There are two common methods in practice:

(a) The lessee agrees to pay a fixed rent *or* an agreed percentage of his gross sales to the lessor, whichever is greater.

(b) The lessee agrees to pay a fixed rent, *plus* an agreed percentage of his gross sales over and above an agreed annual sales figure, to the lessor.

If the rent resulting from a percentage lease is greater than the basic rent, the additional rent paid is called "overage". This can sometimes produce startling and pleasant returns to the lessor, at the same time possibly giving him an inflated idea of the value of his property, but a sophisticated investor will recognize this "overage", not as a fixed return to be used as a basis of true valuation, but something subject to the vagaries of the buying public and the economy of the municipality, and certainly not guaranteed. Buying property leased on this basis, and allowing the "overage" to be used as a basis for additional property valuation, is quite often a calculated risk, and possible gamble.

If you are going to rent an apartment, you will usually be

required to deposit a sum of money with an application equal to one month's rent. The lessor then checks your application to ensure that you will be reasonably able to maintain regular payments of rent. If he approves of you as a tenant, he will invariably shove a document under your nose and say "sign here". *Don't Do It.* Take the document to a lawyer and ask him what it is you are required to sign, and ask him to outline the rights of lessor and lessee in the terms of the document. A responsible landlord can have no valid objection to waiting one or two days while you determine what you are doing.

A Form of Apartment Rent Control that Can Work

If one mentions rent control to a landlord, the suggestion will undoubtedly draw a stern look of abhorrence. On the other hand, if the landlord mentions an increase in rent, he will probably have the look returned.

There could be a solution, and a fair one to both landlord and tenant in apartment buildings.

The owner of a building, having a financial investment at stake, is being reasonable in his assumption that he should receive a fair return on his money.

One of the problems in renting an apartment, especially when it involves a lease, is the landlord's knowledge that his maintenance costs and municipal taxes are surely going to rise during the tenancy, and this is an unknown factor to him.

A commercial lease, which is usually executed for a longer period of time than an apartment lease, will likely contain agreements covering future increases in maintenance and taxes. These agreements are called escalation clauses.

This clause guarantees that the lessor (landlord) will suffer no financial loss by these future increases. If the lessee occupies 10 per cent of the area of the building, he will agree to pay, under the clauses, an increase in rent equal to 10 per cent of any increase in maintenance and taxes charged to the lessor during the term of the lease.

This enables the lessor to give a long term lease to his tenant, by ensuring that the lessor will be reasonably assured of a fixed return on his investment. If he had to bear increased taxes and maintenance over 5 to 10 years without receiving any increase in rent, he would be in a precarious financial position.

So it is with the apartment building owner. When he initially gives one a two year lease, he bases the rent on a projection that will give him a fair return. At the end of the two years, taxes and maintenance costs will have invariably increased, and he is forced to increase his rent to compensate for it.

An apartment tenant can only see the monthly increase. Moving means a new address, which is very disruptive, and inconvenient, and the tenant knows that the costs of moving will often amount to about the same as one year's increase in rent. This results in a feeling that the lessor is taking advantage of him; that the lessor is making too much money. The lessor justifies his demanded rent increases on the strength of increased taxes and maintenance costs, the current yield on money, and little else; unless, of course, he has an insatiable appetite for money.

The rent control that can work is one that the apartment owner imposes on himself and his tenants, by applying the escalation clauses to his apartment leases.

There is no secret about what any increase in taxes will be once the mill rate has been set by the municipality. It is a matter of public record.

In the happy event that a reduction of taxes might occur, the clause could also cover this, thereby slightly reducing the rent, but such a reduction would probably be offset by an increase in maintenance costs.

It could produce interesting results. The yearly statement provided by the lessor to his tenants would clearly outline the tax and maintenance costs for the initial year of the lease (when the tenants' rent is unchanged) and show adjustments to justify any increase in rent.

How could a tenant possibly have any objection to the rent structure under such an agreement; and what objections could a landlord have?

Why, they might even smile at each other!

The Offer to Lease

The balance of this chapter is basically written for lessees other than apartment dwellers. The first document you will sign is an agreement, or "offer to lease". Although the lease will be signed by both parties at a later date, it is well to keep a few points in your mind in your offer to lease. If they are not covered initially, you could be disappointed at a later date after you have made plans to move.

Ownership: It is essential that you determine at the outset just who is the lessor, and verify his authority to lease the property to you. A lease is a conveyance of an estate, and therefore title should be searched by your solicitor in the same manner and extent as though you were purchasing the property. To ensure that you are leasing from proper authority, the identical wording as in an offer to purchase could be used: "Provided the title is good and free from all encumbrances except as aforesaid and except as to any registered restrictions or covenants that run with the land providing that such are complied with".

The reason for establishing title can be obvious if your offer to lease contains the proviso for an option to purchase the property, or your right of first refusal in the event of a prospective sale. Searching title may bring to light registered easements that you may not wish to contend with; and you will most certainly wish to be reassured of your right to possession.

Description of Property: You must first fully determine just what it is you wish to lease. Exactly. Be specific.

For single properties such as a house or small building you wish to lease intact, the municipal address will usually suffice.

Description of a duplex, or triplex, etc., should include your rights for parking, use of the grounds (you may like outdoor barbecues), laundry facilities, and basement area. You might even define your rights of ingress and egress.

Commercial space should include a floor plan of the exact space to be leased, and attached to the offer. It is sometimes advisable to include a survey to properly identify the building and parking spaces, etc.

In *any* offer to lease a *part* of a building, ensure that a proper plan outlining the area, floor number, etc. is included and attached to your offer.

The Rent: Paying the rent is one thing, and knowing what your financial responsibilities encompass is another.

It is advisable to outline exactly what municipal and building operating charges you will pay for, and exactly what your lessor will pay for. Be specific about these charges, *including taxes.*

Check the assessment on the property. If your lease is to contain a tax escalation clause which will require you to pay any *increase* in taxes on your assessed part of the premises, you could be in for a stiff financial jolt if the premises had been renovated and/or improved, and not re-assessed.

Your offer to lease should be checked by a lawyer for your protection and reassurance. He is going to be responsible for ensuring the cognizance of your rights and obligations in the actual lease, so do yourself a favour and let him help you from the beginning. You can be sure that the lessor is going to have a lawyer protect *his* interests!

You and the Landlord

The landlord's basic obligations are (a) covenant for quiet enjoyment, and (b) non-derogation from his grant.

Thousands of pages have been written on the subject of quiet enjoyment, many quoting judgments of higher courts in specific examples.

Basically, it is intended that you, the tenant, should be able to have undisturbed possession and enjoyment of the premises, without being *substantially* interfered with by the lessor. There would be no point in your running to a lawyer and claiming foul because of some minor irritations.

A breach of covenant for quiet enjoyment is almost always the result of some physical interference with the enjoyment of the premises.

While the covenant for quiet enjoyment is applied to a physical interference, the lessor's covenant not to derogate from his grant would be consideration at law for remedy where the covenant for quiet enjoyment would not apply.

The lessee's covenants are usually (a) to pay the rent, with the right of the lessor for re-entry if in default, and, (b) to maintain the premises in good repair. It is well for the lessee to be quite clear about who will pay the taxes, as this may be considered to be a "usual covenant". Spell it out.

On the question of *buying* property, you will find some good advice in the chapter *Caveat Emptor*. When leasing property, take the same attitude. Let the lessee beware! Know what you are leasing. Look the situation over from every angle. Don't take anything for granted, because once the lease is signed, it is signed, and you could find yourself on a sticky wicket.

Remember that a lease has the same effect as a sale of the demised premises for a specified term; in effect, you own the property for the term of the lease. Having the express right of quiet enjoyment, the lessor keeps out unless you agree to allow him access to your leased property, but remember that this places responsibility on your own shoulders, the responsibility that would be yours if you owned the property. The safest attitude to take is that you are in responsible possession; provide yourself with every safeguard — fire and liability insurance, proper maintenance and repair, etc., unless of course it is expressed otherwise in the lease. It is very distressing for a lessee to find that when the leased premises burn down, his business loss not only creates a severe hardship on him, but he is forced to go on paying the rent. The Chinese traders who invented insurance learned their lessons the hard way. All you have to do to protect yourself is call your insurance agent.

Nowhere in real estate is it more important to retain the services of a lawyer than in leasing. This cannot be stressed too strongly.

Check List for Leasing Office Premises
The Location — Check:-

1. Public Transportation (buses, subways, train, airport).
2. Accessibility to Expressway, Parkway and Freeway.
3. Traffic congestion at rush hours.
4. Parking.
5. Restaurants, hotel and convention facilities.

6. Banks, post offices, shopping.
7. Type of neighbourhood. Is it improving, stable or deteriorating?
8. Location of residences of present staff and potential employees.
9. Accessibility for clients, customers and suppliers.

The Space — Check:-
1. Age, quality and image of building.
2. Ownership and reputation of management (are existing tenants satisfied?)
3. Roster of present tenants.
4. How long has space been vacant? Is other space vacant? Why?
5. Number and size of floors, number of tenants (with eye to future expansion, theirs and yours).
6. What is the rental rate per sq. ft.? Is the given floor area accurate? What is the basis used for measurement? Does the measurement include a percentage of common area?
7. Think in terms of cost per month or per annum. An efficient floor layout may well bring a better building within your budget.
8. Allow 150 to 200 sq. ft. per person depending on "Chief to Indian" ratio.
9. Are the following included — if so, are they adequate? heat, water, air conditioning, janitor service, window cleaning, snow removal, landscaping, fluorescent lighting (check candle power), washrooms, elevators, windows (double or single glazed?), window coverings (drapes or blinds?), wiring, soundproofing, floor loading, underfloor ducts, staff coffee and eating facilities.
10. Air conditioning system — does the lessor pay for its maintenance and hydro costs? Will air circulation be effective when partitions are erected?
11. Is there a partition or leasehold improvement allowance? Does the lessor insist on a particular type of partitioning?
12. Who pays for —
    (a) demolition of existing partitions;
    (b) floor tiling, repairs or renewal: does lessee receive a tile credit if he broadlooms instead?
    (c) interior painting of ceiling and walls — does this include interior partitioning?
    (d) changes to air conditioning duct work and lighting;
    (e) power and telephone outlets;
    (f) hydro charges, fluorescent tube replacements, ballasts and starters.

13. In offices previously occupied specify all items to remain for your use, e.g. partitions, counters, shelving, broadloom, drapes or blinds, window air conditioning units.
14. Parking — how many spaces and are they reserved? Are they a part of the lease or can the present monthly cost be increased? Is there additional parking in the area?
15. What is the most desirable lease term? Will longer lease protect against future rent increase or expansion by a larger tenant? Is this type of space in demand so that if necessary could readily be sublet? Has the tenant the right to sublet?
16. If a long lease will the lessor repaint at his cost every five years?
17. Is there an option to renew? If so, at what rental? Is the space under option to another tenant at a later date?
18. Can the lessee be given notice to vacate if the building is sold or demolished? If so, is there any compensation for tenant's improvements?
19. Check if lessee is required to restore premises to their original state on termination of lease.
20. Has the lease a realty tax escalator clause, an escalator clause for operating expenses, or both? What is the base year? In new buildings check how base year relates to extent of completion and percentage of occupancy.
21. Date of possession — check this with the telephone company, contractors, movers, furniture suppliers and allow for delays. Give notice to present landlord. Make sure the tenant has the right of prior entry rent free to prepare the new premises for his use.
22. What are the provisions for signs or identification?
23. What is the position regarding shipping and deliveries? Note if there are charges for use of elevators for furniture, materials or delivery of parcels.
24. Check availability and cost of storage space.
25. Has the building 24 hour access? What time are the doors locked? At what hours or seasons are heat, air conditioning, elevator service curtailed?
26. Note if the landlord levies a fee for the supervision of the installation of tenant's leasehold improvements.

To obtain a copy of the statutes covering landlord and tenant relationships in your province, write the Queen's Printer, as follows:

Address	*Publication*
Newfoundland (St. John's)	The Judicature Act

Quebec (Quebec City)	Rental Commission (An Act to Promote Conciliation between Lessees and Property-Owners)
Nova Scotia (Halifax)	The Overholding Tenants Act
Prince Edward Island (Charlottetown)	The Landlord and Tenant Act
New Brunswick (Fredericton)	The Landlord and Tenant Act
Ontario (Toronto)	The Landlord and Tenant Act
Manitoba (Winnipeg)	The Landlord and Tenant Act
Saskatchewan (Regina)	The Landlord and Tenant Act
Alberta (Edmonton)	The Landlord and Tenant Act
British Columbia (Victoria)	The Landlord and Tenant Act

33

Air and Ground Leases

I don't know who the gentleman was who put the idea of "air rights" into operation, but it is a dandy. It creates municipal income out of nothing, allows larger buildings to be constructed than allowed by current zoning by-laws, and generally seems to please everyone, especially the developers.

A prime example would be the Yonge Street open cut subway of the Toronto Transit Commission. Any regular transit rider on the line would have noticed the sunshine disappearing at a rapid rate, and probably wondered why. The answer is that someone is leasing the air above the big ditch and covering it over. If a developer had, for instance, 50,000 square feet of land located beside this open cut, with zoning requirements allowing him to construct a building containing 100,000 sq. ft. of floor space, he would be boxed in and stuck with it unless he could obtain more land to allow him to erect a larger building.

All he has to do is take a look at that open subway ditch next to his 50,000 ft., measure off 50,000 ft. of horizontal space right over it and work out the details with the Transit Commission, to enable him to double the size of his building. Basically, the 50,000 ft. would be valued as though it were actually 50,000 ft. of land, and if, for instance, the developer's piece was worth $15 a sq. ft., then his air space would be reasonably valued at the same rate, because the rights to use this air space would allow the developer the same allowances for building as his own land next to it.

Once everyone has agreed on a valuation, the leasing of this "air right" is usually agreed on at about 6½ % per year of its valuation, net to the Transit Commission, or lessor. The developer would pay the taxes on it as though it were a piece of land.

He would use the extra zoning rights to increase the size of his building, and then cover the ditch over and use it for outside parking to take care of his additional municipal parking requirements occasioned by the larger building.

Sometimes a building would be erected right over the railway property, and valuation of the space under the building would be in proportion to the size of the building.

The following is an example of the terms the developer might have in his agreement.

(a) If the leasing agreement is contingent upon obtaining municipal rezoning, the applicant would pay the Transit Commission a sum equal to the present municipal taxes on the property during such period of rezoning.

(b) The term of the lease would be for an initial period of 33 to 40 years, with the right to two additional terms with the total lease not running for more than 99 years. The renewals would be on the same terms and conditions except as to rental rate which would be agreed upon, or decided by arbitration at the time that such renewals were negotiated.

(c) On execution of the lease, the lessee would be required to put up about three years' rent in advance.

(d) The lessee would pay all taxes, except taxes levied against the retained rights of the lessor.

There are other aspects of real estate that necessitate leasing by making it impossible to purchase the land. I had once negotiated for some property owned by a hospital in Toronto, only to find that a university had ingress and egress rights covering a *one foot strip* right along the street. By owning these rights, the university was in a position to approve or disapprove of any planned construction on the street because a trespassing law would be violated by anyone crossing this one foot strip of land on the street, which they would have to do to gain entrance to the building. Once the university approved of the projected building, they would grant a "frontage license" to the developer for a nominal sum which would legally allow persons to cross the one foot strip and enter the building. The "frontage license" would be valid for the duration of the life of the building.

Another case was a school board that had a large parking lot. They wanted to expand the parking facilities but were in short supply of the long green, so negotiations began whereby they would grant the air rights to a developer allowing him to construct a building over the parking area, in return for supplying the school board with the required parking facilities.

There is a large insurance company in Toronto that is going to own half the city in 99 years if they continue with their current practice. If anyone approaches them for a mortgage on a proposed building, they agree, providing the owner of the project sells the land to them, and leases it right back from them for 99 years. In 99 years the insurance company owns the land and everything on it, unless they feel inclined to renew the ground lease. The developer is only interested in making money. This plan allows him to attain his goal under favourable circumstances, and he is in business. How could he care what would happen to his building in 99 years? He won't be here, but the insurance company will. This is how it would work, in effect:

In the following situation, the developer has his choice of purchasing land for $320,000 for an apartment building, or selling it to the insurance company and leasing it from them, providing them with an annual return of 7%, or $22,400. The developer proposes erecting the building at a cost of one million dollars.

If he owns the land, he can obtain a mortgage loan of $1,000,-000 against the entire package. If he leases the land, he can expect a mortgage loan of $700,000 against the security of a leasehold mortgage. Both mortgages are at 7½% yearly interest, compounded semi-annually, fully amortized for 30 years.

	Purchased		*Leased*	
Cash Required	$1,320,000		$1,000,000	
Mortgage	1,000,000		700,000	
Equity:	$ 320,000		$ 300,000	
Gross Income:		$220,000		$220,000
Expenses				
Operating	88,000		88,000	
Mortgage Amort.	82,966		58,076	
Leasehold rent	—	170,966	22,400	168,476
Net Return:		$ 49,034		$ 51,524
Net cash flow } % on equity }		15.32%		17.17%
Taxable Income				
Net Return		$ 49,034		$ 51,524
Plus Mortgage } Principal rep'mt }		9,427		6,598
		$ 58,461		$ 58,122
Less Capital Cost } Allowance 1st Yr }		50,000		50,000
Total Taxable:		$ 8,461		$ 8,122

(a) This reflects the first year's operation only.

(b) The book value of the building is $1,000,000.

By owning land, the developer has a gross return (before depreciation) of $58,461 on $320,000, or 18.26% on his investment.

By leasing the land, the developer has a gross return (before depreciation) of $58,122 on $300,000, or 19.37% on his investment.

Well, you say, according to this, the developer only has to put up another $20,000 over leasing, and he can own the whole project. The end result is very similar, so why lease the land?

It boils down to the availability of mortgage funds for the building. If he applies for funds and can't get them at what he considers to be a reasonable rate from anyone, unless he goes along with the lease on the land, then that is what he will do. He will take the best possible solution to his financing problems to give him the best possible return on equity. There are also other instances where the owner of land will only lease it as an investment, and not sell it, which would force the situation.

Look what would happen if the borrower could obtain a larger mortgage under both circumstances, and how it would affect his net return on equity. Even if he had to pay a bonus for the increases, it would probably be worth it:

	Purchased		Leased	
Cash Required	$1,320,000		$1,000,000	
Mortgage	1,200,000		900,000	
Equity:	$ 120,000		$ 100,000	
Gross Income:		$220,000		$220,000
Expenses				
Operating	88,000		88,000	
Mortgage Amort.	99,559		74,669	
Leasehold rent	—	$187,559	22,400	$185,069
Net Return:		$ 32,441		$ 34,931
Net cash flow } % on equity }		27.03%		34.93%
Taxable Income				
Net Return		$ 32,441		$ 34,931
Plus Mortgage } Principal rep'mt }		11,312		8,484
		$ 43,753		$ 43,415
Less Capital Cost } Allowance 1st Yr }		43,753		43,415
Total Taxable:		$ 0		$ 0

If you don't need the total allowable capital cost allowance (depreciation) you don't take it!

The ground rent is very simply established. Once an agreeable valuation has been placed on the land, the owner of the land would lease it to the tenant for a fixed percentage of the valuation per year. For example, land value; $200,000 \times 7\% = \$14,000$ yearly. This rent would be in effect for the first term of the lease, which is usually not more than 40 years. The second and third term rent would be established by mutual agreement, or arbitration by professional appraisal of the land. It is usual not to extend a ground lease for more than 99 years.

The ground lease is not a small document; it may contain from 50 to 100 pages, with many and varied provisions. The following are basically the general terms that you may expect to find.

The lease is a net lease, with the lessee required to pay all municipal taxes and charges on the land. Lessors were formerly in the habit of requiring the lessee to pay his taxes through the lessor, but with tax payments established as they now are in most municipalities on a two-month basis, it is comparatively simple for the lessor to check this, and ensure the lessee doesn't get far behind in his payments. If the lease has a clause requiring the lessee to pay the land tax through the lessor, it would also have a clause ensuring that the lessor promptly remits this money to the municipality.

Before the lease is executed, the lessee's covenant would define, and the lessor would fully understand, the complete details of the proposed building. The lessor would check the proposition carefully, to see that there would be sufficient income reasonably projected to ensure there would be sufficient funds left after the building operating charges to pay the ground taxes and ground rent.

Being a long lease, great detail is paid to the required maintenance of the building in keeping with the quality of the surrounding buildings, wear and tear, and replacement of part or all of the building. A lot can happen over a 99 year period. The lessee, unless otherwise provided for in the lease, is required to replace the building in the event of destruction by fire or other cause; therefore, the lease will usually contain a clause outlining in detail the rights and waivers optional to the lessee during the last few years of the lease. For instance, if the building were destroyed or damaged beyond reasonable repair during the last 10 years of the lease, the lessee may not feel like going to the trouble of rebuilding just to hand it over to the lessor in a few years time. In this event, the lease would be terminated, and the lessor would be compensated by receiving the insurance money.

The subject of possible replacement or major facelifting and alteration will also be dealt with in detail. Other than agreed-upon smaller amounts, any major change will require the lessor's consent, and will usually require the lessee to establish a performance bond covering it before any change took place.

The lessee is usually granted rights to sub-lease and mortgage to the end of the term.

The lessee would be required to carry insurance of a very

broad nature to protect it under the indemnity clause protecting the lessor.

The lessee would be protected by a requirement that the lessor give him proper notice of any default, so that through some error such as not paying the ground rent, the lease would not be automatically terminated and the building handed over to the lessor.

Insurance claims of a minor nature (sums fixed in lease) are settled with the lessee, and repairs made. Large claims would be paid to the lessor, who would release sums as progressive repairs were completed by the lessee.

In cases of expropriation, they are usually settled by arbitration.

The Leasehold Mortgage

Before a builder signs a ground lease, he will have an irrevocable mortgage commitment for his building. The mortgage requires an assignment of the ground lease, or sub-lease, and the terms of the ground lease will be satisfactory to the mortgagee, or there is no loan.

The principal sum of a leasehold mortgage is understandably less than it would be or could be if the mortgagor owned the land.

If the mortgagee takes his mortgage under assignment of the lease a situation is established between the lessor and mortgagee whereby the mortgagee becomes responsible for the terms of the lease, including that of paying the ground rent. The mortgagee would be liable for all breaches of covenant that might occur.

Under a sub-lease arrangement, the requirement would be that the mortgagor would hold the last day of the term of the lease in trust for the mortgagee, in order to allow the mortgagee to control the last day and thereby control the renewable term. This is necessary, because although the mortgage term is usually of shorter duration than that of the lease, it could be possible for the mortgagee to have not received his final payments by the end of the term.

A leasehold mortgagee will most certainly protect himself fully to ensure that there is no termination of the lease, and will therefore have an agreement with the lessor to allow the mortgagee time to remedy any default on the part of the lessee.

The mortgage will contain a clause stipulating that a default by the mortgagor under the terms of the ground lease will automatically become a default under the mortgage.

The leasehold mortgage will require that the lessee pays the ground rent to the mortgagee, who in turn will pay it to the lessor, or require the lessee/mortgagor to produce receipts promptly.

This will answer the question: which has priority, the ground rent, or the mortgage payment?

34

Lease-backs

WANTED

Industrial building, AAA tenant on net lease. 6% return on equity required.

This advertisement was placed in a large metropolitan daily newspaper, and ran for several editions without the slightest response. It was an honest request; the advertiser had the cash in the bank, and he may still be wondering, in view of his modest interest requirement on equity, why he could not place the funds in what is commonly called a lease-back.

This expression has been bounced around so much that practically every situation in which the owner of a building has it leased to one tenant on a net basis automatically is called a lease-back. A true lease-back is a situation whereby the owner/user of an industrial building, for example, sells the land and building to someone and immediately leases it right back from him without moving.

The fellow with the $100,000 had a reasonable request. He wanted to purchase such a building, leased to a firm with a high credit rating for a minimum period of 10 years, with a reasonable expectation of return on his investment. The problem of placing his funds in such a venture is created by the competition from large corporate bodies, such as insurance companies, in the manner in which they handle a lease-back agreement. Basically, where they shove him aside is in their agreement to sell the property back to the original owner at the expiration of the lease (or sooner by agreement, but seldom before the first 10 years) for a very moderate sum, somewhere between 10% and 20% of the appraised value of the property at the time of the initial agreement.

The private investor wants no part of an agreement like this. He wants to buy the property, lease it back, and that's all. He wants to own the property, period. No agreement of resale at the end of *his* lease.

The corporation will probably handle it in this manner:

If the building is new, and was constructed by a reputable

builder, the costs of land acquisition and building will be the figure used to proceed with formal negotiations. If the building is a few years old, a professional appraisal will be made to arrive at its reasonable current market value, and this figure will be used.

If, for instance, the agreed value of the property were $100,000, the owner of the property would be offered this sum, with the following conditions:

(a) The property would be leased immediately to the now former owner on a net basis (he would pay *all* charges against the property) for an agreed period.

(b) The rent paid would be established by (1) the strength of the lessee's covenant (the stronger it is, the less he pays) and (2) by the term of the lease.

(c) The lessor would treat the $100,000 investment as a sort of annuity, and it would be amortized completely, including principal and interest, over the period of time under the term of the lease, which would be what the lessee would pay as rent. The interest rate in such amortization is generally about 1% higher than current, conventional mortgage rates.

(d) The lessee would have the right to purchase the property at the end of the term under lease (when the lessor would have had his investment returned plus interest) for a moderate sum, or earlier by agreement.

In a booming economy, with a rising market, especially in real estate, the option to purchase the property at the end of the lease at a moderate figure would be a very attractive proposition for the owner of the property.

The reason put forth by the buyer for the premium rate of interest would be that it is justified by the fact that 100% of valuation financing is effected.

You might say, why wouldn't he mortgage the property if he needed additional funds for operation and expansion, or use one of the other means open to him such as financing his accounts receivable, borrowing from a bank, issuing shares or debentures, etc. The latter means may not be feasible, or possible, at the time, and the owner of an industrial plant could expect to receive no more than 60% financing by mortgaging. Before any agreement is signed, every financial avenue will be explored, but they will be hard pressed to beat the proposition of the insurance companies, etc.

In addition to the option to repurchase the property, the agreement may contain an option to renew the lease at its expiration, but with a sharp reduction in rent, because the investing body has recovered its capital cost. This is another bonus to the proposed lessee that he would not normally receive from the private investor.

The lease will, of course, be registered, and will also contain a proper and full description of the metes and bounds, which will also show the exact dimensions of the existing building and its location, to ensure a proper and permanent record.

The rental, being based on full amortization of the capital cost to the lessor, will be scheduled to show the breakdown of each payment, the principal, interest, and unrecovered capital cost. The lessee, being on a net lease, and therefore required to pay all municipal taxes, local improvements, utilities, insurance, etc., will covenant to pay these charges as "additional rent", which will enable the lessor to have the same recourse for breach of this covenant as he will have for non-payment of the basic rent.

In the event of loss by fire or other cause, it will be the lessee's responsibility to rebuild, which makes it necessary to detail at length the insurance clause in the lease. He will be required to cover himself, the lessor, and possibly a mortgagee fully with a wide range of coverage. Smaller, agreed-upon claims will be settled by the lessee alone; larger amounts will usually be settled through the lessor.

The most extensive part of the lease probably will be that which concerns the rights and/or obligations of the lessee to repair, renovate, remodel, add to, or even completely replace the building. This will cover such aspects as performance bonds, restrictions under municipal building by-laws, etc., and the building, regardless of the approved changes, will of course remain the property of the lessor. In case of loss or damage when the lessee will be required to promptly remedy this at his own expense, he is usually bound to continue paying the rent during such period, unless otherwise provided for by moratorium in the lease. The stiffness of the requirements of the lessee will soften as the lease approaches expiration, when he will probably have option agreements covering loss during this latter period. For instance, if his lease contains an option to purchase the property at the end of the lease, and the building were damaged or destroyed during this period, he would normally have a clause giving him the option to rebuild, or end the lease by purchasing the property from the lessor, plus indemnifying the lessor for his unrecovered capital cost plus interest. The advantages to the seller, or lessee, are many:

He deals with one body for the full treatment. No middleman looking for commissions in the transaction, which could amount to sizeable sums. He gets his money, and he can do what he wants with it. The rent he pays will be a tax deductible item.

If he had financed by conventional mortgage, the only tax deductible part of it would be the interest on the mortgage. The rent is, in effect, a mortgage, but the principal repayment is considered a part of the rent, and is therefore also tax deductible. An argument put forth here could be that the lessee would lose his rights of capital cost allowance, or depreciation, but don't forget that this would be allowable on buildings only, not the land, and would in any event be recoverable at a later date.

One disadvantage would arise in the event that the seller had depreciated his building to any great extent. The income tax would have to be immediately paid on its recapture, during the calendar or fiscal year of sale.

Conventional mortgaging would give him about 60%, against the 100% he would receive under lease-back.

It gives the lessee greatly increased immediate working capital, which is frequently uppermost in the company comptroller's mind. It turns the property into a fluid bank account, which in turn can increase the company's business and profits, which is why it is in business. Sometimes a healthy bank balance looks better on financial statements than the same amount tied up in a building.

The ace in the hole, of course, is the option to purchase the property from the lessor at the expiration of the lease at a very nominal sum. By that time, who knows what the market value of the property might be?

Is the purchaser/lessor happy?

Naturally, he isn't going to enter into any such agreement unless he satisfies himself that the covenant is satisfactory, and once he does, he gets a bonus interest rate on his capital outlay, plus a bonus at the end of the term when the lessee exercises his option to purchase the property, or renews the lease.

He is receiving an effective bonus on the investment of about one percent over conventional mortgage rates. Assuming conventional mortgaging were at 8%, and he received 9% under the agreement, this would be his bonus on an investment of $100,000, over 30 years, fully amortized loan, compounded semi-annually.

9% yearly	$9,514
8% yearly	8,697
Bonus Yearly	$ 817

Which is an increase on return of 9.39%.

Is everybody happy? They must be, because this type of lease-back arrangement has become very popular.

There is one alternative to all this, which would be worth exploring. It would be a calculated projection for five years.

Assuming there is a reasonably strong covenant on the part of the property owner, he could expect to obtain a first mortgage loan of 60% on the $100,000 property. This would carry at 8%, over 30 years amortization of principal and interest, semi-annual computation, for $5,218 per annum. Subtract this sum from the 9% proposition of

$9,514 of the proposed buyer/lessor, and it leaves the property owner with $4,296.

He would now have his $60,000. The balance of the required sum, $40,000 could possibly be obtained by giving someone an equitable mortgage at a high rate of interest, such as 15%. This mortgage would have to be projected for interest only on the principal, with no principal payments.

Assuming this equitable mortgage could be arranged for a term of 5 years, and it just might be possible with good covenant, it would produce the following results for the property owner:

(a) He would have his $100,000.

(b) He would still own the property, subject to mortgages.

(c) It would mean an additional outlay of cash per year over the 9% proposition of:

9% Proposition:		$ 9,514
1st Mortgage:	$5,218	
2nd Mortgage:	6,000	11,218
		($ 1,704)

or $8,520 outlay over 5 years.

Probably, being a corporation, the property owner could not take advantage of the Interest Act regulations requiring a mandatory "open" privilege at the end of the first five years' life of his first mortgage, so he would have to protect himself by ensuring that a prepayment clause were inserted in the mortgage allowing this, even with some penalty, to ensure that he could pay it off, or discharge it, in 5 years' time.

The property owner would have to decide:

(a) Would his property value increase 8.52% in five years to justify the increased expense under this projection of $8,520?

(b) The principal credit to him on the first mortgage would amount to just $50 per thousand for the first five years, due to its lengthy amortization, which would give him a credit of $3,000. Would this be enough to take care of the bonus penalty in the mortgage in its discharge at the end of the five year period, in the event that he wished to go along with a lease-back at that time?

If, in 5 years' time, his business hadn't prospered to the point of enabling him to discharge the second, or equitable mortgage, or if he were unable to renew or refinance it, he would then be in a position of having to negotiate a lease-back at a minimum $108,500, instead of today's $100,000.

All you need is a sharp pencil, a good accountant, and faith in the future to come up with the right answers!

35

Speculation

Some people view a speculator as a man who sits hovering like a vulture waiting for the poor old widow to find herself all alone in the world, thereby becoming fair game, in his eyes, for him to pounce on her with a pittance for her cherished nest of memories and force her into the old folk's home. Well, I suppose it has happened, but in my memory the only "poor old widow" who I wanted to have moved out of her $14,000 house ended up getting $32,500 for it. The dear old soul was the last holdout on the street and therefore my principals coughed up and said no more, because they had to have the house.

A speculator doesn't have to have any particular house. He can roam all over the city, or back forty, picking and choosing; he is a theorizer. He theorizes that he can buy an old pile of lumber and mortar someone calls a house, spend some money on it putting it in top condition (thereby improving the neighbourhood and municipal tax coffers), and make a profit. That's what he does.

How does he find all these hot buys? He constantly reads the newspaper ads, he constantly calls dozens of real estate salesmen, he constantly looks and looks and looks at houses, and he makes offers. My how he makes offers! He theorizes that if he makes enough offers, at his price, some of them have to be accepted. And they are. I remember receiving a phone call from a sign on a $28,500 house I had listed. I had never before spoken to the man who called me and he ended up instructing me to present his offer on the house at $21,000. Not only that, he wanted the seller to accept a mortgage of $15,000. I thought he was nuts, and I was sure the owners would think I was nuts for bringing his offer to them but the man was very insistent and that was his offer. I couldn't get him up another nickel. When I presented the offer I apologized to the owners for bringing such a low offer, but they took one look at it, said they wanted to leave the next day on an extended vacation, and signed it. The purchaser later sold the house for close to $30,000.

You can do the same thing, and even do it with your own house if you want to move and it looks a little scratchy. Don't sell it the way it is; smarten it up. Why, even a fresh coat of good paint on the verandah, steps and front door could be worth an extra three hundred dollars to you; and smarten up the lawn. First impressions are lasting. When someone is going to inspect your house, they are going to have to ring the doorbell. If your property presents a good front, keep them waiting a few minutes. They aren't going to stare at the wall, they are going to stand there and look around, and all there is to look at, at this point, is the verandah, steps, front door and lawn. Once you have gone this far, don't let them down by opening that cheery entrance and having them walk in on a scratchy, unkempt interior.

The first thing to do inside the house is to forget it is your home with grandpa's moth-eaten bear rug on the floor and junior's old tricycle in the corner. Be objective. The buyer doesn't have any sentiment for such chattels so get them out of the way. Spring clean from *top* to *bottom*. Every piece of junk goes out into the garage. Not into the basement.

Now go to work. Closets first. If you have a good sized closet, make sure it is clean and nearly empty, and install a good light in it; let them see it. If it is a small closet, take the light out of it.

The bathroom and kitchen are next. The person who will make about 90% of the decision in buying the house will be the purchaser's wife. She'll spend a lot of time in that kitchen and she will want her guests to be impressed by her bathroom. I'm not going to go into great detail on what to do to all these rooms; you'll just have to keep in mind that you are selling something to a man and a woman who like things to be clean and presentable. Don't forget, it is easy for you to live with a cracked sink and broken tile, because you *have* lived with it, but the man who's buying it, oh no!

Check all the walls. Maybe they can pass with a good washing; maybe you'll have to use some paint and wallpaper. Modern paints and wallpapers are easy to apply yourself, but stick to neutral colours and stay away from over-bright splashy decorating.

Check all the woodwork, including the floors. If you have old floor coverings, store them in the garage, rent a sander, and get to work.

Dust everything. Books, shelves, pictures, ceilings; get rid of the kid's crayon marks; clean the inside of lighting fixtures, fireplaces and around the radiators; don't leave cobwebs in the corners; cupboards must be spotless. On and on and on. Boy, are you going to be busy.

Make the house look like a home. If you don't subscribe to magazines, buy the current issues of *Time, Holiday, Saturday Night, Macleans* and *Chatelaine*. Place them around the room with unpremeditation. Get some fresh flowers, a couple of new scatter rugs, and coverings for the worn spots on the furniture. Don't spend a lot of cash you havn't got, but use your head.

Last, but not least, the basement. Clean it. Spray air freshener around. Whitewash the walls if they need it. If your heating unit is in sad shape, have a new one installed on the never-never plan and let the home buyer assume your covenant for payment. I'll never forget the couple who went so far they painted their furnace, pipes and all, a powder blue.

All this dressing up will take one good hard week's work, but it will be worth it.

So much for your own home. Back to speculation.

If you want to pick up a couple of thousand dollars or more a year you can do it and learn a lot at the same time. Do what the speculator does. Get to the real estate salesman, and *look*, *look*, *look*. One real estate salesman isn't enough.

Get half a dozen salesmen with half a dozen firms on the lookout. Don't use more than one salesman with the same firm, because there is a danger of your name getting bounced around. Let each one think he is your confidential agent. The multiple listing services offered by realtors is an excellent service, but don't forget every firm has exclusive listings they don't bother to tell other brokers about, and that is one more reason you should have half a dozen on the go.

There are three important things to look out for in your house hunting:

1. Location
2. Location
3. Location

Everyone needs transportation, so this must be a prime factor. Make sure it is near a bus stop, preferably near one that will take you right downtown. This is especially important if you are going to buy a small bungalow, because your purchaser will probably be a retired couple who need the close transportation. If you get a three-bedroom house, someone with children will be your buyer; the kids have to go to school, and the closer the school the better. And make sure the little darlings don't have to cross a busy thoroughfare to get there! You can't have it close to everything, but always have the potential buyer in mind.

Don't bother looking at houses that have just been all spruced up. Someone else has done this, and they have upped the price. This is what you are supposed to do. Pretty soon you will know what is and what isn't a good buy. The three most important things in buying a house for speculation are the heating plant, the plumbing and the roof. If these are in good shape the rest can be easy.

If you buy a house with $2,000 down at a price of $20,000 (and it is done quite often) and you immediately sell it "as is" for 10% more than you paid for it, you will realize a gross return of 100% on equity, but if you pay cash for it and sell it when it appreciated 10%, you have just made 10%. The secret of any venture like this in a stable and rising market is to buy with as little cash as possible.

The truly best financing to look for in a speculative venture is where the owner of a property is willing to receive a mortgage from you for the balance of the purchase price. Don't forget that this means no conventional loan application, no appraisal fees, very seldom a credit check, and lower legal fees.

So get yourself a paying hobby. Buy a property at the price you want to pay for it, and you *can* if you toss around enough offers on enough properties. Buy it at market price (considering its condition), doll it up, creating a new market price, and sell it. Then do it all over again. Three rules:

1. Don't put more cash into a house than 15% of the purchase price.

2. Don't spend more than 5% of the purchase price fixing it up. If you have to, it is too shot to bother with, so go on to another one.

3. Sell it for a modest and fair profit. Don't be greedy. Don't forget that if you just do this three times a year at a profit of $2,000 each, you have added $6,000 to your yearly income. And learned a lot.

There is another thing you can do with a house. I met a railway yard foremen in 1964 who owned 42 houses. *Forty-two!* He still worked at the yards. This was his hobby; but what a hobby! When I asked him to tell me about it, he said that when he found himself with $1,500 lying in the bank at 3%, he told his wife that he wanted to buy a house he had heard about that he could get for $1,000 down, fix it up and rent it. His wife told him that it was okay by her, but his house hobby could never interfere with his regular work in the yards. He agreed. From that humble beginning, 16 years later he owned 42 houses, and he bought them all with from one to two thousand down, usually with one mortgage for the balance. He still brings the paycheck home from the yards, but if this man wanted to cash in he would be worth at least a million dollars! And he started the whole thing with $1,500.

Someday maybe you'll give me a ride in your new Cadillac?

Land Speculation: I recently read an article on financing written by someone who has a certificate in real estate from a major university, is an instructor of real estate seminars, and is active in counselling and estate building. I can only say that I am very pleased that I was not the one being counselled.

This expert cited an assumption of purchasing a vacant lot for $20,000 and selling it for $24,400 four years later, with the following result:

Profit:	$4,400
Legal fees and Brokerage:	1,400
Leaving:	$3,000

There is just one thing wrong with this; someone forgot to sharpen their pencil and enter the debit. The $20,000 involved in the purchase price of the lot is worth a modest 6% a year. 6% of $20,000 $\times$ 4 years is $4,800. This is a debit. On top of this, the owner of the lot had to pay municipal taxes for four years. A reasonable tax would be approximately $300 a year on such a lot, which is $1,200 for the four years. If this counsellor had presented an accurate picture of the profit it would have looked like:

Profit:		$4,400
Legal fees and Brokerage:	$1,400	
Taxes:	1,200	
Interest on $20,000 @ 6%	4,800	7,400
Leaving a let *loss* of		($3,000)

Instead of having a pretty profit of $3,000, we have turned it into a nasty loss by remembering our expenses.

The point of the example is that speculation in land is speculation in its highest sense. *There is no income from raw land* (unless you lease it to a passing circus or some such thing) and therefore you have to be very very sure in your own mind that there will be an almost immediate appreciation in its value; otherwise it will start to eat a hole in your bank account.

A common method of land speculation is to obtain an option on the property for a minimum period of one year. The cash consideration given to the owner of the land will be about one per cent of the agreed price in the option. Then the would-be purchaser scrambles around during the option period trying to find a buyer at a higher price or to arrange for rezoning of property to greater density use, creating a higher value. If he is successful, he has made money and, in some cases, a great deal of it. If he is not, and feels he is close to something, he would consider the advantages of extending the option for a further cash consideration. If all fails, he drops it and, learning his lesson, goes on to another one or to something else.

If the speculator had a property optioned for $100,000, and has put up $1,000 cash, he is really out of pocket just the $1,000 plus the interest earning power of the money. This is much better than sinking a great chunk of money into such a scheme by buying the property outright, which could be disastrous.

The truly big winners in land appreciation are the farmers on the fringes of the urban areas, the men who live on the old homestead and work the land. If you or I obtained a piece of land for $10,000 and someone came along and offered us $15,000 for it soon afterward, we would probably take it. This purchaser in turn would probably behave in the same manner, so that over the years the value of the land could appreciate tremendously, with the profits spread through several hands. The farmer, on the other hand, living and working with the land, possibly with his sons, resists initial bids on his land, but as time goes by and his land value soars, possibly when he is ready to retire he would realize the entire appreciation built up over the years.

Summarizing it; if you intend to speculate with land, be very careful not to get in too deep, and do it preferably on an option basis. You won't get stung too hard if you fail.

Making It With Land

As I have quoted, the late Will Rogers was fond of advising all to buy land, "because they are not making any more of it".

There are millions who made a bundle by taking this advice. But what kind of land to buy, and for how much?

The moose-pasture variety is almost as bad as a windswept stretch of sand with no water. On many of my television appearances I was asked where to go for land investment, and my answer was invariably to go north, away from the urban centres, where the land *with water frontage* and good access from public roads could be found at comparatively reasonable prices.

The soaring market values of such land during the past few years has proven that I was right, and I still recommend this as an excellent investment.

Money-wise Americans are swarming over the border, joining urban Canadians in their search for cleaner air, water and land. They are going north, to the resort areas, and potentially future resort areas.

Access is a big consideration. Local rough roads do not deter a camp or cottage owner, providing he has first class roads to get to the area.

In searching for your land, get to the *local* brokers, preferably ones who have been working your chosen area for a few years. They know local market values, trends, and can offer helpful advice.

The author has carefully researched this aspect of land investment for years, and, after careful deliberation, I have zeroed in on what may be the last great frontier of resort land available at reasonable prices. When I say reasonable, I mean from $50 to $100 an acre, *with water frontage.* It's in Ontario, it's available — a real sleeper.

If I disclosed this freely, there would be a land rush on. I want this information known, but I do not want to be responsible for what could be a massive inflation of land values. You bought this book in good faith, and so I will reveal this to you in good faith.

You will be provided with a large scale map of the area, with my recommendations on how to go about finding your land and buying it. This will cost you $100. The money will be used to help defray the costs of research and time to be spent on future editions of this book, which in the past have been astronomical.

In the next edition of this book, I'll include a chapter telling about buying and selling pieces of this land by my recommendation, using factual information, which I expect will enable me to say, "I told you so!"

Write to Richard Steacy, P.O. Box 222, Willowdale, Ontario, Canada.

Commercial Buildings: There are about five reasons why anyone would speculate on a commercial property.

1. The present income on the property is just obviously too low, the leases are about ready to expire, and the situation could be drastically improved.

2. The building is in terrible condition, but structurally sound, and could be renovated to attract higher income.

3. The land under the building is obviously worth more than the entire parcel.

4. There is a good, very good, chance that the area zoning could be changed to create an inflated price on the land.

5. He can buy it for a song.

As for the commercial building itself, there is a limit to the income it will realize, and this is the true determining factor in the value of any such property, if its use is to remain constant. Income less expenses leaves you what? That's the question.

Incidentals: There are many other ways that people have speculated in real estate.

1. Getting a lease in a good location for less than the going rate, and sub-letting the vacant property at a higher figure.

2. Installing a do-it-yourself laundry or other such service shop in a good location, again sub-leasing it profitably.

3. Picking a house or small building in an expanding commercial or high rise apartment area and sitting on it for a couple of years. (This is only reasonable if you can buy it at a price that will enable you to sell it again, without loss, under its original use if the anticipated area expansion does not materialize. If the area does boom, you could take a trip around the world on your profit.)

Anything else? Take a good hard look at the property. Remember the debit. What can you do to improve it? Who would buy it from you? Why are they selling? Whatever you propose buying, make sure it is a condition of your purchase that there are no outstanding work-orders against the property from any municipal department, and that its present use and your proposed use are allowed by the by-laws of the municipality.

I can think of no more exciting way to put a couple of thousand extra dollars to work than speculating in real estate, but remember that I said "extra" dollars. Don't speculate with money you can't afford to lose. It hurts.

36

The Oklahoma Offer

One of the meanest financial flim-flams devised and used by money-grabbers is the "Oklahoma Offer".

It is slick, professional, and to the untrained eye hard to spot. It enables one to purchase property with nothing down and make a substantial and immediate cash profit.

Unfortunately, it leaves a vendor (property seller) stuck with a mortgage, most of which is not worth the paper it is written on. If you are selling property, watch for it — here is an example of how it works:

The following are briefly the financial contents of an offer to purchase property:

1. Purchase Price: $47,000.
2. Deposit with Offer: $ 2,000.
3. Purchaser agrees to pay vendor $30,000 on closing.
4. Vendor agrees to hold second mortgage for $15,000.
5. Purchaser agrees to arrange, at his own expense, a first mortgage of not less than $30,000.

The innocent vendor adds it up:

Deposit:	$ 2,000
Cash:	30,000
Mortgage:	15,000
TOTAL:	$47,000

If the offer is accepted, the purchaser can go to work and arrange a first mortgage of not $30,000 but $40,000. Remember, it was agreed that the first mortgage will be *not less than $30,000*.

Out of this $40,000 first mortgage, the purchaser will pay the vendor the agreed $30,000, give himself $2,000 to get back the deposit, and put $8,000 profit in his pocket.

Proof?

First Mortgage:	$40,000
Second Mortgage:	15,000
	$55,000
Purchase Price:	47,000
Profit to buyer:	$ 8,000

The vendor, having agreed to hold a second mortgage of $15,000, is now in the unenviable position of having $8,000 of the $15,000 mortgage *exceed* the purchase price of the property.

If the purchaser is a corporate shell with no assets, it could then walk away with the $8,000 profit and forget the property.

If the vendor (now the second mortgagee) ended up owning the property again, he would owe $40,000 to a first mortgagee. Here is the spot he would be in:

Property worth	$47,000
Owing	40,000
Equity worth	7,000
Cash received	32,000
	$39,000
Selling price:	47,000

Net loss to vendor: ($ 8,000)
(plus headaches and legal fees)

What this means, of course, is that it will cost the vendor (mortgagee) $8,000 out of his own pocket to regain possession of the property.

This money-making scheme is triggered by a clause in the agreement that will allow the purchaser (mortgagor) to increase the principal amount of the first mortgage "without necessarily applying the increase to reduce the principal amount of the second mortgage", which allows the purchaser to arrange and secure the $40,000 mortgage.

If questioned on this nocuous point, a glib person will say something to the effect that money obtained from such an increase will be required to improve the property, resulting in greater security for the second mortgagee (vendor). Which is hogwash! Watch it!!

Also, the purchaser may ask to assign the agreement to a third, unnamed party. This will release the purchaser from his covenant, and the assignee could be a corporate shell with no assets.

And, in *any* agreement of purchase and sale, here are two warning signs:

Be careful about accepting an offer from a buyer who shows the words "in trust" after his name.

"In Trust" could be a corporate shell with no money, and when the time comes to close it would be useless to attempt to legally force a closing if the purchaser decided not to close.

It is tantamount to giving the purchaser an option on the property. Therefore, a serious consideration must be the amount of the deposit made with the offer and the length of time to close the sale. If the purchaser defaults, the vendor could retain the deposit money, which should be an amount considered to be fair compensation for the length of time the property was tied up . . .

When selling an older property, be careful about agreeing to warrant that there will be no municipal or other legal work orders registered against the property on the date of closing.

A sharp purchaser, under such an agreement, could have the property inspected by municipal fire and building departments resulting in unheard of orders to repair and/or improve the property. The vendor would be stuck with the bill.

Agree only to there being no work orders registered against the property on the date of acceptance of the agreement.

Caveat emptor? Let the buyer beware?

Let the *seller* beware!

37
Selling Your House

There is a bit more to selling your house than having a real estate agent hammer a "for sale" sign on your front lawn.

Before you get involved in *any* real estate transaction that requires financing, you *must* understand mortgaging. Review the mortgage chapters.

Quite often the sale of a property requires the seller to become a mortgagee in agreeing to receive a mortgage as a part of the purchase price, either a mortgage on your property (the one you are selling) or a mortgage on another property the buyer is willing to assign to you as part of the agreement.

If the buyer asks you to receive a mortgage on your own property as part of the agreement, be quite sure you fully understand:

(a) The principal amount
(b) The interest rate and computation
(c) The method of repayment
(d) The term

and other proposed conditions and clauses.

If the property you are selling is free and clear of financial encumbrances, and no cash buyers appear, the method of obtaining all cash can be effected by discounting a second mortgage.

In a $30,000 sale, for example, the buyer will have his agent or lawyer arrange a first mortgage of about $20,000.

The buyer will put up about $5,000 cash.

You will be asked to be the mortgagee in a second mortgage for $5,000, which will be sold for you by your agent or lawyer at a discount.

You will receive:

Cash from buyer:	$ 5,000
First mortgage funds:	20,000
Proceeds of 2nd mortgage:	4,000
	$29,000

The proceeds of the sale of the second mortgage will vary, and depend on such things as the term of the mortgage and the rate of interest, but you will get all cash, without an all cash buyer, for about a 3½% discount off the original price. And the buyer gets his $30,000 home for $5,000 down.

If there is already a financial encumbrance on your property, there will, of course, be variations of this, but the end cash result could be achieved by selling a mortgage at a discount.

Another method of providing a seller with all cash is by the buyer arranging a high ratio mortgage loan, which can be as much as 95% of the purchase price.

If there is little cash involved in the transaction, and you are becoming a "first" or an equitable mortgagee, ensure that the purchaser's covenant, or probable ability and strength to repay your loan, is checked thoroughly. Under these circumstances, you could agree to sell your property under a sales agreement whereby the purchaser does not obtain title to the property until a later date, when he has paid you a further sum of money under the agreement. This forestalls the annoyance, expense, time and trouble involved in the event of possible foreclosure proceedings.

It is advisable, as a mortgagee, to obtain a mortgage repayment schedule from your lawyer or a commercial firm that computes mortgages, which will clearly show your position, every month right to maturity, to the penny.

If the purchaser asks you to accept a mortgage on another property as part of his cash consideration, take a good, hard, long look at the mortgage. Your lawyer is really your best guide as to the acceptability of this, because he has the means and experience to check it thoroughly.

How much is your property worth?

Surprisingly, there are a few hundred thousand property owners in Canada who haven't a clue. They must depend on *someone* to establish a reasonable market value for their property.

Here is a good way to do it. Call the offices of three brokers who have shown evidence of being active *in your neighbourhood*. Don't call them all at once. Tell the three offices you are seriously considering putting your property on the market. Make appointments with the three of them on three different half-days. Get each reaction. Each valuation. Assess the person from each office. Then put the three situations on your scales.

The price tags will very seldom be the same, although they probably will be close. Sometimes you may be unfortunate and find that one of the price tags will be much higher, and out of proportion, to the other two. I say unfortunate, because this could be the work of a salesman who is giving you an inflated price with a view of impressing you with the dollar sign, obtaining the listing, and figuring on bringing you down to earth at a later date. Reputable salesmen will be pleased to show you comparable sales records to justify their appraisal. An inflated price could also be the result of inexperience on the part of the salesman.

When you have decided on the firm that you would like to handle the sale of your property, give the firm a listing agreement. Once you have decided to sell, get on with it, and a listing agreement at a fair market price means you are well on your way to selling.

You may want the sale handled quietly by one broker, or you may want to give the property full exposure, which will mean having the broker co-operate with other brokers to expedite matters. By giving a listing to a broker you place him under obligation to work on your behalf, and you have someone to rely on. If strangers should call you personally, you just naturally refer them to your broker.

Agents are immersed full time in the real estate business every day, are constantly in touch with buyers and sellers and are fully aware of market trends. One of the distinct advantages of listing with an agent is the possibility that the agent (or a sub-agent) has the waiting buyer for your property, which is basically why some properties are sold in a matter of hours.

When you have listed your property for sale, and thereby retained the services of a broker, remember that you have agreed to let *him* sell it. You can help a great deal by not only making your property as attractive as possible to a potential buyer, but also by doing your best to be as inconspicuous as possible during your agent's showing. Don't volunteer any information; it may be something the buyer doesn't want to hear. Make yourself available for answering questions, nothing more. Leave the negotiating to the agent.

Make every bit of information about your property available to the broker. Mortgages, site plans, surveys, municipal tax bills, heating bills, receipts for any major repairs, roof and other guarantees and contracts, and leases. It would be a nice gesture also to provide your own list of preferred neighbourhood shops, servicemen, and suppliers.

The majority of real estate salesmen are sincere and straightforward businessmen just doing their best to make a living as most of us are. However, you may find a few cuties in the barrel; the just might resort to subterfuge in the presentation of offers to purchase your property. Examples I could cite would be instances where the purchase price in the offer was altered *after* the offer was typed, in an attempt to impress you:

(a) If your house were listed for $25,000 this figure would be inserted in the typed offer, then changed in ink, and initialled by the purchaser. The salesman might tell you that here is proof that he tried his level best to get them to sign at the full price, but you can see that they just wouldn't go for it, and this is the best he could do.

(b) If your house were listed at $25,000, a figure, for instance, of $20,000 might be inserted in the typewritten copy, and then changed to $22,000 initialled by the purchaser. The salesman might tell you that all the purchaser was willing to offer for your property was $20,000 but you can see that through his good efforts, and after exhaustive arguments, he managed to bring them up another two thousand!

A salesman might present an offer at 8:00 p.m. with an irrevocable date reading midnight the same day in an effort to force you into an immediate decision. Sometimes this is done for a valid reason. I have known buyers to have their eye on two houses and if they didn't get an answer on one immediately, they would have an offer presented on the second one the next day.

You might find the closing date on the offer too soon for comfort in your plans to move. If you can manage to close early, fine, but if you can't, contact the purchaser through the salesman and discuss it with him. Perhaps the salesman was just trying to hurry things up a bit to get an early pay cheque. (The sooner he gets his, the sooner you get yours.)

If a purchaser inserts a condition in his offer, such as a condition to purchase *your* property providing he sells *his* property before the closing date on his offer to you, don't be too hasty in rejecting it. You can always cover this by agreeing to the condition providing you have a 48 or 72 hour escape clause that will allow you to entertain other offers. In the event that one does come along that you would like to accept, the first purchaser would have the 48 or 72 hours' time in which to remove the condition. If he doesn't, you could accept the second offer.

Conditional offers are sometimes excellent offers, and conditions do become erased much to everyone's satisfaction; so don't knock an offer simply because it isn't as sweet and clean as you would like it to be. Give it a chance.

O.K. Someone has produced a bona fide offer to purchase your property. Deposit cheque certified? Signatures in order and under seal properly witnessed? Price and terms attractive? You would like to accept it? Now, you just take a good solid piece of advice — take the offer to your lawyer. If you can't see him personally, or are pressed for time, read it to him over the phone. No matter how simple an offer may look, there just might be something adverse about the situation your lawyer could spot immediately that you couldn't, or had overlooked. You are going to retain him to effect the eventual closing of the sale, so you should give him the opportunity to look after your interests right from the start.

In the offer from the buyer, there will be an irrevocable date for acceptance on the agreement of purchase and sale. If you agree to accept the offer, subject to certain changes, and sign the document, make sure the irrevocable date is changed to read from *you* to the *buyer,* with your agreed date for limiting the time of his acceptance of your counter-offer.

Here Are the Real Estate Agent's Duties to a Vendor:

1. Give the vendor a true copy of the listing agreement immediately after the execution of the agreement.

2. The agent shall give the owner an honest effort to sell the property and promote and protect his client's interest by proper guidance in matters of price, law (with limited application) and shall render conscientious service.

3. He shall offer the property at one price only, the listed price.

4. He shall accept the standard commission payable by his principal.

5. He shall inform the vendor of any and all offers to purchase the property.

6. The agent shall declare any personal interest in any transaction.

7. The agent shall be honest, loyal to his principal and shall not be negligent.

38

Your Property as an Apartment Site

The Value of the Land: Just what is a piece of land worth? All land has value, and this value is governed principally by its logical, legal and most economical use, or potential use. This applies to land regardless of where it is located. However, if you own a piece of land and you know a permit can be obtained to erect a ten storey office building on it, but no one wants to erect a ten storey office building on it, then it cannot, at present, be valued as a site for a ten storey office building.

Now, if you insist that this land is still worth its value as an office building site, you must wait until someone agrees with you to the point of paying you a sum of money based on this. If you exhaust all means of disposing of it under this valuation, and are unsuccessful, then what? You can wait, and wait, and wait, or you can lower your sights and entertain offers, possibly based on some alternative use. If you receive offers that are less than you had hoped they would be, and turn them down, then you are simply "buying it yourself" for the value of the offers that were unacceptable to you. So *a piece of land is really worth what someone is willing to pay for it.*

We are concerned here with land as a site for an apartment building. To be forewarned is to be forearmed, and if you read this chapter carefully, study it, and apply the same ground rules to your own property, you will be in a very good position to sensibly evaluate any financial proposition that comes your way.

Let us assume that you live in a house with a lot that has a frontage of 30 ft. and a depth of 150 ft., and you can reasonably expect to receive $23,000 for it on the market. One day you are approached by a developer with an option or offer to purchase your property for $29,000, subject to certain conditions. He says there is a redevelopment underway in your block, so how about running through the details and signing. Well, what do you do? You know the offer, on the surface is attractive. You hadn't thought about moving, but here is a chance to make some money, perhaps buy a better home, take a trip, pay all the bills, move into an apartment, or any one of numerous reasons. You are suspicious. Why would this man offer you more money than your house is worth? If he will offer you that much, perhaps he will offer you considerably more. Why is he offering you $29,000? Why not $30,000, or $28,000?

The answer is very simple. He is trying to make the offer as attractive as possible to you, and you can be assured that at the same time it will be attractive to him. No developer will fire his best shot the first time he takes aim because you are a moving target that has to be steadied. A developer is inclined to get heartburn in his pocketbook if he has his initial offer accepted, because he is always left with the nagging doubt that he might have obtained it at a lower price. We are going to examine this situation, and you are going to learn why, in this case, the developer could very well afford to pay you, and reasonably so, not $29,000, but $36,000!

The Initial Approach

Before we go into the mechanics and arithmetic of this, let's examine the most probable approaches that will be made to you and the pitfalls, by the use of one of the following documents.

Option to Purchase: This is simply an indenture between you, as the Vendor, and a second party, the Purchaser, whereby you grant to the purchaser the sole and exclusive option, irrevocable within a certain time limit, to purchase your property at a sum of money agreed upon by both parties. It will contain the following:

(a) A cash consideration to you, which will be credited to the purchase price on closing. If the purchaser does not exercise his right to accept the option by a date agreed upon, you retain this money, and the option becomes null and void.

(b) The stated and agreed upon purchase price.

(c) A stated sum of money to be paid to the agent upon acceptance of the option by the purchaser, which will be held in trust until completion.

If the purchaser is going to proceed with the transaction, you will be advised by letter before the time limit has expired, and the sale will be completed within a prescribed period of time from the date of such notice of acceptance on the part of the purchaser. If you do not receive such advice, the option is null and void.

There are two especially important points to bear in mind in this document. Let us say that you agree to grant the purchaser an option to purchase your property, and the option granted will be open for acceptance by the purchaser up to, but not after, a date six months from now. The document will state in writing that the contract arising from the acceptance of this option will be completed, let us say, 30 days after the date of acceptance of the option, at which time, of course, you will have sold your property and moved out. But read this carefully. This does not mean that you have 6 months (plus the 30 days) to further enjoy living in your home. The purchaser could legally accept the option 48 hours after you have granted him the option, in which case you will have 48 hours (plus 30 days) in which to kiss the old homestead good-bye.

People have found themselves in an awkward position because of this, and it is for this reason that I shall spell out very clearly the two points I have just mentioned. Read them carefully:

Point One: The option hereby granted shall be open for acceptance by the purchaser up to, but not after, the__day of____19__., and may be accepted by a letter delivered to the vendor or to the aforesaid agent or left at the agent's usual place of business. In the event that such option is not accepted in manner aforesaid this agreement and everything herein contained shall be null and void and no longer binding upon any of the parties hereto and the vendor shall be entitled to retain the said sum given as consideration for the granting of this option. In the event of and upon the acceptance of this option by the purchaser in manner aforesaid this agreement and the letter accepting such option then become a binding contract of sale and purchase between the parties and the same shall be completed upon the terms herein provided for.

Point Two: The contract arising from the acceptance of this option shall be completed__days after the date of the acceptance of the option as hereinbefore provided, on which date the vendor will convey the said lands to the purchaser or his nominee by a good and sufficient deed thereof in fee simple, free and clear of all encumbrances and dower rights, save as aforesaid, and shall deliver vacant possession of the said lands to the purchaser free of all tenancies unless the real property is rented, in which event the purchaser is to accept any present tenancy and be entitled to the receipt of the rents and profits thereafter.

The option then goes on into the detail of adjustments on completion, etc.

If the price in the option is the fair market value of your property *under its present use and zoning,* you have every right to expect financial compensation for such an option, *but* if the price in the option is based on the fair market value to the developer after he has gone to all the trouble and expense of obtaining municipal authority for his project, thereby creating an inflated price for your property over its present value, you should not expect to receive financial compensation over and above the minimum legal requirement, which is usually $2.00. By financial compensation, I mean the cash you will retain in the event that the purchaser does not accept the option by the time limit you have agreed upon.

Now don't sit there and jump up and down saying that you wouldn't give anyone an option on your property for $2.00. Be fair about it. You can't expect to have your cake and eat it too. Remember, by his concerted efforts the developer, and he alone, is attempting to make it possible for you to receive a much higher price for your property than its current market value.

Offers to Purchase: Whereas the option is straightforward and to the point, an offer to purchase your property, which is an agreement of purchase and sale, is straightforward all right, but it takes quite a while to get to the point due to the conditions you will find in it.

Where it is necessary for a developer to apply to municipal authorities for a change in zoning, the following are basically the conditions you can expect to find in an offer.

(1) Purchase agreements to be obtained on specific properties in your block by a certain date, usually within 90 days. This will allow the purchaser to know where he stands, how much land he will have, etc., and whether or not he can proceed with his application for rezoning. Remember, no one can apply for rezoning if he has no agreement of purchase on the subject property.

(2) Subject to application for rezoning being approved by the provincial municipal board by a fixed date, usually in about 12 to 18 months. It takes time, money and work.

(3) The offer will contain an agreement to deposit a sum of money in trust pending completion of the sale. If the conditions are not fulfilled, this money is returned to the purchaser, and *not* to you, and the agreement is null and void.

If you receive an offer subject to rezoning, ask a few questions about the "coverage" the purchaser intends to go after. It may be stated in the offer and it may not be. It may simply say something about a building density acceptable to the purchaser, without being specific. If you decide to sell based on a fair price against, for instance, 200% coverage, and the developer receives 250%, you could stipulate in your agreement that your price will be adjusted accordingly. Get it? Think, and think with a sharp pencil.

Time for Your Sharp Pencil: A developer will have a projection in mind of what he can hopefully expect to build on your land, and that of your neighbours. As you have read, one of the conditions in his offer to purchase your property will be that he must be successful in obtaining a change in zoning from the municipal and provincial authorities to fit in with his projected plans. To explain this I shall use the zoning by-laws of the City of Toronto for an example.

At the present time the zoning for residential buildings is:

Zone 1   35%   coverage
   "   2   60%   "

"	3	100%	"
"	4	200%	"
"	5	250%	"

which simply means that if you are now in Zone 2, and the developer intends to apply for a change in zoning to a Zone 4, and is successful, he will be able to erect an apartment building in Zone 4 that contains a maximum gross floor area equal to 200% of the area of the land in question. In other words, if he had a site containing 40,000 sq. ft. of land, he would be allowed to erect a building containing a gross floor area of 80,000 sq. ft.

This is then broken down into a square foot allowance for apartment suites to make his estimates simpler to work with. If the developer decides that a fair measurement for the average suite in the proposed building would take up 800 sq. ft. of the area of the building, he would simply divide his gross floor area by 800 to arrive at the number of suites the building will contain. This does not mean that the average size of the suite itself would be 800 sq. ft. It is a *gross* allowance of the total building area. In the case of an 800 sq. ft. allowance, for instance, the size of the individual suites would be approximately:

Bachelor suite	400 sq. ft.
1 Bedroom suite	600 sq. ft.
2 Bedroom suite	800 sq. ft.

Other municipalities have their own zoning by-laws, which may stipulate the number of suites in an apartment building allowable for each acre of land, or the number of sq. ft. of floor area, but the end result is the knowledge by the developer of the size of his project. He will usually break this down into a fixed number of suites based on an average, such as the 800 sq. ft. His offer to purchase land will therefore naturally be based on what he expects to be able to do with it.

To arrive at his projected land costs, there are 3 factors the developer must ascertain:

Income: By looking at current rents in the immediate area of his project, the developer can reasonably assess from this information what he could expect to receive in renting his new building. If, for example, he finds that it would be reasonable to expect an average of $2.75 per sq. ft. gross income from the building, and his plans show an average gross allowance per suite in the building to be 800 sq. ft., this would mean that his average rental per suite would be 800 × $2.75, or $2,200.00 per suite per year.

Current Operating Expenses: Let us assume that he found that at the time of his projection, the total operating costs for his building would amount to 40% of his gross income. Operating costs include:

Taxes	Insurance
Heating	Management

Utilities	Superintendent
Maintenance	Vacancy Allowance
Supplies	Misc. & Audit

Current Construction Costs: If, by experience and advice from quantity surveyors, he finds that he can expect to construct his building for $12.50 per sq. ft., this would again be broken down into the cost per suite, which in our case would be 800 × $12.50, or $10,000 per suite.

Sometimes a municipality will require him to pay something towards sewer costs, etc., and this is all taken into consideration in his estimates.

Now he has these three factors:

1. Income:	$2,200 per year, per suite
2. Operating Costs:	40% of gross income
3. Construction Costs:	$10,000 per suite

Now I'll show you why he can afford to pay you $36,000.00 for your property:

Rent per suite:	$2,200
Less Operating Expenses (40%):	880
Net Income:	$1,320

He is figuring that he must receive 10% return on his investment; therefore, this net income of $1,320 represents 10% of the total cost of the project per suite, land and buildings, or $13,200.

He knows that the construction costs are going to be $10,000 per suite, so this leaves him:

	Per Suite
Total cost of project:	$13,200
Construction costs:	10,000
Available for land:	$ 3,200

Well, what does this mean insofar as his ability to pay you $36,000 for your property is concerned? Just this: Remember, he is projecting this on 200% coverage. His average allowance per suite is 800 sq. ft. For every square foot of land he obtains, he can put two square feet of space in his building. Your lot, being 30 x 150, contains 4,500 sq. ft. This is worth 9,000 sq. ft. in his building. With an allowance of 800 sq. ft. per suite, this means:

$$\frac{9000}{800} = 11.25 \text{ suites}$$

We know he can allow $3,200 per suite for his land, so 3,200 × 11.25 equals his ability to pay you $36,000.

Using this same yardstick, he will make his estimates on land offers simple by breaking it down to an allowance per square foot of land:

$36,000 divided by 4,500 square feet equals eight dollars per square foot.

He will then use this figure as a basis for all his offers to the property owners in your block that he would like to include in his plans. In your own case, of course, your 4,500 sq. ft. × $8.00 is $36,000 again.

Another way to prove this is to multiply the average allowance for his suites (800 sq. ft.) × $8.00 = ($6,400) per suite, divided by his "coverage", which in this case is 200%, or twice:

$$\frac{\$6,400}{2} = \$3,200 \text{ per suite}$$

He can also arrive at land costs by sticking to the square foot, instead of figuring by the suite:

Income:	$2.75
Operating costs 40%	1.10
Net return:	$1.65

This $1.65 will again represent 10% of his investment, or $16.50 sq. ft. for his building, including land costs. Construction costs being $12.50 sq. ft., this will leave him:

	Per Sq. Ft.
Total cost of project:	$16.50
Construction costs:	12.50
Available for land:	$ 4.00

However, this $4.00 must be multiplied by *two* because you will remember he has obtained 200%, or double coverage, which gives him our land allowance of $8.00 per sq. ft.

Now, instead of waiting for someone to come along, let's assess your own land:

(1) Go to the office of your municipal clerk, check the zoning book, and find out what "coverage" or sq. ft. of building has been generally allowed in your neighbourhood.

(2) By a little snooping, you can find out from some big-hearted real estate salesman what land in your area has recently sold for "per suite", and he will probably tell you the sq. ft. allowance per suite.

With this ammunition, if you find, for example, that land has sold in your area for $2,800 per suite at 900 sq. ft. average, and the coverage was 225%, why, just do the following to find out what your land could be worth.

$$\frac{2800 \times 225}{900} = \$7.00 \text{ sq. ft.}$$

That's the formula! Here's the proof:

$$\frac{900 \text{ sq. ft.} \times 7.00}{2.25} = \$2,800$$

If no redevelopment has recently been established near you, then you'll have to make some speculative estimates, which you can work out from the arithmetic I have given you, but in any event, if an offer or option does come your way, you will be in a better position to understand what it is all about.

However, you must remember a few things. Unless you own a very large piece of land, the developer will have to obtain purchase rights to other properties to make the proposal worthwhile. Ideally, he would like to get the whole block. Municipal authorities are beginning to frown on spot zoning (less than one block) and if he does get the whole block and receives a favourable response to his application for rezoning, the developer can look forward to a possible bonus, which may be in the form of an increase in the size of his building, or possibly the addition of a number of "town houses" to his main building.

He will work on averages. If he can obtain an agreement to purchase 5,000 sq. ft. at $6.00 per sq. ft., and he knows he can afford to average $8.00 per sq. ft., then he will have an allowance in reserve of $2.00 per sq. ft., for 5,000 ft. He needs this. You might be the rough guy and demand $10.00 per sq. ft. for your property. He would then be able to pay the price.

You are going to hold out for a big fat price? Sometimes you'll get it, sometimes you'll kill the proposed development, or possibly you might be left with a house in the middle of nowhere, which has happened. It is your property and only you can sell or refuse to sell it to a private party.

But whatever proposal you get, take it to your lawyer and have him explain the legal implications fully to you, regardless of how simple it looks. I cannot stress this too strongly. Your lawyer is a trained legal expert. You are not. An offer, or option, to purchase your property is a legal document. Your lawyer's fee for advice is a minimal factor compared to the headaches he can save you.

You might wonder about the value of a parcel of raw land and its use. Basically, whether it is intended by the municipality to have its use designated housing, industrial, or commercial, its value will be determined on the following basis:

(a) Current market value of serviced land
(b) Less cost of servicing

To illustrate this, let us assume that a ten acre parcel of raw land is zoned for residential use, and it were determined that a serviced lot would be reasonably worth $10,000 to a builder. If it cost $4,000 to service each lot, that is, to supply sanitary and storm sewers, roads, etc., this would leave a value of $6,000 for the raw land per *lot*.

If the zoning called for four lots per acre, then simply multiply the $6,000 by this zoning, and the raw land would be worth $24,000 per *acre*.

39

The Selling Commission You Pay

Real estate boards have a commission and fee tariff which is adhered to by its members. If a member broker accepts a selling commission or fee below the board's tariff, the broker can be penalized by a fine set by the board.

Some board members have undoubtedly charged less without being discovered, but generally the tariff is firm.

If you wish to sell your property through an agent at a fee lower than board charges, the only alternative is to try agents who are not members of a real estate board. There are agents who are qualified to serve you, and who may charge a lower selling fee, but maximum property exposure demands the cooperation of as many agents as possible, which is what a real estate board member can offer.

The greatest exposure your property can get is through the multiple-listing service offered by real estate board members. This service provides every broker/salesman member of the real estate board with a photograph and details of your property.

A basic thing to remember about a real estate agent is that he is in business for the same reason anybody else is in business — to make money (which is a reasonable observation).

You may wince when you have to pay an agent $1,500 for selling a $30,000 property, but what if the agent doesn't sell it after working diligently on the listing? Remember, it costs money to operate a real estate office; especially the advertising crunch, which is inexorable.

Who pays the agent for working on your behalf without effecting a sale? Somebody has to pay the overhead, and that somebody is the vendor whose property the agent has sold.

When an agent lists ten properties and sells five, the five sales carry the five no-sales, and the no-sales are fortunate in having an agent work on their behalf for nothing, which is only possible because somebody else has provided the agent with the expense money to work for nothing on behalf of the no-sales. If it were possible to be absolutely certain that all listings would be sales (which it isn't) then the costs to the vendor would undoubtedly be much lower.

The author has gone through a period of criticism of standard real estate charges, considering some of them to be too high. I have even gone so far as to offer my services to property owners to sell property for a fee of $1,000 regardless of the price of the property. This plan, however public-spirited it may have been, didn't work.

To effectively sell property an agent needs the cooperation of other agents, and other agents were understandably reluctant to work on listings that produced small financial returns. If an agent agreed to work on one of the "thousand dollar specials" his office would receive 50 per cent of the fee. By the time the office deducted its share for overhead, the selling agent would be left with about $250 which really isn't enough for effecting, say, a $60,000 sale.

There is a large international real estate organization based in New York City that has established a very sound method of selling propery throughout the world. Its system is not suited or geared to handle the local neighbourhood property, but to larger properties (including homes) that could conceivably attract buyers from all parts of the world.

The firm charges the owner a listing fee equal to 2 per cent of the appraised value of the property, which is paid immediately upon signing the listing agreement. Then the property is photographed and full details listed in a monthly publication which is mailed to brokers all over the world. The brokers, in turn, deal directly with the owner, and if a sale is effected, the owner pays a further fee to the selling broker. And in case you don't think that this is such a hot idea, it is interesting to note that each year hundreds of millions of dollars worth of real estate is listed by this method.

So here we have thousands of property owners each year willing to pay to have their properties listed. If the average homeowner were asked to pay a 2 per cent listing fee he would recoil in horror. The accepted practice is "sell it and I'll pay" — no sale, no pay.

Therefore, it is the agent who is willing to take you and your property on, realizing that he could work without cost to you, who is performing and offering a distinct service to your advantage. So remember, when you pay a selling commission, you are also paying for the no-sales, and when your property is not sold, somebody else's sale paid your freight.

At least one real estate organization in Toronto has an overhead of One Hundred Thousand Dollars a month! Think of it. If the office split the income with its selling agents, this means that, at 5 per cent, the firm would have to sell about fifty million dollars worth of real estate each year just to break even.

The broker with about 20 or 30 salesmen can have problems. All salesmen are not top producers; it costs money to train a man, not knowing if he will be a firecracker or a dud. The modest broker doesn't need very many months of poor performance to go under.

Some people apparently think that getting a broker's license is tantamount to having a license to print money, buy fancy cars, drink the best champagne, take her nibs on luxury cruises and keep the family wallowing in luxury. Nothing could be further from the truth.

A relatively few succeed, and very few become large successful brokers. One would be more assured of success by investing in a well located donut shop than trying his hand as a real estate broker.

The next time you list your property for sale, and the agent, after working diligently on it, produces no sale, ask yourself this question; would *you* work for nothing? When you pay a selling commission, pay it and thank the agent. His job is no sinecure.

40

Insurance

Insurance secures protection against property loss in consideration of a payment proportioned to the risk involved.

Property insurance includes real property, buildings and contents, machinery, merchandise, household furnishings, valuables, automobiles, boats, aircraft, ships and cargoes, and in fact any insurable object in which a person has an insurable interest.

When you are going to have property insurance placed, don't call your cousin Joe and ask him for his advice, unless he happens to be in the profession of placing property insurance. Consult a properly qualified insurance agent.

In the process of obtaining property insurance, you bump headlong into a matter of good faith between you and your agent. If you know something materially affecting the acceptability of the risk, and do not tell the insurer about it, that is called a "non-disclosure"; and if you tell the insurer something that is not in accordance with the facts, that is a "misrepresentation". Your non-disclosure or misrepresentation of material facts when the insurance is applied for makes the contract voidable, at the election of the insurer, upon his discovering the situation.

You must have an *insurable interest* in property, without which your insurance contract is void. An insurable interest in property is when you stand in such a legal relationship to it that you may be prejudiced by its loss or damage and stand to benefit by its continued existence. If you simply took out a policy on property belonging to somebody else in which you have no financial interest, you are merely making a bet with the insurer that the property will not be lost during the policy period, and such a contract would be void.

You do not, of course, have to be the owner of property to have an insurable interest in it. For example, those who have possession of the property of others, such as bailees, pledgees, pawnbrokers, warehousemen, carriers, jewellers, furriers, tenants, etc., have an insurable interest. Their interest arises out of their potential liability to make good loss or damage to the property in their care. Others with an insurable interest are executors, administrators and other trustees, mortgagees, lienholders, vendors under conditional sales agreements; and lessees and other users of property which they employ for gain and who may therefore suffer business loss if it is damaged or lost.

Your indemnity, up to the limit of the policy, is to be fully indemnified for what you have actually lost in money value, but you can make no profit out of the occurrence in case of loss. Your loss is the cost of restoration or repair in the event of partial loss, with due allowance for betterment, and, in the case of total loss, it is the depreciated actual cash value of the property at the time of loss — the insurer pays the true *pecuniary* loss, no more, no less.

A *valued policy* is one covering loss or damage to chattels under which, on *total* loss of the insured property, a fixed sum is payable which has been agreed upon between you and the insurer at the inception of the contract. Generally speaking, and subject of course to gross or fraudulent over-valuation, the stated amount is payable by the insurer without reference to your actual monetary loss. Generally, your insurer requires you to obtain an independent valuation of the property before entering into such a contract.

The first form of insurance was marine insurance on ships and cargo. Next came fire insurance, and today fire insurance accounts for about 20% of all insurance business written in Canada.

A fire insurance policy will cover you in the event of your property being destroyed or damaged by fire, lightning, or an explosion of natural, coal or manufactured gas, without allowance for any increased cost of repair or reconstruction by reason of any ordinance or law regulating construction or repair, to an amount not exceeding, *whichever is the lease,* of:

(a) The actual cash value of the property at the time of destruction or damage.

(b) The interest of the insured in the property.

(c) The sum set opposite an applicable item in the policy, and subject to any pro rata provisions.
The policy will not cover:

(a) Loss or damage to goods while undergoing any process involving the application of heat, whether fire ensues or not.

(b) Loss or damage caused by riot, civil commotion, war, invasion, act of foreign enemy, hostilities (whether war be declared or not), civil war, rebellion, revolution, insurrection or military power.

(c) Loss or damage to electrical devices or appliances caused by lightning or other electrical currents, unless fire ensues and then only for such destruction or damage as results from such fire.

(d) Loss or damage caused by contamination by radioactive material directly or indirectly resulting from an insured peril under the policy.

(e) Money, books of account, securities for money, evidence

of debt or title, and automobiles, tractors and other motor vehicles.

(f) Loss or damage to the building or its contents during alteration of or addition to the building and in consequence thereof; normal repairs being allowed without permission.

(g) While the building insured or containing the property insured, is, to the knowledge of the insured, vacant or unoccupied for more than thirty consecutive days, or being a manufacturing establishment, ceases to be operated and continues out of operation for more than thirty consecutive days.

The cardinal principle being that the contract of property insurance is a contract of indemnity, you will not recover more than the actual value of your property at the time of the loss.

A provision of your fire policy is that in no event shall the insurer's liability exceed what it would cost you to repair, or replace, the property with material *of the same kind and like quality*. This is not the proper measure of damages which you may invoke, but, rather a limitation on the insurer's liability.

The term "value" is difficult to define with exactness, and as a result several interpretations have developed. Establishing value is, to some degree, a matter of opinion, but several concepts are useful in arriving at the true meaning of value as used in insurance contracts. One of the basic concepts of value is "actual cash value", which is defined as replacement cost less depreciation. This concept is useful in that it establishes a value which is designed to restore you to the same financial condition you were in prior to the loss.

A problem arises here because you usually must replace the damaged or destroyed property at full cost, and so must pay for the cost of the depreciation at that time. On certain types of property it is often possible to avoid this situation by insuring on a *replacement cost basis* so that the value will be determined on the actual amount required to restore your property without having to take into consideration the item of depreciation.

Interrelated to actual cash value and replacement cost are the concepts of : (1) value in use, and (2) value in exchange. Value in use refers to the benefits you derive from property in the form of shelter, income, health, or pleasure. Value in exchange is a measure of goods which can be valued in terms of the price at which the property would have sold, not exceeding the cost of replacement.

There are two primary and fundamental obligations which you must assume if a fire insurance contract is to be effective and binding upon the insurer. You are responsible for the determination of the amount of insurance for which the policy is written, and for proving a claim in case of loss. Unless you meet these obligations, the effectiveness of the policy is jeopardized and its purpose is materially affected.

Misunderstanding by you as to your responsibility for these two points would probably be partly due to the fact that insurance is future indemnity; purchased today against loss, which may or not be realized. Loose thinking could also be a factor. The amount of a fire policy relates to the value of the property to be insured. You should insure for the full value of the property in order to get the best protection. At the time the contract is purchased a properly qualified appraiser should enter the picture.

Remember that your insurance policy will cover you to the extent of the actual cash value of your property at the time of loss, but not exceeding the amount which it would cost to repair or replace the property with materials of the like kind and quality, and not exceeding the amount of the insurance you have effected. You must realize that premium cost for the protection is based not only on the value you put on your property, but also upon its type and character. Indemnity payable at time of loss is based upon a specified type of value at that time.

Judges and lawyers have expounded on the meaning of actual cash value, but are still confronted with new and exceptional interpretations of it. It is not book value, historical cost, purchase cost, trended costs, nor the result of cube or square foot computation, although this information when properly applied can assist in its determination. Remember that the intention of the contract is to place you in the same position after the loss as you were before.

In many instances when an insured business suffers a severe loss from fire and additional perils that may be covered, the insurance settlement falls short of the loss. Primarily the reason for claim settlements coming into this picture are (a) insufficient coverage against the background of the present day values and (b) the insured's misunderstanding of the basic fundamentals of a standard fire contract.

There are several advantages in securing an appraisal beyond the point of satisfying an insurer's enquiry as to whether insurance to value has been written. Primarily, appraisals for fire insurance are invaluable for the following reasons; (a) to insure proper coverage without over or under insurance; (b) to provide immediate proof of loss in the event of fire, as required by the conditions of the fire policy, and (c) to facilitate settlement of claims through availability of a written record covering inventory of destroyed property with itemized values. Appraisals will also help you in the following:

(a) Sale or purchase — to assure the seller that he is receiving a reasonable price under current market conditions, and to provide the purchaser with an analysis of the value of the property, both from the standpoint of current market and long term investment value.

(b) Financing — to provide the lending institution with an unbiased statement of value which could be accepted to expedite a loan.

(c) Expropriation — to ensure adequate compensation for actual value of property taken in whole or in part for public improvement, or expropriation.

(d) Reorganization or merger — to establish, through the opinion of a disinterested appraiser, a fair value of the assets, thus assuring equitable distribution of the assets to the interested parties.

(e) Litigation — to provide an expert opinion as to the value of the property to assist the Court in ascertaining value, and the assurance of the availability of expert testimony if required in the process of litigation.

(f) Liquidation — to provide accurate estimate of the sum that may be realized from liquidation of assets.

(g) Accounting — to provide an estimate of the cost of replacing assets under current conditions, and to establish present worth of assets.

The appraisal will be paid for by you, and if you don't have it done, you are being "penny wise and pound foolish". Without it, in the event of partial or total destruction of your property, you will undoubtedly find that to furnish a proof of loss, stating the exact value of the property to the satisfaction of the adjusters, may present a serious problem.

You should review your insurance coverage periodically. *All of it.* It is something we are sometimes guilty of ignoring until it is too late. Place a bookmark in this page to remind you to call your insurance agent. Or, better still, never mind the bookmark. Call him now!

41

Fire Protection

When I was a boy it was a great thrill to chase the "fire-reels" because we knew that at the end of the chase there was going to be a real show; but unfortunately it very seldom had a happy ending, because I remember that most of the houses burned right to the ground.

I haven't seen a house burn to the ground for years, undoubtedly due to the increased efficiency of fire-fighting equipment, and maybe because I don't chase the trucks any more, but we do still have fires and plenty of them. In 1971, for instance, there were 51,333 residential fires in Canada, and as I light my cigarette I am reminded that 42% of them (21,592) were caused by smokers' carelessness.

Read this chapter carefully, and when you have read it, read it again. It could save your life, and the lives of your loved ones.

In Case of Fire

Shout "Fire": to arouse persons nearby if you see fire, or smell smoke or gas. If you believe the fire to be in a room, a cupboard or in a basement section, keep the doors closed. Quickly shut any doors and windows that will help confine the fire, cut down the draft and prevent spread of deadly gases. This will give everyone more time to escape.

Out You Go: Save lives by getting everyone out of the building involved as quickly as possible. Don't wait to dress yourself or children — wrap them in blankets.

If you have to go upstairs or away from exits to rescue children and you are unable to return to the ground floor, or if you are otherwise trapped, get to a room with a window, quickly shut the door between you and the fire, and shout for help. Don't jump from upper storey windows except as a last resort — wait for help.

Remember, the air is usually better near the floor in a smoke-filled building.

Summon the Department: by telephone *only* after all are out.

Never go back into a burning building. It can be totally involved in flame in seconds.

Try to hold the fire in check with equipment at hand while the fire department is responding. Fight the fire only if you are not endangered.

Don't waste time or your life.

Plan in Advance: Have your plan of escape from fire worked out in advance. Everyone should know the plan, and the reasons for each part of it.

Alternate escape routes are a *must* because one or more of the ways out may be blocked off by fire.

Escaping from one-storey buildings is relatively simple — there are alternate routes through any of the windows to the outside. But remember, storm and screen windows may be difficult to get through. Make sure there is something such as a chair available to smash them out.

Two-storey buildings require more planning because the stairway may be blocked off by fire, smoke or hot gases. Be prepared to use upper windows, perhaps to the roof of an adjacent building, by having ladders strategically located, or by means or a rope with knots at every two feet anchored to the inside of windows.

Remember, in the event of a fire during sleeping hours, a closed bedroom door may save your life.

If conditions permit, gather everyone together into one room before attempting to escape. Children are easily lost in the confusion.

When escaping *never* open the window before the door is closed behind you. This cuts down the draft which would help to spread the fire into your area of escape.

Fire drills should be carried out often enough so that everyone's role becomes automatic.

Methods of evacuating children and sick or aged persons should be studied particularly.

Everyone, including children, should know how to telephone the fire department and the number to call.

If in doubt, have your local fire chief check over your escape plan with you.

How to Fight Home Fires: When you blow out a match you extinguish a fire. It is easy to do at this stage. However, small fires can grow and join to destroy an entire city. The first five minutes are vital. Keep calm, don't panic! Remember, each fire is different.

Clothing Fires: Don't run, it fans the flame. Act quickly to smother the fire. Make victims lie down, then roll them up in a rug, coat, or blanket with the head outside. Gently beat the fire out. Give burn or shock first aid.

Cooking Fires: (involving fat, grease or oils): Turn off the stove or appliance and cover the pan, or close the oven, or pour baking soda on the fire, or use an approved type of fire extinguisher. Never use water! It will spread the flame.

Electrical Fires (motors, wiring, etc.): Unplug the appliance if possible. Use an approved type of fire extinguisher, or throw on baking soda. Never use water on live wiring, or you may get an electrical shock.

Fires in Ordinary Combustibles: Keep near the door so that you can escape if necessary. Stay low out of heat and smoke. Aim a stream at the base of the fire. For floor fires sweep from the edge in, for wall fires sweep from the bottom up. Stay outside closets, attics, etc., and shoot the stream in. Ventilate the area only after the fire is out. Remember, if the fire is large, get out and close the doors behind you.

Home-type fire-fighting tools are very effective against small fires. Brooms, or mops soaked in water, blankets, rugs, buckets and garden hoses are good examples. A threaded hose connection on each floor of the house (in bathroom, kitchen and basement) and a good length of garden hose properly coiled is a good fire protection.

There are numerous fire extinguishers on the market suitable for home use. Make sure that you use a type listed and labelled by a nationally recognized fire testing laboratory, such as the Underwriters' Laboratory. Otherwise you cannot be sure it is reliable.

Home fire-fighting equipment will not be of any help unless you know how to use it. You will not have time to learn how after a fire breaks out. Read the instructions on the fire extinguisher *now* and be sure that everyone in the house knows how to use it and the other equipment as well.

The equipment is of no use unless it is in good working order. Check with the dealer or your local Fire Chief regarding maintenance of your type of extinguisher.

Do not risk your life unless it is to save another life. The house can always be rebuilt, and unless it is a small fire you probably cannot extinguish it by yourself anyway.

Instruct Your Babysitter: During your absence the babysitter is responsible for the safety of your children and your property. Impress upon her that in the event of fire, the first and most important thing to do is to get the children out quickly and stay with them. Tell her to wrap them in blankets, not take time to dress them. The following rules will assist you in advising her:

Show her through your house so that she will be familiar with each part of it, and leave *your* municipal address by the telephone.

Be sure she knows the quickest way out for the children if she has to get them out because of fire.

Show her the alternate escape routes in case the regular route, such as the stairway, is blocked off by fire.

Show her how to control the heating equipment in case this should be necessary.

Give her the telephone number of a nearby friend who can

come to her assistance quickly, as well as one where you may be reached if possible.

She must call the Fire Department as soon as possible from a neighbour's house.

A Safety Fire Test

Can you answer "yes" to all these questions? Questions which receive a "no" answer indicate potential danger spots which need prompt attention and correction. Inspect your home yourself — today!

In Case of Fire: Is the number of the nearest fire department posted near the telephone?

Have you instructed your family in a plan of action if fire breaks out?

Have your family been instructed and drilled on the location of exits from the house and how to close all windows and doors in case of fire?

Do you keep exit routes clear — especially of such things as room heaters and stoves which might start a fire and block your escape?

Are bedroom windows large enough and sufficiently unobstructed to serve as emergency exits?

Care of Children: Do you make it the rule never to leave small children alone or unattended?

Do you show your babysitter the escape routes from your home, and give instructions on the right way to call the fire department?

Do your babysitters (and you) know the first rule of safety in fire emergencies: get everybody out fast, and don't go back in?

Are your children trained to keep a safe distance from flame and spark sources?

Electrical: Has wiring been checked by a qualified person since installation?

When new appliances were added to the load, was wiring inspected and any necessary new wiring installed by a qualified electrician?

Do you check your fuse box regularly to see that only specified sizes are being used?

Are all electrical appliances in good condition; are they being properly operated?

Are all electric motors kept oiled, clean and free from dirt accumulation?

Lightning Protection: Has your radio or television antenna been equipped with a properly grounded lightning arrestor?

Heating Equipment: Have your stoves, furnace, chimney and smoke pipes been checked and cleaned where necessary within the past year?

Are furnaces and stoves at least 18 inches from any exposed woodwork?

Do any stove pipes run through attics or concealed spaces?

Are smoke pipes, when running through combustible partitions, protected by a double ventilating metal thimble?

Do you prohibit the use of gasoline or kerosene for starting or quickening fires in your home?

Does your fireplace have a metal screen in front of it to prevent sparks from flying onto the carpet or furniture?

Are all portable heaters of a type listed by the Canadian Standards Association?

Is your portable oil heater always placed on a level floor to ensure proper operation?

Do you always refill the fuel tanks of portable heaters out of doors and in the daylight?

If you use a wick-type portable oil heater, do you trim the wick and clean it regularly?

Do you always turn your portable oil heater out upon retiring at night or when moving it from one part of the house to another?

Flammable Liquids: Are small quantities of gasoline stored in safety cans?

Have you made it a rule never to use flammable liquids like gasoline or kerosene for cleaning clothes or starting fires?

Are oil saturated or paint rags properly disposed of or stored in metal containers?

Smoking Habits: Are approved design ash trays provided?

Is smoking in bed strictly against the rule in your home?

Do you make a bedtime check for smouldering butts lodged in chesterfiields and also upholstered furniture?

Are you careful how you dispose of cigarettes, cigars and pipe ashes?

Are matches and lighters kept out of the reach of children?

General: If you use L.P. gas, are the cylinders outside the buildings on a solid foundation and located away from windows and basement doors?

Do you keep rubbish cleaned out of the attic, basement, closets, garage and yard?

Do you use extreme care when using lighter fuel to ignite your barbecue?

Do you spray your hair only away from open flames or lighted cigarettes?

Fire Protection: Have your fire extinguishers been checked and recharged if necessary within the past year?

Do you have approved fire extinguishers?

Do members of your family know how to use your fire extinguishers?

Do you have enough garden hose supplying water?

Like many of the tragedies in life, fire, or at least its worst effects, can be avoided if we only think about it beforehand, and act wisely. Remember — if you learn the rules, and never need them, you lose nothing: If you never learn them and need them, when fire occurs, you may lose everything — including your life.

Hundreds lose their lives each year in Canada as the result of fire — most of them children.

42

Physical Protection

"It can't happen to me!"

What this really means is: "It *hasn't* happened to me."

About ten years ago I was living in a very smart apartment building in a top Toronto location. One of the "nice" neighbourhoods. Nothing could happen there!

One evening I arrived home in good spirits, looking forward to the pleasant task of entertaining friends. When I opened my apartment door I was temporarily stunned. Everything but the two chesterfields, a large chair and the T.V. set was strewn all over the place. If I had employed professional mess-makers they couldn't have done a better job.

Someone had very neatly entered my premises, filled a large suitcase (*my* suitcase) with everything of conceivable value that could be carried in it, and disappeared.

His method of operation was my one piece of luck. The burglar had done the same thing to other apartments on lower levels, and my suitcase with its entire stolen contents (with the exception of a watch) was found in another apartment. The picking was apparently much better there, so he helped himself, dropped my belongings, and fled.

Don't think for one minute that it can't happen to you!

The first thing you must do to start protective measures for your home is make a note of your police department telephone number. Keep it near the telephone, clearly visible. In an emergency dial "O" ask for police and immediately give them your name and address.

Protection of the home begins with you. In the home. It cannot be effectively carried out without your assistance and co-operation.

No home, whether apartment or house, can be burglar-proof. However, the security of every home can be improved to the point that a burglar will not risk the chance of detection which is ever-present in a well protected home.

1. Have your doors mounted so that the hinge bolts are not exposed on the outside.

2. Have your locks properly mounted, of good quality, and able to be dead-locked.

3. Have your doors equipped with a chain-type doorstop, to prevent the door being pushed open suddenly when unlocked.

4. You should know where all the keys for your locks are distributed, and don't distribute them indiscriminately.

5. Don't leave a key under the welcome mat at your front door; a stranger might take it literally. Don't "hide" it outside the door. It won't be hidden from a burglar.

6. It is not a good idea to have car and house keys in the same key case, if your name and address is in the case. In case of loss, and discovery, someone knows where they can gain easy access to a home.

7. If you have lost or mislaid keys, you should have your locks changed.

8. Have your window locks and catches in good working order, and be sure to use them.

9. Windows that provide easy access to your home should be protected with extra locks.

10. When inspecting your home for weak points, keep in mind that burglars will use ladders, garbage pails, trellises and low roofs to reach windows and doors that are not normally accessible.

11. Consider also these other openings into your home:
(a) The milk chute which may allow someone to enter by crawling through, or which may provide access to the door-lock.
(b) The coal or wood chute, again a way of entering.
(c) Openings which contain air-conditioning units or exhaust fans which can be pushed in to gain entry.

12. Your garage should be kept locked to prevent burglars using your tools and equipment to break into your home, and to prevent theft.

13. When going out for the evening, leave lights on in one or two areas in your home, *and a radio playing.*

14. When going away for extended periods of time, you should:
(a) Arrange with your neighbours to watch your home, and notify the police department if they see anything suspicious.
(b) Arrange to have all deliveries stopped, including bread, milk, newspapers, and in addition, *have a neighbour pick up handbills and circulars.*
(c) Have some type of equipment, such as an automatic timing device, to turn light on and off at designated times.
(d) Arrange to have the grass cut regularly.
(e) Leave instructions with a neighbour or your building superintendent where you can be reached in an emergency.

In other words, when you are going away, leave your home so it has that "lived-in appearance", which helps to frighten off the burglar.

15. If you are an apartment dweller, you should:

(a) Refer unknown persons seeking entrance to your building to the superintendent and never let them in with *your* key.

(b) Let your superintendent know at all times when your apartment is usually vacant.

(c) Report the presence of suspicious persons to the superintendent or to the police department.

16. If you live in a house:

(a) Have a close neighbour who knows when your home is usually vacant who could report to the police any suspicious person around it.

(b) You should report the presence of suspicious persons or automobiles in the neighbourhood to the police department.

17. If your doors are solidly constructed, have a "peep-hole" device which will enable you to identify a caller without opening the door.

18. Your valuables and extra cash should be kept in a safety deposit box at your bank or trust company.

19. You should keep a record of serial numbers and other identifying marks on your valuables in the event they are stolen.

20. Do not trust your memory with such things as license numbers. Write them down.

21. Always verify the identity of hydro, gas and other service men who seek entry to your home.

Now that you have read this chapter, there are two things you can do right now.

(a) Place the telephone number of your police department on your telephone, clearly visible.

(b) Read this chapter again, and check the points one by one to see how much safer you can make *your* home for you and for your family.

General

43

Quick Appraisals

An appraisal of real property is an opinion of its value. The logical arbiter of an appraisal is the buyer.

It can be said that there will be one of three price tags on every bit of privately owned property in Canada.

(a) The lowest would be that of an owner who suddenly finds he absolutely *must* sell and sell quickly, for any one of a number of reasons.

(b) Next we have the owner who wishes to sell, but is prepared to wait until the property has been exposed on the market for a reasonable length of time before accepting what he considers to be a fair price.

(c) The highest price tag would be on the property that is *not* for sale. Period.

The three basic approaches to appraising real property are (1) comparable sales, (2) replacement value, and (3) capitalizing a cash flow from an investment (rental property).

There are well trained, professional real property appraisers from coast to coast, and if you want the last word in appraising done, call one of them. However, there are times when you don't want to be stuck with a fat appraisal fee because all you want is a general idea of the approximate market value of property as a potential buyer or seller. This chapter can help.

Appraising your land for an apartment site is covered in a separate chapter. Here are a few other examples of the value of an appraisal.

Land Value For Commercial Buildings

Permit: Obtainable to construct an office building containing a gross floor area of 120,000 s.f. (square feet).

Question: What is the land worth?

There are three things to know in addition to the above, and with them you have the problem solved.

Income: You must be able to have a reasonably assessed rental income figure. This can be determined by finding out what rents are generally acceptable and applicable in the area of the project in buildings comparable to the one proposed. If you find that the figure is $5.00 per s.f. per year, you must remember that this figure refers to *net* rentable space. The net rentable area in an office building is about 15% less than the total area of the building, so in order to arrive at a gross figure you have to deduct 15% from the $5.00, which will leave you with an average figure of $4.25 for the *entire* building area. So we'll use $4.25 for our figure.

Operating Expenses: You will be safe in assuming that the operating expenses (including taxes) will amount to 50% of your gross rentable income. It is quite a common practice today for lessors to require lessees to agree to tax *and* maintenance escalation clauses, which naturally means that this 50% will seldom be exceeded, and guarantees the lessor a fixed return on his investment.

Construction Costs: This figure is easily obtainable from a firm of quantity surveyors. For our example we are going to assume the construction costs to be $19.00 per s.f.

Step One

Deduct the operating expenses from the income:

Income: 120,000 ft. × $4.25	$510,000
Operating Expenses: (50%)	255,000
Net Return:	$255,000

Step Two

The developer wants a 10% return on his investment, so this $255,000 represents 10% of $2,550,000, which is the allowable cost for the project, including land.

Step Three

Deduct the construction costs from the allowable cost:

Allowable:	$2,550,000
Construction (120,000 × $19.00)	2,280,000
	$ 270,000

This $270,000 is the allowance for the land. If the land is to cost more, or construction costs are higher, the rental income must be adjusted. If this cannot be done, you might be in trouble. This is a quick guide, and can be used in any commercial construction venture.

There is an old rule of thumb in real estate that says the land is worth "one year's gross income of the commercial building".

This is how it works, but of course is dependent on building costs and market value of space. For example, the following would be a good stab at downtown bigtown — you can work your own figures very easily to suit particular cases:

Per Square Foot

Gross Income:	$ 10.00
Operating Expenses: (50%)	5.00
Net return before financing:	$ 5.00

($5.00 capitalized at 10% is $50.00)

Building Costs:	$ 40.00
Land Costs:	10.00*
	$ 50.00

*This figure is multiplied by the density.

If the zoning allowed a building density of 12 times the land, the land would be worth $120.00 per square foot.

Gross Income: ($10.00 × 12)	$120.00
Operating expenses: (50%)	60.00
Net return before financing:	$60.00

($60.00 capitalized at 10% is $600.00)

Building Costs: ($40.00 × 12)	$480.00
Land Costs:	120.00 (*per sq. ft.*)
	$600.00

Appraisal of Existing Commercial Buildings

The value here is again based on income and operating expenses. Anyone investing money wants to know what he can expect to receive on his investment. In this I shall include apartment buildings, and start right in with a statement on one that sold recently for $1,180,000.00. The following are actual figures for an audited annual statement:

Gross Income			
(89 suites)		$169,464	
Laundry machines		1,920	$171,384

Expenses			
Maintenance & supplies	$ 4,800		
Taxes	26,852		
Heat and Hydro	17,000		
Water	2,410		
H.W. Tanks (rental)	1,121		
Gas heat (garage area)	600		
Elevators (contract)	1,500		
Insurance	670		
Superintendent	5,000		
Vacancy allowance	5,140		
Management	5,000		70,093
Income Before Debt Charges			$101,291

When you look at the end result, the net income of $101,291, you will immediately realize that this is not 10% of the selling price, so that if an investor wanted to receive 10% on his money, he wouldn't get it here because this building just shows a net return of 8.58% on a cash basis. Buildings like this are not purchased for cash, and if they are they are financed at a later date. You will note that the net income shown was "before debt charges" which means charges for mortgage repayment. This property had 2 mortgages on it, totalling $1,100,000. The combined interest and principal carrying charges on the two mortgages totalled $91,848 a year, and when this figure is deducted from the $101,291, it leaves us with a net return of $9,443. The purchaser bought the property for $1,180,000 with $80,000 cash and assumed the two mortgages. This left him with a net return on his investment of:

$$\frac{9,443}{80,000} \times 100 \quad \dots \dots \dots \dots \dots \dots \quad 11.8\%$$

If you wanted to work on a straight basis of giving an investor 10%, then you would appraise this investment to be worth 10 times the net return figure of $9,443 or $94,430 cash to the existing mortgages. All this, of course, is on the assumption that the buildings are in good repair.

Any other type of commercial building, whether it is a large office building or a corner store with an apartment upstairs, will be appraised basically in the same manner. Everything will be gross income less total expenses, which will leave you a net figure representing a percentage return on your invested capital.

The foregoing is the generally accepted way of doing it, but mortgages can make such a difference in the end result of such an appraisal that it is advisable to compare the net figures on a mortgaged property with the results of capitalizing the cash flow *before* mortgaging (which is how the government does it for estate appraisals — it ignores mortgage charges).

Appraisal of an Industrial Plant

This one is easy. You forget about the possibility of anyone buying the plant. You assume it is vacant and estimate what can be realized by leasing it on a *net lease* basis. A net lease is one where the lessee pays all charges pertaining to the property, including municipal taxes, maintenance and repairs, insurance, etc., thereby giving the owner a fixed return on his investment.

For example, if it is assumed that you could expect to receive 85¢ per s.f. per year in income from the property, and the building contained 10,000 s.f. of rentable floor area, then the yearly fixed income would be $8,500.

The next thing to determine is what an investor would expect to receive on his money, and this can vary with the strength of the company to which the property will be leased. If it can be leased to an AAA Dun and Bradstreet rating, then it is conceivable that the investor would be satisfied with an 8% return. This establishes the value of the property:

$8,500 is 8% of $106,250

If the credit rating of the company isn't this good, the investor would probably want a 10% return.

$8,500 is 10% of $85,000

So the industrial plant would be worth somewhere between $85,000 and $106,250.

An investor will not purchase a vacant building, unless he believes he is getting a real bargain. The property must be leased, and then his purchase price will depend to a great extent on the covenant of the tenant.

If the property is being appraised just as bricks and mortar for an estate, or for reasons other than outlined above, then it is again a matter of arithmetic. Add together construction costs (determined by a firm of quantity surveyors) and land costs (determined by recent sales of land in the area), and then deduct the cost of necessary repairs to put the building in top shape to arrive at its current value. But in the end, the appraisal will have a direct relationship to the income that may be expected from the building.

Appraisal of Your House

If you want a price tag put on a house, it is a piece of free cake. Just call the local office of your neighbourhood real estate broker, ask them to send over someone who has been selling properties in the area for at least three years, and let him tell you. You can do this two or three times with different brokers and they will be pretty close together in their estimates.

Real Estate Boards don't like their members advertising "free appraisals" but I have never met one who would refuse to give one. It's good business for them. If they can't get your house listed for sale right away, they may make a favourable enough impression on you to be remembered and possibly recommended to one or two of your friends who might be making a move. The appraisal will be verbal, or it might be written on the back of a salesman's card. Don't expect anyone to give you a written appraisal for nothing. This costs money, and so it should.

Appraisal costs can range from a house appraisal of about $75 to fee appraisals starting at $175 per day.

If your house is a fairly standard plan, the appraisal will be more accurate. Sales comparisons are easy. If your house was constructed with the original owner in mind and has some odd-ball nooks and crannies, or something different about it, then don't forget that in selling the property someone has to be found who will go along with such things, and this has to be taken into consideration in the appraisal.

I firmly believe that the best person to appraise your house is a real estate sales person who has been actively working in your neighbourhood for the last three years.

A Farm: Mostly based on recent sales for comparable land plus allowances for buildings and equipment. A good farm broker is your best guide, and if you are a farmer working your farm you *know* what it is worth. Farmers are like that. The minute a farm is sold, the party lines start buzzing, and the most recent sale, with all the details, is well known for 9 miles as the crow flies.

House Building Lots: Sometimes a man will pay $15,000 for a lot that should normally be worth $10,000. But what is normal when it comes to location in building a man's dream house? I am not talking about sub-division lots but about odd ones that come on the market unexpectedly in built-up areas. They are snapped up immediately, usually by builders who are tipped off by alert real estate salesmen. If you want a building lot in such an area, you have to do a lot of ground work yourself. Get in the car and systematically drive through your selected neighbourhoods, noting all the addresses of houses that have unusually large lots beside them. Check the ownership through the assessment office; they will for the most part, be owned by the owner of the house next door. If you spot one that is particularly appealing to you, check the zoning by-laws first to ensure there would be enough land for construction. *Don't phone the owner* . . . knock on his door and speak to him personally. He just might have a reason for wishing to entertain an acceptable offer on the vacant lot at the time of your call. In any event, your personal visit will be remembered in case he might think about it, whereas a phone call is just a phone call. Sometimes this approach produces wondrous results, and it is about the only way to do it.

The appraisal of the lot then is done by you and your builder and the owner. Your builder will give you a very good idea of what the lot should normally be worth,, but if you can't get it for that, then you have to ask yourself what it is worth to you to be located there. This can be where an appraisal is thrown right out the window and the heart takes over.

Other Properties: If you want a price put on a business venture, call a broker who spends most of his time specializing in the sale of businesses. If you want a price put on a summer cottage, call one who is actively engaged, as evidenced by his "for sale" or "sold" signs, in the resort area. Pick the broker. Don't call a commercial broker if you want to sell grannie's old homestead, and don't call a residential broker if you want some help of a commercial nature.

Real estate brokers are very active, alert to changing values and can provide you with a straightforward appraisal of anything that can be called real estate, but whatever your reason for calling on one to assist you in an appraisal, ask him for his reasons for the amount of his appraisal.

44

Capital Gain Tax Appraisal

A capital gain tax is payable only when one actually realizes a gain (profit) through disposal of real estate by selling, by giving it away, or by dying. If you leave the country the Government will have something to say about that also.

Valuation Day (V-day) applies to real estate owned on December 31, 1971. When determining gains or losses on disposal of such real estate, if valuation day value and selling price were the only figures used to calculate gains or losses, the calculation would sometimes result in greater gain or loss than actually occurred over the period of ownership, because the V-day value could be greater or less than the cost of the property, and the property could be sold for a gain or loss over its cost.

To be fair about this, a taxpayer can elect to use a "median" rule, to determine gain or loss, which is fully explained and illustrated in a readily available booklet titled "Valuation Day". This can save you money, and is available by writing to the Department of National Revenue, Ottawa.

No capital gain tax will be paid on one's "principal dwelling", if its sale reflects a profit. This includes up to one acre of land. Farmers may use this rule or deduct $1,000 per year from gain on sale of home and farm land.

All other real estate owned and sold and producing a net financial gain to the owner will be subject to a capital gain tax. Although any new tax law is often considered to be a "foot in the door", the current tax is not as bad as one might assume.

Fifty per cent of the net profit realized in selling real estate subject to the tax is free of tax. The other fifty per cent is to be added to your taxable income for the year of the sale. If you are lucky enough to find yourself in a 50% tax bracket, it means that the Government gets 25% of the net profit on the sale.

Remember, I said "net" profit. You may deduct legal fees, real estate selling commissions, improvements and other legitimate costs in selling.

If you lose on one sale and gain on another, half the losses may be deducted from the gain. If there is a loss balance left, you may deduct up to $1,000 of the unclaimed portion each year in the future from *any* income. Losses not deducted in the tax year may be carried back one year, and carried forward indefinitely.

As for V-Day, time presses on, and some time in the foreseeable future, most privately owned real estate in Canada will change hands. When that time comes, will you and/or your estate be able to present adequate and sensible evidence to the Department of National Revenue concerning the reasonable market value of your taxable real estate as of December 31, 1971?

For those actively engaged in the business of buying and selling real estate, profit is still profit, and the net profit will not be subject to a capital gain tax, but will be *all* taxable. But for the millions of Canadian property owners not in the real estate business, how is a value to be determined for V-day?

If your home (principal dwelling) is located on more than one acre of land, the excess land will be subject to tax when the property is sold profitably.

One might assume that the value to be placed on this excess land can be determined by referring to the municipal assessment of the property. For example, assume a property having a home and four acres of land is assessed as follows:

House:	$20.000
Land:	$5,000
Total:	$25,000

The land being 1/5 the value of the property.

If the property is sold at a figure that produces a net profit to the seller of $10,000, the taxable portion of the gain would be:

$$\frac{10,000}{5} = \frac{2,000}{4} \times 3 = \frac{1,500}{2} = \$750 \text{ taxable}$$

Although this system has been popularly used in the past, the income tax department has found that the use of the ratio of land and buildings used for municipal assessment purposes is not reliable in many cases in determination of the market value of either land or buildings. Furthermore, many municipalities no longer provide a breakdown of the assessment between land and buildings.

So you'll need an appraisal.

For the owners of homes, cottages, hunting lodges and other personal-use property, and small investment holdings such as houses and duplexes, the valuation for the record will be fairly simple. If the properties were purchased during the latter part of 1971, use the purchase price as valuation.

If one thinks he got a real bargain and bought under the market price, or if the property were purchased prior to about July 1971, it will be advisable to obtain a proper appraisal to determine V-day value.

An unsupported letter of opinion from a real estate agent can be quite helpful to a taxpayer in estimating the value of his property, but it has *limited value* in cases when the opinion is challenged, particularly when the person who gave the opinion is not available to explain the basis used to arrive at his conclusions. The one who would do the challenging of course, is the income tax department.

Do not assume for one minute that the Government will accept your own V-day opinion of value, or that of your neighbourhood real estate agent unless it is supported, which means an appraisal. One would be well advised to ignore the opinions of those who advise against obtaining proper appraisals by qualified experts. The money spent on an appraisal is a sound investment, and it must be done in the near future while V-day values can be readily determined.

For the owners of investment properties, it can be a bit confusing. Houses, for example, generally have a higher market value than capitalization of the investment cash flow would indicate. To capitalize something is to convert it to capital. One Hundred Dollars capitalized at 10% produces a capital value of One Thousand Dollars. Just divide the annual return by the required annual rate of interest and multiply by 100 to arrive at a capital value of the investment.

For example, assume one owns a house which is rented for $200 a month.

Annual gross income:	$2,400
Less taxes, etc.	750
Investment cash flow:	$1,650

Capitalizing this cash flow at 10% would indicate a value of $16,500. Capitalizing it at 9%, $18,333 and at 8% $20,625. The house, could be well worth more than any of the three figures, so here one would logically have the property appraised for fair market value *as a house*, and not as a so-called investment property. The income tax department will undoubtedly agree that the use of an income approach for a single family home is not a practical method in most cases.

Small multiple dwellings such as duplexes and triplexes command higher prices than an "investment property" because of their popularity. So have them also appraised for market value and forget about capitalizing the cash flow in determining their value as an investment.

Owners of multiple dwelling units, living and maintaining a home in one of the suites, will only be able to treat the owner's lived-in portion of the building as the principal dwelling, tax free. The rest of the building will come under the provisions of the capital gain tax.

However, if you own a rooming house jammed to the rafters with roomers, it would probably produce a higher market value figure by capitalization than by a house appraisal. If so, use the capitalization for value, but by doing this, one must remember that the income figures would probably have to be substantiated by an income tax return.

Appraising larger investment properties is usually done by employing qualified appraisers. Owners of these larger properties will also have their own auditors.

A question often raised is "what capitalization rate can be used?" As the foregoing illustrates, the higher the rate, the lower the value of the property, and conversely, the lower the rate, the higher the value of the property. Rates vary with the size, type and quality of investment property; a proper appraisal will support the rate used in determining value.

Appraising by replacement value is often done for insurance purposes. Reviewing your insurance policy with your agent, and having him arrange an appraisal of the property will serve a twofold purpose: appraisal, and no arguments about insurance claims.

Many farm properties close to urban centres will appear to present a difficult assessment of value. The owner of a farm who sold to a housing or other subdivider will undoubtedly have received a price out of proportion to that of the farm as a farm. What about the farm owner next door? His land could still be zoned agriculture, and he can be forgiven for hungrily eyeing the fat price obtained by his neighbour.

Unfortunately, zoning will of necessity have a bearing on value, because if it did not, a chain reaction of inflated values could set in from farm to farm, and where would it settle down? If you own such a farm, be prepared to pay plenty of taxes on a possible future high price to a developer.

Procrastination is a way of life. Get the value recorded and substantiated. Don't panic, but get it done. It can save you or your heirs a headache at a later date.

Differences of opinion between taxpayers and the Department of National Revenue on valuation matters are not uncommon, and when they occur all reasonable effort is made to negotiate a value acceptable to all concerned. When it is not possible to reach agreement the final decision will rest with the Tax Review Board or a higher court.

Taxpayers may visit, telephone or write their own District Taxation Office for help. In many instances the regular information staff will be able to answer your questions.

But some taxpayers will have what may appear to be difficult and complex problems. These will be referred by the regular information staff to the Informal Consultation Service which is staffed by officers in each District Office with special training. The experts, in turn, will be in ready touch by telephone with a central group of experts.

As soon as an answer can be provided by this Informal Consultation Service, the taxpayer will be contacted by telephone or by the quickest possible means. The advice will not be binding on the Department, but will be the best opinion that can be given without the detailed documentation that would be required for a binding Advance Income Tax Ruling.

So you see, you will have plenty of help.

45

Checking on the Neighbours

Have you been curious about your neighbours? What did they pay for their house? How much did they get when they sold it? How big is their lot? Do they pay less taxes than you do? How much do they owe on the house? How old are they?

It is amazing what you can find out about your neighbours without asking them or anyone else one question. The answers to these and many other questions are a matter of public record, and all you have to do is locate the right office of your municipality, open a book, and there they are.

The average Canadian assessment office has a standard system of keeping records relating to the ownership of property and its details. If you want to find out the details of Mr. & Mrs. Jones' property, all you have to do is go to your assessment office armed with the municipal address of their property, give the address to the clerk on duty, and he will provide you with a large assessment volume which will answer all your reasonable questions.

The assessment office will not tell you about the purchase price or the selling price of a property, mortgages, liens, etc. This information will be supplied to you through the public records of the Registry Office or the Land Titles Office, whichever is applicable.

In a large Canadian city you can expect to find the following information in the assessment office about any particular property:

(1) Municipality

(2) Ward Number

(3) Division Number of Ward

(4) Book Number of Ward

(5) Assessment roll number

(6) *Dash number*, which will indicate the number of tenants in building.

(7) The class of property, as designated by:

R / Residential	VR / Vacation Resort
PC / Professional & Commercial	SW / Slash & Wasteland
MI / Manufacturing & Industrial	F / Farmland
PCMI / Combination of above two	C / Corporation

(8) The property address

(9) Lot frontage in feet and inches right down to 1/8 of an inch

(10) Lot depth in feet and inches right down to 1/8 of an inch

(11) Names and addresses of owners, lessees and tenants. If the owner lives at the property, it will indicate this. If the owner is an absentee owner, it will provide you with his address

(12) Owner's occupation

(13) The marital status of the owner, as designated by:

MW / Married Woman

   S/Spinster

   W / Widow or Widower

   B / Bachelor

If it is not designated, the owner is a married man.

(14) The "OLTFV" Column, which will indicate:

   O / Owner

   L / Lessee

   T / Tenant

MF / Municipal Franchise

   V / Vacant property

   U / Unfinished property

   E / Other than above

(15) Citizens Status column, which will indicate:

          A / Alien

Not designated / Citizen

(16) School support Column

S / Separate School supporter

P / Public School supporter (if Roman Catholic)

If nothing is designated, it will indicate a public school supporter (OTHER than Roman Catholic)

(17) Religion Column

E / Anglican (C. of England)	AM / Armenian
AE / Atheist	B / Baptist
BH / Bahaism	BU / Buddhist
CH / Chinese	CR / Christadelphians
CS / Christian Scientist	CC / Church of Christ
E / C. of England (Anglican)	C / Congregational
DI / Disciples of Christ	EO / Eastern Orthodox
EV / Evangelical	GT / Gospel Tabernacle
GC / Greek Catholic	GO / Greek Orthodox
J / Hebrew	HN / Hindu
IB / Int. Bible Student	IS / Islamic
IB / Jehovah's Witnesses	J / Jewish
LS / Latter Day Saints	LU / Lutheran
MO / Mohammedan	MR / Mormon
MS / Moslem	PL / Pentecostal

PN / Polish National
PR / Protestant
RC / Roman Catholic
7D / Seventh Day Adventist
SP / Spiritualist
UT / Unitarian

P / Presbyterian
QU / Quaker
SA / Salvation Army
SI / Sikh
UK / Ukrainian Catholic
UC / United Church

(18) Year of Birth

(19) Particulars of Amount of Assessment:

"T" indicates Tenant's portion, then it will show:

Land
Main Building
Other
Total Taxable or)
Portion not exempt)
Exempt
Portion Unfinished
Partial Exemption

(20) The dollar assessment liable for tax rate, broken down as:

Residential)	Residential)
Public)	Separate)
Commercial)	Commercial)
Separate)	Public)
Business)	Business)
Assessment)	Assessment)
Public)	Separate)

(21) Date of Delivery of Tax Notice

(22) Number of Residents

(23) Number of dogs

If you wish to know the taxes in dollars and cents on any property, and want it to the nickel, just walk over to the tax department, and they will probably give the figure to you. You can also get an idea by simply multiplying the assessed value of the property by the current mill rate in its property category, such as residential or commercial, but be sure you deduct the exemptions.

Concerning yourself with such things as the selling price of property, mortgages, liens, etc. is another matter.

To obtain this information you must first ascertain the system of registering property in your neighbourhood, and where it is registered. When you have determined this, and have the required details to properly identify the property, the rest is simply a matter of *searching title*.

Searching under a land titles system of registration will be comparatively simple because everything pertaining to one individual piece of property will be on one page. Searching under the registry office system will take much more time, especially for city properties;

you might have to jump from page to page and book to book. There will be a small fee for obtaining the proper abstract books to do your searching, and when you have pinpointed the property and information you want, you can go further into it by requesting to examine the instruments, or actual documents pertaining to such entries as title and mortgage deeds, registrations, assignments and discharges of mortgage deeds, liens, leases, etc.

There are some things that even a registry office cannot tell you. For instance, if a property owner were the mortgagor in a $20,000 mortgage deed, he might have whittled it down considerably, but the records won't indicate it. This can be only verified by checking with the mortgagee. Of course the records will give you the complete details of the original loan, its repayment schedule, and maturity date.

A trip to a registry office is an education, and its activity is also a good barometer of the real estate market.

46

Mechanics' Liens

Provincial statutes provide protection to suppliers of material, or workmen who have supplied material or services in the construction of real estate. Basically, materialmen, that is people who supply material in the erection of buildings, and persons who render services can have a lien upon the property to the amount of the value of their particular services or material. This is called a Mechanic's Lien, and can be enforced by court action.

A good example of how it is governed would be the following notes on the Mechanics' Lien Act of Alberta.

1. The act provides protection by way of a statutory lien in favour of mechanics, material suppliers and wage earners for improvements to land.

2. A labourer, a manager, officer or foreman whose wages are not more than $25.00 cannot waive his lien.

3. The lien cannot be for more than the sum due to the contractor. The lien arises when the work is begun or the first material is furnished.

4. The lien has priority over any unregistered mortgage or any mortgage that is registered. Where a mortgage has been registered before the lien, the lien has priority to the extent of the increase in value as a result of the improvements, and a lien cannot be barred or foreclosed in any proceedings under the mortgage.

5. A judge can order a sale of the premises and the distribution of the proceeds is made according to the Act.

6. A lien for the wages of a labourer has priority to the extent of six weeks' wages over all claims.

7. A lien has the same claims to the proceeds of insurance as against the land.

8. An owner can retain 20% of the value of the work done if less than $15,000 or 15% if over $15,000 for certain periods outlined in the act, and the balance can be distributed. A mortgagee can retain out of periodic advances the same percentages as an owner.

9. The right of a lienholder may be assigned by an instrument in writing and if not assigned, passes upon his death to his personal representative.

10. A lien may be registered with the land titles office by completing a statutory form and it ceases to exist if the lien is not so registered within 35 days of the completion or abandonment of the contract or sub-contract. This time limit is extended to 120 days for an oil or gas well or an oil or gas pipe line.

11. A lien may lapse after service of a notice as provided for in the Act.

12. A lien ceases to exist 6 years from the date of registration unless renewed.

13. A court can order the registration of a lien to be cancelled upon the giving of security or payment into court.

For full reference to a particular province, it is suggested that you write to the Queen's Printer of that province for a copy of the Mechanics' Lien Act.

47

Dower Rights

At common law, dower is the right of a wife to an estate for life in one-third of certain freehold estates of her deceased husband. During the life of her husband, a wife has an interest in his real property which cannot be alienated or interfered with by her husband without her consent.

Dower attaches very strongly, and even if the legal estate rests in the husband briefly, it cannot be removed except by the wife's release.

Common law right to dower has been retained in Ontario and the Maritime Provinces.

In Newfoundland, there are no dower rights. All lands, tenements and hereditaments are chattels, and are handled by an executor as personal property.

In the western provinces, dower is restricted to a wife's estate in lands of her husband's "homestead". In Alberta, the husband and the wife have the same dower rights in each other's homesteads, which will surprise many who are of the opinion that a dower right belongs only to the ladies. They include:

(a) The right to prevent disposition of the homestead by withholding consent.

(b) The right of action for damages against the married person if a disposition of the homestead that results in the registration of title in the name of any other person is made without consent.

(c) The right to obtain payment from the Assurance Fund of an unsatisfied judgment against the married person in respect of a disposition of the homestead that is made without consent and that results in the registration of the title in the name of any other person.

(d) The right of the surviving spouse to a life estate in the homestead of the deceased married person.

(e) The right of the surviving spouse to a life estate in the personal property of the deceased married person that is exempt from seizure under execution.

"Homestead" means a parcel of land:

(a) On which the dwelling house occupied by the owner of the parcel as his residence is situated, and

(b) that consists of:

(*1*) Not more than four adjoining lots in one block in a city, town or village as shown on a plan registered in the proper land titles office, or

(*2*) Not more than one quarter section of land other than land in a city, town or village.

The Alberta Act provides statutory form for consent to a disposition of a specific homestead or for a general release, or a release for a consideration. The Act also provides for dispensing with consent by a judge in certain cases i.e., where a married person and his or her spouse are living apart, where whereabouts of spouse are unknown, where there are two homesteads, etc.

The forms must be strictly adhered to and should be prepared and executed before a person who knows the Act.

There are remedies in the event one spouse disposes of his homestead without a consent or an order of the court dispensing with consent.

A spouse can elect as to which homestead she or he claims dower.

Where a husband and wife are joint tenants or tenants in common, both have to sign the disposition so that the dower rights are released.

Instruments releasing dower or consenting to a disposition must be acknowledged before a commissioner for oaths, a notary or a solicitor.

The acknowledgement must be signed freely and voluntarily without any compulsion on the part of the husband or the wife. The usual practice is for the husband or the wife to sign apart from the other spouse.

In the Province of Quebec, dower is covered by the civil code. There are two kinds of dower, that of the wife and that of the children, and are either legal or customary, or prefixed or conventional.

Legal or customary dower is that which the law, independently of any agreement, and as resulting from the mere act of marriage, establishes upon the property of the husband, in favour of the wife as usufructuary (the use and enjoyment of lands or tenements without the right to alienate such), and of the children as owners.

Prefixed or conventional dower is that which the parties have agreed upon, by the contract of marriage.

Conventional dower excludes customary dower; however, it is lawful to stipulate that the wife and the children shall have the right to take either the one or the other, at their option.

The option made by the wife, after the opening of the dower, binds the children, who must remain satisfied with whichever dower she has chosen. If she dies without having made the choice, the right of making it passes to the children.

If there be no contract of marriage, or if in that which has been made the parties have not explained their intentions on the subject, customary dower accrues by the sole operation of law. But it is lawful to stipulate that there be no dower, and such a stipulation binds the children as well as the mother.

Dower, whether conventional or customary, is not regarded as a benefit subject to the formalities of gifts, but as a simple marriage covenant.

The right of conventional dower accrues from the date of the contract of marriage, and the right to customary dower from the date of the celebration, or from the date of the contract if there be one in which it is stipulated.

Customary dower consists in the usufruct for the wife, and ownership for the children, of one half of the properties which belong to the husband at the time of the marriage, and of one half of those which accrue to him during marriage from his father or mother or other ascendants.

Property which the husband has contributed (as movable under a clause of mobilization) in order to bring them into the community, is not subject to customary dower. Neither are properties by fiction, composed of movable objects which the husband has reserved to himself by the clause of realization in order to exclude them from the community.

For full reading of dower rights in all Provinces, write the Provincial Queen's Printer and ask for the following:

British Columbia (Victoria)	Wife's Protection Act and Homestead Act.
Alberta (Edmonton)	An Act respecting the Interests of Married Persons in each other's Homesteads.
Saskatchewan (Regina)	Homestead Act
Manitoba (Winnipeg)	The Dower Act
Ontario (Toronto)	The Dower Act
Quebec (Quebec City)	Quebec Civil Code
New Brunswick (Frederiction)	The Dower Act
Nova Scotia (Halifax)	The Dower Act
Prince Edward Island (Charlottetown)	The Dower Act
Newfoundland	No reference

48

Title Insurance

Title insurance is corporate indemnification against title losses, whether arising out of matters of public record or matters not of record, such as forgery, fraud, concealed marriages, etc. The insured may be anyone who has an interest in real estate including home owners, mortgage lenders, industries and leaseholders.

From a legal standpoint, it may be defined as a contract of indemnity against loss or damage arising out of defects in, or liens upon the title to real property. A definition would be "the application of the principles of insurance to risks incident to real estate titles".

Title insurance is not a gamble, nor is it guesswork. Just as the life insurance company bases the issuance of its life policies upon physical examinations made by competent doctors, so does the title insurance company base the issuance of its title policies upon careful examinations of titles made by experienced title lawyers.

Every lawyer who examines titles is aware that there may be defects in titles of which he cannot take cognizance in his opinion: defects arising from fraud, forgery, conveyances by minors or persons of unsound mind, demands of missing heirs, dower, rights of divorced persons, deeds by defective corporations, errors in registration and copying and many other like curcumstances that are liable to occasion serious financial loss to investors in real estate or real estate securities. Title insurance is protection against financial loss through such defects as these and all other matters adversely affecting the title as insured.

Under the terms of a title policy, should the title be attacked, the insurance company through its approved lawyers will defend it in court at its own expense. Should loss be suffered, the insurance company must protect the assured.

There are three basic policies available:

Owners Policy: This policy is generally used in insuring all estates of ownership, occupancy and possession and remains in force as long as the insured or his heirs have any interest in the property. In addition, when the property is sold the owners policy continues to protect the insured against any action for recovery by a subsequent purchaser.

Mortgagee Policy: This policy is used to insure estates or interests held by lenders as a pledge or security for the payment of a debt. Such estates or interests exist in many different forms, dependent largely under the laws and customs of the local area. Liability upon the mortgagee policy is reduced as payments upon the mortgage are made, and terminates upon satisfaction of the debt, whereas liability upon an owners policy is perpetual and indeterminate.

The coverage of the mortgagee policy is designed to meet the security needs of mortgage lenders. This coverage is broader than that of the standard owners policy.

The mortgagee policy provides continual protection to each successor in ownership of the mortgage. Loss payable under a mortgagee policy is automatically transferred to the assignee of the debt and security. In the event of foreclosure and purchase by the holder of the security, the policy automatically becomes an owners policy and insures the purchaser as owner of the fee, against loss or damage arising out of matters existing prior to the effective date of the policy.

Leaseholder Policy: This policy protects a leaseholder against loss or damage sustained by reason of eviction or curtailment of his leasehold interest through title difficulties. Such policies are usually written on long term industrial or commercial leases.

Premiums for most other forms of insurance are recurring and must be paid periodically. Title insurance policies continue in effect for a *single premium.*

There are many practical advantages of title insurance which arise directly as a result of title defects against which a lawyer cannot or would not certify, and for which he is not responsible in the event of a loss suffered by real estate investors.

The possibility of human error that may result in financial loss is always present. Registry office employees can easily err in copying and indexing deeds, mortgages and other instruments that affect the titles to real property. Nor is any lawyer infallible. In spite of the high reputation enjoyed by that profession, to err is human. Because of the growing number of exposures to risks due to pressure and complexity of present-day real estate conveyancing, title insurance can provide for safety, security and complete insurance indemnification.

After deliberate consideration, no broadminded counsel can for a moment believe that his own opinion of title, based upon a search however properly made, can give his client the security that a title insurance policy will provide.

No lawyer, regardless of his ability, can assure his client that all signatures affixed to the instruments making up a chain of titles are genuine, or that none of the signatures affixed to instruments constituting a chain of title was fraudulently or wrongfully obtained, but a title insurance policy insures against forgery, fraud, duress and misrepresentation.

Some people may be of the opinion that a title insurance policy would not help under the "Torrens" or "Land Titles" system of registration, but it is interesting to note that approximately 50% of title insurance policies isued in Canada cover titles registered under this system. A policy provides indemnity against the following matters, for which compensation may not be available without it under provincial land titles acts.

(a) Provincial taxes, succession duty and municipal taxes, charges, etc.

(b) Any right-of-way or other easement.

(c) Adverse possessory title by encroachment.

(d) Leases not exceeding three years.

(e) Mechanics' liens.

(f) Expropriation rights and public highways.

(g) Errors in survey or description.

(h) A prior certificate of title.

(i) Instruments executed by legally incompetent persons.

(j) Fraud, when not participated in or known to the insured.

(k) Any amount due in excess of that recoverable from the fund.

(l) All costs and legal fees involved in any action or preparation therefor regardless of the success or otherwise of the action or preparation therefor, being related to title matters within the coverage of the title insurance policy.

What does it cost?

Generally speaking, you can expect to pay approximately $4.00 per thousand dollars of protection up to the first fifty thousand dollars, which is ⅖ of 1%, which makes it a bargain considering that the premium is paid just once. A policy on a $25,000 property, for example, would cost you just about $100. On protection above fifty thousand dollars, the charge is less per thousand.

It is well worth serious consideration.

49

Selling Real Estate as a Career

I am not going to attempt to tell you *how* to sell real estate. There are a great many people in Canada much better qualified to do that than I am, and this is not a real estate salesman's handbook. However, I would like to give you something to think about in your attitude and deportment as a salesman.

The days of the old fast-talking, slippery salesmen are numbered and just about obsolete. If you follow the ground rules I have laid down in this chapter, you cannot help but be a better man for it.

Take the word salesman. Look at each letter in the word and imagine that they represent the following words: sincerity, ability, logic, energy, self-control, manners, amiability, name.

Now see what great men have said on the subjects.

Sincerity:
> *Sincerity is to speak as we think, to do as we pretend and profess, to perform what we promise, and really to be what we would seem and appear to be.*
>
> John Tillotson (1630-94)
> Archbishop of Canterbury

When you have a prospect in your car, what are you thinking about? The possible sale? Naturally. But before you get to the point of a possible sale you have to spend some time with the prospect, and this is where a glib tongue is going to get you in trouble and lengthen the distance between success and failure with the prospect. If the prospect is new at the business of associating himself with real estate salesmen, possibly through the potential purchase of his first home or investment, you will frighten him with a lot of blah blah and you will not gain his confidence. If he is an old pro at talking about real estate, your blah blah won't impress him one bit. So be sincere. Being sincere also means being truthful. It's nice to use a little varnish in life once in a while, but before we apply the varnish the surface should be smooth and free of impediments. Get the ground work straight, present the straight honest facts about the property, good and bad; let your prospect know he is dealing with a man who is sincere in his attempt to present a true, clear picture of the property. Don't assume anything about the prospect. Let him come to his own conclusions during the presentation. Once the facts have been made clear, then you can go into the details and advantages of why the man should buy what you are offering him. The real estate sale is not a hit or miss affair, or a one shot deal. Not many prospects buy the first property you show them. So remember, you are competing with other salesmen. Let *them* scare him away.

Ability:

> *Men are often capable of greater things than they perform. They are sent into the world with bills of credit, and seldom draw to their full extent.*
>
> Horace Walpole (1661-1724)
> English Author

Being a real estate salesman means having the competence, aptitude, talents, faculty, skill, power and capacity to work with a multitude of subjects. An example is zoning. This is the imposition of specific limitations on the use of land and the construction and use of buildings in a defined section of a municipality. It is very important to understand it. I remember a very embittered lady who was selling her house. She told me that she bought it to use as a child day-care centre. The salesman who sold her the property told her the particular section of the city in which the house was located was zoned to allow such an operation, and she believed him. He told her a half-truth. It *was* zoned that way all right, but the child day-care centre could be operated only in a building that was specifically constructed for that purpose. The salesman was one of three things: (a) ignorant (b) half-educated (c) a money-grabbing liar.

Let's give him the benefit of the doubt and say he just didn't read the rest of the page in the zoning book and therefore was just ignorant in not telling the woman that she would be making a serious mistake. This sort of salesmanship is inexcusable. Don't let it happen to you. Know your zoning.

Every time you list a property for sale you should thoroughly investigate the zoning. What is its present legal use? What could you do with the property? If the building were demolished, what could you erect on the site? These are not difficult facts to ascertain, but they are important.

Zoning has a great bearing on land values regardless of the present use of the structure. I had a case where I was driving a client back to his office, and on the way he pointed to a modest three storey apartment building and said it was his. Next to the apartment building were three houses. I knew that people had tried to purchase the houses and couldn't afford them because of the zoning restrictions as to the size of a building you could construct. It immediately occurred to me that my client's building had been erected *before* the present zoning by-law, and his small building wasn't utilizing the full building allowance of the zoning. It would not be economical to demolish his building, but what he did do was purchase the three houses, which he was able to do because he added his already unused allowance from his present adjoining property to the allowance he legally had on the site of the three houses. He now owns a very nice brand new 35 suite building in a very desirable area, right next door to his older one. One superintendent looks after them both. It all happened because I just happened to know and understand zoning.

If you know your zoning, believe me, it will add to your income, which is why you are in business.

Another important area is arithmetic. If you are slow in this department, get additional training by attending night classes or obtaining private tuition. It is better to start right from scratch because you have probably forgotten a great deal about the fundamentals of the subject. Here are two simple questions; see how fast you can answer them. If you can't do them in your head, you need a refresher course.

(1) I invest $15,000 in a property that nets me $2,250 yearly. What is my return (%) on investment?

(2) I am paying $1,860 per year rent. This represents a 6% net return on the lessor's investment, which would be what?

You don't have to be a whiz at it, but you should know the basics. I met a real estate salesman one day who had been selling for years. He did *not* know how to establish the unpaid principal balance of a fully amortized loan at any given year, despite the fact that he always carried with him a 224 page book showing monthly amortization tables. The answer to his problem was clearly outlined in the back of his book under a few charts of loan progression. He never bothered to look in the back of the book. He is not a very successful salesman. Play with arithmetic. Doodle with it. Obtain quick finding charts and tables and keep them handy.

Your ability is your responsibility. Learn all you can about your business. Study your provincial and municipal laws, and your real estate board rules. Don't feel discouraged if your manager is obviously lacking in his own knowledge of the business. Work somewhere else. Once I went to a great deal of trouble and a bit of expense obtaining interest factor tables, tailor-made to suit real estate. I had several copies printed and gave one to my manager. He brushed it aside saying, "What good is that?" *Everything* you can learn about your business is helpful.

If you are constantly alert and learning, learning, learning all the time, you will amass an enormous fund of automatic facts at your fingertips. You won't use them all the time, but they will be there when you need them, and you will always have that edge on the competition.

Logic:

It was a saying of the ancients, that "truth lies in a well",
and to carry on the metaphor, we may justly say, that
logic supplies us with steps whereby we may go down to
reach the water.

Isaac Watts (1674-1748)
English divine and hymn writer

Logic is the science of reasoning. You use it every day in the most mundane things you do. It has been said that the basic difference between a monkey and mankind is that a monkey does not have the power of reasoning. He apes things very well. Don't be a monkey in your business; it will save you a lot of time.

Young couples love looking at new houses, regardless of their bank balances. If you are holding "open house" in a $30,000 home and in walks a young couple after hopping out of their 10-year-old jalopy, what do you do? Do you look at them and go back to the racing form? Be logical. Reason.

(a) They *are* looking at houses.

(b) If this one is too much for them, you could possibly steer them into a nice $21,900 job.

(c) The jalopy could be there because the young man is *saving* his money, not because he hasn't got any.

Talk to them. Be friendly. Remember, you are the one who is supposed to know the business. How long have they been married? Both working? Renting? Living at the in-laws? Looked at many houses? A little probing will do wonders, and produce sales.

I well remember a Cadillac and Oldsmobile dealer telling me about one of his salesmen. A man walked into the showroom, looked at a snappy Cadillac convertible and asked the "salesman" how many miles he could get to the gallon with the car. The salesman looked at him and said, "If you have to ask that question about a car, you'd better look at an Olds 88 over here." The man turned to another salesman and repeated the question. The second salesman was logical. He realized that the man obviously must have had some reason for asking the question, and whatever the reason, it required an answer, so he promptly answered the question and just as promptly sold the man the Cadillac.

Don't try to play a guessing game with people when you are selling. Ask questions, and be logical and orderly in your mind about what the answers could or could not mean. If a man is speaking to you about investments, for instance, qualify him quickly by asking him *how much money he would like to invest*, not *how much money he has*. The latter is none of your business. The former is.

When you are listing properties for sale, one of your first

logical questions should be "Why are you selling?" Quite often the reason for selling can be more important than the price. I'll take an overpriced listing any day if I know the owner is moving to Shanghai in six weeks.

Be orderly in your thinking, and this will automatically produce logic.

Energy:

> *Energy will do anything that can be done in the world;*
> *and no talents, no circumstances, no opportunities will*
> *make a two-legged animal a man without it.*
>
> Johann Wolfgang von Goethe (1749-1832)
> German philosopher and dramatist

This is inherent to successful salesmen. They thrive on it. The following salesman's report card on one day's work is a little extreme, but illustrative of how to fail.

9:10	Got up.
9:30	Shaved, listened to news.
10:00	Arrived at office, glanced at paper.
10:15	Had coffee with the boys, discussed 2nd world war.
11:00	Looked over listings other salesmen brought in. (no good)
11:30	Called girl and made date for dinner and drinks. (real doll)
11:45	Called 3 prospects. (nothing doing)
12:00	Out for lunch with the gang.
1:30	Haircut.
1:55	Stopped to supervise manhole operations in street.
2:00	Argued with foreman about moving my car.
2:30	Back at office.
2:45	Coffee break. Read paper. Like to know what's new.
3:15	Argued with client about his lack of knowledge about real estate. Real dumb cluck.
3:30	Criticized wording in offer being prepared by salesman next to me. He's new at the business.
3:45	Double checked on date.
4:00	Nothing doing today so went home. Tough day. Can't understand how that dumb guy next to me had two sales last week.

The "go-go" expression must have been swiped from observing successful salesmen at work. They really go-go. They plan their day's work the night before; then work their plan. When the alarm goes off they put 'er in high gear and are on the job looking forward to a good hard day's work. Their energy is boundless. It is directed.

They know the secret of getting started, and it is really very simple. The best way to do anything is *do it*. To illustrate this, if you are, for instance, going to do some cold canvassing on a street, you might find yourself sitting in your car thinking about it. You simply mechanically open the door, get out, walk up to the first house and knock on the door. Once you have performed this mechanical act you have found yourself forced into a situation because someone is going to answer that door and you are going to have to speak to them. The next knock will be easier and shortly you will find yourself working with a head of steam.

Remember always that selling time is money. You only have so many hours in each day to earn your living, and one of the dangers about real estate selling is your freedom. You are free to knock off for a couple of hours any time, or a couple of days, or a couple of weeks. But you only hurt yourself and your family if you abuse this freedom.

If you are sitting in the office with an hour's break ahead of you, use it. Get on the phone. Talk to people. Talking is energy. Keep talking; your tongue will last as long as you will. Use your 9 to 5 hours for listing, meeting buyers and sellers, and putting them together. Do your paper work and studying at night, when you must plan your next day.

If you put in a good, hard, constructive, honest day's work, you will feel better when you get home. You won't feel that you or anyone else has been cheated. You owe it to yourself and your family.

Self Control:
> *It is the man who is cool and collected, who is master of his countenance, his voice, his actions, his gestures, of every part, who can work upon others at his pleasure.*
> Denis Diderot (1713-84)
> French author

Some people, unfortunately, just do not understand the meaning of this, and probably never will. Self control is:

Keeping quiet when someone else is explaining something to a group of people when he obviously knows less about the subject than you do.

Keeping your temper when your client's little darling drips her ice cream cone on your car upholstery.

Restraining yourself when a potential purchaser is argumentative, bellicose, loud, and has B.O.

Swallowing your pride when your boss sounds off because he thinks you muffed a sale, when you know he is wrong.

Patiently waiting for a late client to keep an appointment, when you "know" he is going to be a no-show.

Smiling when you lose a sale because you sincerely felt the vendor was too greedy.

Being cheerful when your competitor beats you out in obtaining a listing. And sells it.

How is *your* self-control? When was the last time you flew off the handle? Was it worth it? Did it impress anyone? You have to impress people in selling, so easy does it man.

Manners:

> *There is a policy in manners. I have heard one, not inexperienced in the pursuit of fame, give it his earnest support, as being the surest passport to absolute and brilliant success.*
>
> Henry Tuckerman (1813-71)
> American art critic and author

Your carriage, bearing, conduct, deportment, polite, decorous behaviour can be wrapped up in a neat parcel called manners. No one ever had to apologize to anyone for having good manners. I would like just to remind you of a few quotations on the subject:

> *Good manners is the art of making those people easy with whom we converse; whoever makes the fewest persons uneasy, is the best bred man in company.*
>
> — Swift
>
> *Always behave as if nothing had happened no matter what has happened!*
>
> — Arnold Bennet
>
> *Cultured and fine manners are everywhere a passport to regard. They are the blossom of good sense and good feeling.*
>
> — Samuel Johnson
>
> *Good manners are made up of petty sacrifices.*
>
> — Emerson
>
> *Manner is one of the greatest engines of influence ever given to man.*
>
> — Whately
>
> *Nothing is more reasonable and cheap than good manners.*
>
> — Anon
>
> *Good manners are a part of good morals, and it is as much our duty as our interest to practice both.*
>
> — Hunter
>
> *Manners easily and rapidly mature into morals.*
>
> — Mann
>
> *There is no policy like politeness, and a good manner is the best thing in the world either to get a good name, or to supply the want of it.*
>
> — Bulwer
>
> *In manners, tranquility is the supreme power.*
>
> — 2nd wife of Louis XIV

Amiability:

*Amiable people, though often subject to imposition in
their contact with the world, yet radiate so much of sunshine that they are reflected in all appreciative hearts.*

Madame Deluzy (1747-1830)
French actress

When I was a student salesman, I once tagged along behind a
co-worker as he was showing a couple through a house. The prospect
wanted to have a few notes jotted down as he talked, and my friend
handed a pen and piece of paper to the man. I was puzzled by this
gesture, and thought my fellow salesman should have done the jotting.
It wasn't until months later that I realized why he had done it. He
couldn't spell c-a-t. This man was a whiz. A top producer. He had an
I.B.M. mind. He was extremely successful because of his one outstanding trait. He was one of the most amiable and immediately likeable
men I have ever known.

He was one smart cookie. He knew he didn't have all the fine
formal education of his competition, so he made use of the one great
asset he had that shone like a beacon. To be amiable is to make us
unwilling to disagree with those with whom we are on harmonious
terms. That's what he did. If he ever felt like disagreeing on a point, he
would side-step it and go on to other features about the property.

This is a difficult mode of deportment for some of us, but I
know a salesman who worked hard at it by smiling all the time. My,
how that man smiled, and if you didn't have to look at it all day, it was
all right.

So try your best to be agreeable. Give a little on the little points;
it will give you some glue for the bigger ones. Don't be a nit-picker
about details, leave your grouch at home and go to the office armed
with a beaming happy personality. I had a boss once who used to come
charging into the office glaring and snorting like a bull every morning.
He apparently thought this was the way to get people steamed up for a
good day's work. I still remember him as a snorting bull.

Name:

*A good name lost is seldom regained. When character
is gone, all is gone, and one of the richest jewels of life is
lost forever.*

Joel Hawes (1789-1867)
An American clergy

The last of our letters, but one of the truly most important.
A man's name.

I remember driving past a man who was hammering on a "For
Rent" sign. I stopped and asked him if I could help him lease the

property. During our conversation, he began cursing the name of an acquaintance of mine, repeating that he was a crook. I didn't press the subject and left. Later in the day, I phoned my acquaintance and told him there was a man running around town telling everyone he was a crook. He asked me who said it, and when I told him, he said, "Aw, forget it."

That's what he thought of *his* name. Protect yours, it's the only one you have.

In the opera *Aida*, Aida was the daughter of the King of Ethiopia. Sales forces the world over have taken her name, but not in vain, to illustrate the four successful steps to sales.

A	attention	(get it)
I	interest	(arouse it)
D	desire	(create it)
A	action	(sell it)

Good luck. It is no sinecure.

"I expect to pass through this world but once. Any good therefore that I can do, or any kindness that I can show to any fellow creature, let me do it now. Let me not defer or neglect it, for I shall not pass this way again."
Stephen Grellet (1773-1855)
Quaker of French birth.
Also credited to Emerson, John Wesley,
William Penn, Thomas Carlyle.

Memorize it, and try it on for size.

Mr. L. G. Taylor, a widely known and respected Toronto Realtor, has a nine year old charmer named Leslie, who sold 94 boxes of Brownie cookies. This was the Brownie pack record.

When I asked Leslie how she sold 44 boxes more than her nearest competitor, she observed that "it was because of the fun of it".

Successful salesmen enjoy their work! Remember that.

50
Real Estate Definitions

Abstract	A written, condensed history of title to a parcel of real property, recorded in a land registry office.
Abuttals	The bounding of a parcel of land by other land, street, river, etc. A boundary.
Acceleration Clause	On mortgage payment default, the entire balance of the loan is due and immediately payable.
Administrator	One who has charge of the estate of a deceased person who died without a will, or one who did not appoint an executor. Appointed by Court order.
Adverse Possession	When someone, other than the owner, takes physical possession of property, without the owner's consent.
Agent	One who legally represents an individual or corporate body.
Agreement of Sale	Written agreement whereby one agrees to buy, and another agrees to sell, according to the terms and conditions in the agreement.
Agreement to Lease	Written agreement whereby one agrees to lease real property to another, according to the terms of the agreement.
Amortization	To extinguish a loan by means of a sinking fund.
Appraisal	A written estimate of the market value of real property, made by a qualified expert.
Appreciation	Increased market value of real property.
Appurtenances	Additional rights that are an adjunction to real property.

Assessed Value	Value of real property set by a municipality for taxation purposes.
Assessor	Person employed by a municipality or other Government body empowered to place valuation on property for taxation purposes.
Assignment	Legal transfer of interest in real property or a mortgage from one person to another.
Assumption Agreement	An agreement whereby a person other than the mortgagor covenants to perform the obligations in the mortgage deed.
Attornment of Rent	Taking of rents by Mortgagee in Possession to protect his rights in case of default by mortgagor.
Blanket Mortgage	Single mortgage registered to cover more than one parcel of real property.
Bond	A binding agreement to strengthen the covenant of performance.
Broker	A person who legally trades in real estate for another, for compensation.
Certificate of Charge	Provincial Government acknowledgement of registration of mortgage in a Land Titles office.
Certificate of Title	Provincial Government acknowledgement of registration of title deed in a Land Titles office.
Chattels	Moveable possessions, such as furniture, personal possessions, etc. A furnace, before it is installed, is a moveable possession. Once installed, it is not.
Chattel Mortgage	A mortgage on moveable possessions, personal property.
Closing	The time at which a real estate transaction is concluded legally in a registry office.
Cloud on Title	An impairment to title of real property, such as executed judgment, mortgage, lien, etc., registered legally against the property.
C.M.H.C.	Central Mortgage and Housing Corporation, a Crown agency administering Canada's National Housing Act.

Commission	Financial remuneration paid to an agent for selling or leasing property, based on an agreed percentage of the amount involved.
Consideration	Something of value for compensation.
Contract	An agreement upon lawful consideration which binds the parties to a performance.
Conveyance	Transmitting title of real property from one to another.
Covenant	Solemn agreement.
Convenantee	Lender in a (mortgage) deed.
Covenantor	Borrower in a (mortgage) deed.
Date of Maturity	In mortgages, the last day of the term of the mortgage.
Deed	A document containing an agreement that has been signed, sealed, and containing proof of its delivery; effective only on the date of delivery. (Mortgage deed, title deed, etc.)
Demise	To transfer or convey an estate for a term of years, or life.
Deposit	Money or other consideration of value given as pledge for fulfillment of a contract or agreement.
Depreciation	Reduction in market value of property. Also used to indicate capital cost allowance.
Derivative Mortgage	Mortgage on a mortgage. Mortgagee assigns his mortgage to lender to secure loan.
Dower	Rights of wife or widow in freehold property owned by her husband.
Easement	A right acquired to use another's land or buildings, generally for access to some other adjoining property.
Encroachment	Undue or unlawful trespass on another's property, usually caused by a building, or part of a building, or obstruction.
Encumbrance	Any legal claim registered against property.

Escheat	Conveyance of property to the Crown (Government) due to intestate person dying and leaving no heirs.
Escrow	A deed or contract delivered to a third party to be held until the payment or fulfillment of the agreement by the grantee.
Estate	One's interest in lands and any other subject of property.
Equity	The financial interest of a property owner in excess of any encumbrances, limited by its market value.
Executor	Person legally appointed by testator to carry out the terms of his will.
Exclusive Listing	An agreement granting sole and exclusive rights to an agent to sell property.
Fee Simple	Absolute ownership of property.
Fee Tail	Property ownership, limited to some particular heirs.
First Mortgage	One that takes precedence over all others. (Mortgage seniority established by date and time of registration.)
Fixture	Permanent improvements to property that remain with it.
Foreclosure	A legally enforced transfer of real property ordered by a Court to satisfy unpaid debts. The most common is a foreclosure by a mortgagee.
Freehold	Property held in fee simple (untrammelled tenure) or fee tail (for the term of the owner's life).
Frontage	Property line facing street.
Gale Date	The date on which interest is charged.
Grant	An instrument of conveyance transferring property from one to another.
Grantee	Person to whom a conveyance is made; one who receives legal transfer of property from another; the buyer.

Grantor	Person who makes a conveyance; one who transfers property to another; the seller.
Hereditament	Property that may be inherited.
Hypothec	Lien on real estate (Quebec).
Hypothecary Creditor	Mortgagee (Quebec).
Hypothecary Debtor	Mortgagor (Quebec).
Indenture	An agreement between two or more parties. Originally, indentures were duplicates placed together and cut in a wavy line, so that the two papers could be identified as being authentic by corresponding to each other.
Instrument	A writing instructing one in regard to something that has been agreed upon.
Intestate	Not having a will.
Joint Tenancy	Ownership of real property by two or more persons; when one dies, his share automatically passes to the survivor(s).
Judgment	Binding decision of the Court.
Landed Property	Having an interest in and pertaining to land.
Landlord	A lessor. One who allows another to occupy his land or building for a consideration.
Lease	Binding contract between a landlord (lessor) and tenant (lessee) for the occupation of premises or land for a specified period of time, and a financial or other consideration.
Leasehold	Property held by lease.
Leaseholder	Tenant under a lease.
Lessee	The tenant. One who pays rent.
Lessor	The person granting use of property to another.
Lien	A legal claim affecting property.
Lis pendens	Notice of commencement of Court action, recorded against title of property.

Market Value	The Courts have defined this as being the highest price estimated in terms of money which a property will bring, if exposed for sale in the open market, allowing a reasonable time to find a purchaser who buys with knowledge of all the uses to which it may be put, and for which it is capable of being used.
Mechanic's Lien	A lien filed and registered against property by a person or corporate body, for labour and/or materials supplied for the improvement of the property.
Moratorium	Provincial statute deferment of mortgage principal payments during depression. Non-existent now.
Mortgage	Read chapter 4 in this book.
Mortgage Bonds	Bond holders are represented by trustee, who is the mortgagee. Bonds can be traded, making them more flexible than individual mortgages.
Mortgaged Out	Situation whereby total mortgage debt on property equals or exceeds market value of property.
Mortgagee	The lender in a mortgage deed. The one receiving the mortgage.
Mortgagor	The borrower in a mortgage deed. The one giving the mortgage.
N.H.A.	National Housing Act.
Option	An agreement whereby one has the exclusive right to purchase another's property at a specified price, with a time limit.
Personalty	Personal property, chattels.
Postponement Clause	In mortgaging, the agreement of an equitable mortgagee to allow the mortgagor to renew or replace a senior mortgage that becomes due before such equitable mortgage.
Power of Attorney	Legal authority for one to act on behalf of another.

Prepayment *Clause*	In a mortgage, an agreement giving the mortgagor the privilege of paying additional sums off the principal balance over and above the agreed payments.
Principal	A person or corporate body employing an agent.
Principal *Balance*	In a mortgage, the outstanding dollar amount owing on the debt.
Quit Claim *Deed*	A full release of one's interest in property to another, usually executed between mortgagees and mortgagors.
Real Estate	Landed property (land).
Real Property	Land *and* buildings thereon, and rights thereof.
Realtor	Certification mark being the property of the Canadian Real Estate Association. Designates broker-member of Association.
Realty	Real Property.
Rest	The date upon which the amount between the parties to a mortgage is altered. It is not necessarily the date upon which payment is made, unless so agreed in the mortgage deed.
Sales Agreement	Purchase of property without obtaining title deed until a specified further sum of money is paid to the vendor.
Socage	A tenure of land held by the tenant in performance of specified services or by payment of rent, and not requiring military service (history).
Straight Loan	In mortgaging, a mortgage with no principal payments. Interest only.
Survey	Surveyor's report of mathematical boundaries of land, showing location of buildings, physical features and quantity of land.
Tenancy in *Common*	Ownership of real property by two or more persons, whereby on the death of one, his share is credited to his own estate.

Tenant	The one who pays rent for the right to occupy land or buildings.
Tenant in Tail	Holder of an estate limited to the heirs of his body. The line of heirs is called entail.
Tenement	Property held by tenant.
Tenure	The right of holding property.
Title Deed	Proof of legal ownership of property.
Title Search	Research of records in registry or land titles office to determine history and chain of ownership of property.
Usury	An unconscionable and exhorbitant rate of interest.
Zoning	Specifiel limitation on the use of land, the construction and use of buildings, in a defined section of a municipality.

51
Interest Rates

Remember . . . The more frequent the compounding, the *greater* the yield to the *lender*.

To determine the interest payable on any payment date, take the following steps:

1. Establish the frequency of compounding the interest.
2. Locate the interest rate for the appropriate payment period. Example: 10% loan, compounded semi-annually, payable *monthly*: the interest rate is .816485
3. Multiply the outstanding principal balance of the loan by the interest rate to determine the interest to be charged, or paid, for the month.

viz: Balance owing $12,432.00
                                   12432.00
                                     .816485
                            10150.54152000
       Interest: $ 101.50

NOTE: If the payments are more frequent than annually, then the columns under "Payable Annually" indicate the *effective* annual yield. Study the chapter Knowledge of Interest for explanation of "effective" yield.

If the payments are annually, then the columns under "Payable Annually" indicate the actual, or true yield.

Compounded Monthly	Payable Monthly	Payable Quarterly	Payable Semi-Annually	Payable Annually
7 %	.583333%	1.760228%	3.551440%	7.229008%
7½	.625000	1.886743	3.809084	7.763260
8	.666667	2.013363	4.067262	8.299951
8½	.708333	2.140088	4.325975	8.839091
9	.750000	2.266917	4.585224	9.380690
9½	.791667	2.393852	4.845009	9.924758
10	.833333	2.520891	5.105331	10.471307
10½	.875000	2.648036	5.366192	11.020345
11	.916667	2.775285	5.627592	11.571884
11½	.958333	2.902640	5.889533	12.125933
12	1.000000	3.030100	6.152015	12.682503
12½	1.041667	3.157665	6.415039	13.241605
13	1.083333	3.285335	6.678605	13.803248
14	1.166667	3.540992	7.207371	14.934203
15	1.250000	3.797070	7.738318	16.075452

Compounded Quarterly	Payable Monthly	Payable Quarterly	Payable Semi-Annually	Payable Annually
7 %	.579963%	1.750000%	3.530625%	7.185903%
7½	.621134	1.875000	3.785156	7.713587
8	.662271	2.000000	4.040000	8.243216
8½	.703374	2.125000	4.295156	8.774796
9	.744444	2.250000	4.550625	9.308332
9½	.785481	2.375000	4.806406	9.843828
10	.826484	2.500000	5.062500	10.381289
10½	.867453	2.625000	5.318906	10.920720
11	.908390	2.750000	5.575625	11.462126
11½	.949293	2.875000	5.832656	12.005511
12	.990163	3.000000	6.090000	12.550881
12½	1.031001	3.125000	6.347656	13.098240
13	1.071805	3.250000	6.605625	13.647593
14	1.153314	3.500000	7.122500	14.752300
15	1.234693	3.750000	7.640625	15.865042

Compounded Semi-Annually	Payable Monthly	Payable Quarterly	Payable Semi-Annually	Payable Annually
7 %	.575004%	1.734950%	3.500000%	7.122500%
7½	.615452	1.857744	3.750000	7.640625
8	.655820	1.980390	4.000000	8.160000
8½	.696106	2.102889	4.250000	8.680625
9	.736312	2.225242	4.500000	9.202500
9½	.776438	2.347447	4.750000	9.725625
10	.816485	2.469508	5.000000	10.250000
10½	.856452	2.591423	5.250000	10.775625
11	.896339	2.713193	5.500000	11.302500
11½	.936149	2.834819	5.750000	11.830625
12	.975879	2.956301	6.000000	12.360000
12½	1.015532	3.077641	6.250000	12.890625
13	1.055107	3.198837	6.500000	13.422500
14	1.134026	3.440804	7.000000	14.490000
15	1.212679	3.682207	7.500000	15.562500

Compounded Annually	Payable Monthly	Payable Quarterly	Payable Semi-Annually	Payable Annually
7 %	.565415%	1.705853%	3.440804%	7.000000%
7½	.604492	1.824460	3.682207	7.500000
8	.643403	1.942655	3.923048	8.000000
8½	.682149	2.060440	4.163333	8.500000
9	.720732	2.177818	4.403065	9.000000
9½	.759153	2.294793	4.642248	9.500000
10	.797414	2.411369	4.880885	10.000000
10½	.835516	2.527548	5.118980	10.500000
11	.873459	2.643333	5.356538	11.000000
11½	.911247	2.758727	5.593560	11.500000
12	.948879	2.873734	5.830052	12.000000
12½	.986358	2.988357	6.066017	12.500000
13	1.023684	3.102598	6.301458	13.000000
14	1.097885	3.329948	6.770783	14.000000
15	1.171492	3.555808	7.238053	15.000000

52

Depreciation Allowance Tables

This is a 30 year table covering the maximum capital cost allowance (depreciation) permitted for income tax purposes on a class 3 (brick) building — 5% reducing on One Million Dollars for the example.

It is easy to use for your own purposes. For example, if you wish to do some advance figuring on the maximum depreciation allowable over the first 15 years, you will find that your undepreciated balance is 46.3291% of the original capital cost of the building. Looking at it another way, you will have depreciated your building by 53.6709% of its original cost.

Year No.	Maximum Allowance	End of Year Undepreciated Balance
1	50,000.00	950,000.00
2	47,500.00	902,500.00
3	45,125.00	857,375.00
4	42,868.75	814,506.25
5	40,725.31	773,780.94
6	38,689.05	735,091.89
7	36,754.59	698,337.30
8	34,916.87	663,420.43
9	33,171.02	630,249.41
10	31,512.47	598,736.94
11	29,936.85	568,800.09
12	28,440.00	540,360.09
13	27,018.00	513,342.09
14	25,667.10	487,674.99
15	24,383.75	463,291.24
16	23,164.56	440,126.68
17	22,006.33	418,120.35
18	20,906.02	397,214.33
19	19,860.72	377,353.61
20	18,867.68	358,485.93
21	17,924.30	340,561.63
22	17,028.08	323,533.55
23	16,176.68	307,356.87
24	15,367.84	291,989.03
25	14,599.45	277,389.58
26	13,869.48	263,520.10
27	13,176.01	250,344.09
28	12,517.20	237,826.89
29	11,891.34	225,935.55
30	11,296.78	214,638.77

HOUSING PRICE INDEX FOR CANADA (1961 — 100%)

(rounded to the nearest point)

Date	Total Housing	Home Ownership	Property Taxes	Homeowner Repairs	Mortgage Interest	New Houses	Dwelling Insurance	Rents	Household Operation
1961	100	100	100	100	100	100	100	100	100
1962	101	103	104	100	104	103	101	100	100
1963	102	106	106	103	108	106	104	101	101
1964	104	110	110	107	111	112	110	101	101
1965	106	115	114	111	115	117	117	102	102
1966	109	120	119	116	120	123	125	104	104
1967	113	127	124	123	125	132	133	107	108
1968	119	136	132	130	137	141	143	112	111
1969	125	148	144	136	156	152	152	116	113
1970	131	161	154	148	177	161	161	120	116
1971	140	181	161	163	205	181	237	123	121
1972	146	195	161	176	226	202	255	125	125

(Compiled through courtesy of Statistics Canada)

54

Every Home Needs a Budget

A budget is something you make and remake until it works for you, and you are satisfied with the results.

There is no magic formulae.

Budgeting does not necessarily mean pinching pennies and recording every cent spent.

It is a way to get what your family wants most, whatever that may be.

If you do not have money to pay bills when they are due or cannot accumulate enough for a vacation trip, a budget can ease worry about money and start you on a savings programme.

Making and following a budget help all members of your family to understand how and where to use money. That is a cornerstone of education for modern living.

The first step in making a budget is to set goals. Some goals are for the distant future. Some are for next year. Some are for right now.

Decide what your family's needs and wants are. List them in order of importance.

Add to the list — and also substract from it the items that time makes unimportant.

Do not let long-term goals get lost in day-to-day demands. Too many T-bones steaks this month may crowd out a new dishwasher next year.

Define your goals clearly. Then they will be easier to reach. An example: Long term goals may be paying off the mortgage, establishing a fund to cover the children's schooling, or saving for retirement. Your goal for the next year may be a new car, a living room rug, an encyclopaedia, or a new T.V. set.

The next step is to estimate how much money you will have available to spend for the planning period.

The planning period may be a month, a year, or any period. A year is the usual time for which to plan, but you may wish to set up a trial budget for a shorter period to see how it works out.

Start by considering your income in two ways — before taxes and after taxes. Income after taxes is the true amount available to spend and save. Thinking only of the amount before taxes may lead you to buy more than you can afford.

Write down all the income you expect to receive. Include wages or salary, net money earned from a farm or business, interest from a savings account, dividends, extra money that may be earned from odd jobs — everything.

Then estimate your income tax and subtract it from your total expected income. Write the answer down. That is the figure to keep in mind in making the budget.

Now estimate your expenses. You can recall some expenses well enough to make an estimate. Cancelled cheques or stubs, receipts, and old bills are good reminders for some items.

For other items (food, clothing, household operation, recreation), a record of present spending to see where your money is going is more helpful.

You might buy a form for keeping records or draw up your own. Rule off a form on a sheet of paper or in a looseleaf notebook. Allow a separate column for each category of expense that you want to keep track of. Leave enough space to enter the the items you bought and their cost. Add up the amounts at the end of a week or a month.

Keep the record for a month or two. Use it as a guide in estimating expenses in your plan for future spending. In the estimate, make any changes you think are needed in order to get the things your family needs and wants most.

At this point you are ready to set up your plan. The plan needs to be based on your goals, income and expenses. There is a sample form you may wish to use at the end of the chapter.

Start by planning to save something for a purpose or toward a goal. Decide on an amount and treat it as you do any other bill that must be paid.

You should build up an emergency fund for illness, repairs that unexpectedly become necessary, accidents, and so on.

After you have an emergency fund, start saving for your other goals.

If saving for retirement is a long-time goal and a certain percentage of your salary is being withheld to be applied toward retirement, count it as part of your savings goal.

Some of your expenses occur once or twice a year or every month. Some of them have to be paid in definite amounts at definite times.

In setting up your plan for future spending, list the items that come up once or twice a year, such as taxes, insurance, vacation, and perhaps certain debt payments. Divide these expenses to arrive at a monthly average and set aside the required amount every month. Thus you spread the cost and have the money to meet them when due.

Next, list the expenses you expect to be the same from month to month, such as rent, car and mortgage payments, installment on furniture and appliances, contributions to church, etc.

After you have estimated your savings and regular expenses, you are ready for the day-to-day expenses.

Estimate how much to spend for food and beverages, clothing, transportation, and all the other budget groups. Go back over the records you kept and see what you spent for each of the budget groups. You may decide you need to spend more on some and less on others.

Remember to allow some leeway for unexpected or forgotten items.

A personal allowance for each person that need not be accounted for, even if it has to be small, is a good thing.

Now work in the items you and others in the family have listed as your immediate goals.

With the information you have now, you are ready to add the totals and compare your planned outgo with your estimated income for the planning period.

If your income covers your savings and expenses, you have no problem. You can add any surplus to savings for future goals or use to satisfy some immediate wants or desires.

If, as more likely will be the case, you have planned for more than your income will cover, you will need to take a new look at all parts of your plan. You will have to decide which of your wants are less important, important, and very important. Look at the day-to-day expenses. Try to trim them. For example, you may be able to defer some of them, or substitute a cheaper item, or paint your house yourself instead of having someone else do it, or take advantage of free community activities and services instead of going to the theatre, or stretching the life of clothing instead of buying new, etc.

Scan your regular expenses too. Perhaps you can reduce some of them. Look at things realistically. Is that new car as important as the really big things you want, such as security, education, and the means whereby you attain your ambitions?

After trimming here and cutting there, if your budget still does not balance, you may have to consider ways of adding to your income.

Once your budget is made, try it out. You must keep records to see how the budget works, and remember that records are also helpful when it comes time to make out your income tax. Check them weekly and monthly.

At the end of the budget period, compare what you actually

spent with what you planned to spend. Were you fairly close? Were you satisfied with the results? Did you spend more than you planned? If so, why? Did you buy on impulse?

Your first try at budgeting may not be completely successful, but each time you try means improvement. Even if your first budget is "perfect" it will need adjusting from time to time. Through a budget, however, you can plan to get your day-to-day needs and future dreams.

A Budget Plan

Savings: (Annual)
Future goals and emergencies .... $____
Seasonal and large irregular expenses .... ____
Regular Monthly Expenses:
Rent or mortgage payment .... $____
Utilities .... ____
Installment payments .... ____
Other .... ____
Total: .... $____ (× 12) ____
Day-to-Day Expenses: (Monthly)
Food and beverages .... $____
Household operation and manitenance .... ____
Housefurnishings and equipment .... ____
Clothing .... ____
Transportation .... ____
Medical Care .... ____
Education and reading .... ____
Recreation .... ____
Personal and Miscellaneous .... ____
Gifts and Contributions .... ____
Other .... ____
Total: .... $____ (× 12) ____
Total: .... $____
How does this compare with your estimated income after taxes?

55

How to Complain about a Bad Deal

Real estate agents have a remarkable record of behaving themselves in their conduct with the public.

I am not suggesting that an agent is granted a halo with his license to be in business, because serious and very legitimate complaints are made from time to time. Such complaints usually receive prominent coverage in the press, undoubtedly the result of editors seeing something they consider to be newsworthy — a real estate agent in trouble.

The majority of real estate complaints are not made against agents, but against the builders of new houses who are guilty of shoddy workmanship, or fail to rectify construction defects after a buyer has found that he has not moved into his dream home.

Complaints against an agent can often be satisfied by confronting the agent and/or his employer. Nobody wants any flack in his business.

If this route fails, take the matter to your local real estate board, if the offending agent is a member. Real estate boards are very conscious of the ethical responsibility of its members, and tolerate no nonsense.

If the agent is not a member of a real estate board, or if he is and you are not happy about the result of your complaint, here are the addresses of the Provincial Government officials responsible for the licensing of agents. Your complaint will be handled with dispatch.

The Commissioner of Real Estate,
Dept. of the Attorney General,
10621 - 100th Avenue,
Edmonton, ALBERTA

The Secretary,
B.C. Real Estate Council,
608 - 626 West Pender St.
Vancouver,
BRITISH COLUMBIA

The Registrar,
The Real Estate Brokers Act,
The Public Utilities Board,
379 Broadway Avenue,
Winnipeg, MANITOBA

The Regional Planning
  Technician Supervisor,
Community Planning Branch,
Dept. of Municipal Affairs,
Centennial Building,
Fredericton, NEW BRUNSWICK

Registrar of Direct Sellers,
Govt. of Newfoundland/Labrador,
Department of Provincial Affairs,
St. John's NEWFOUNDLAND

Superintendent under The Real
  Estate Brokers' Licensing Act,
Dept. of Provincial Secy.
Box 998, Halifax, NOVA SCOTIA

The Registrar,
The Real Estate and Business
  Brokers Act,
Ministry of Consumer &
  Commercial Relations,
555 Yonge Street, 5th floor,
Toronto 284, ONTARIO

The Superintendent,
Dept. of Financial Institutions,
  Companies and Cooperatives,
Real Estate Brokerage Branch,
Hotel Du Gouvernement,
Quebec City, QUEBEC

The Superintendent of Insurance,
Legislative Building,
Regina, SASKATCHEWAN

Registrar,
Real Estate Trading Act,
Dept. of Provincial Secy.,
P.O. Box 2000,
Charlottetown, P.E.I.

For the unhappy owner of a new house having complaints against the *builder*, here are the addresses of Provincial Government Consumer Protection Bureaus who will give you a sympathetic ear. However, if you write a complaining letter to a Government office, remember that it can only act within statute authority — but it is possible that if enough complaints are received concerning a particular subject, this authority could be enlarged.

The Director,
Consumer Affairs,
Consumer Affairs Branch,
Department of Labour,
Room 502, I.B.M. Building,
10808 - 99 Avenue,
Edmonton, ALBERTA

The Consumer Affairs Officer,
Dept. of Attorney-General,
Parliament Buildings,
Victoria, BRITISH COLUMBIA

The Director,
Consumers Bureau,
Dept. of Consumer and
  Corporate Affairs,
270 Osborne Street North,
Winnipeg, MANITOBA

The Director,
Consumer Bureau,
Dept. of Provincial Secretary,
Room 346, Box 32,
Centennial Building,
Fredericton, NEW BRUNSWICK

The Director,
Consumer Services Bureau,
Dept. of Provincial Secretary,
Box 998,
Halifax, NOVA SCOTIA

The Registrar,
Direct Sellers,
Govt. of Newfoundland/Labrador,
Department of Provincial Affairs,
Confederation Building,
St. John's, NEWFOUNDLAND

Registrar,
Real Estate Trading Act,
Dept. of Provincial Secretary,
P.O. Box 2000,
Charlottetown, P.E.I.

Director of Licensing and
Investigations,
Dept. of Consumer Affairs,
1739 Cornwall Street,
Regina, SASKATCHEWAN

The Director,
Consumer Protection Division,
Dept. of Financial Institutions,
Companies and Cooperatives,
Government of Quebec,
117 Rue St. Andre, Room 343,
Quebec City, QUEBEC

The Registrar,
The Consumer Protection Act,
Dept. of Consumer and
Commercial Relations,
555 Yonge Street,
Toronto 284, ONTARIO

Furthermore, don't forget the *Federal* Government, which recognizes that if Canadians are to get the best results from the market system, they must feel confident that they are making an intelligent, effective and satisfying choice when they exercise their purchasing power.

The Federal Department of Consumer and Corporate Affairs was established in December, 1967, and since that time thousands of Canadians have rapidly responded to the invitation to write:

THE CONSUMER,
BOX 99, OTTAWA.

with questions, suggestions, or *complaints*.

Of the hundreds of complaints received by the Department in the real estate housing industry, the great majority related to (1) the purchase of new dwelling units, (2) building additions for existing dwelling units, and (3) repairs to existing dwelling units.

And, the author would also like to hear your complaints. Perhaps they could add constructively to the chapter "Caveat Emptor".

56

Bits and Pieces

Why 640 acres to a section, and why is a square mile a section?

An Order-in-Council dated September 23, 1869, containing instructions to a Colonel Denis for the survey of townships in the west states that the townships "were to consist of 64 squares of 800 acres each".

This standard of measurement was altered by virtue of Order-in-Council 874 dated April 25, 1871, which stated that henceforth, "Townships shall consist of 36 sections of *one square mile each.*"

The Statutes of Canada, 1872, Chapter XXIII entitled *An Act Respecting the Public Lands of the Dominion* Section 15, states that in legal descriptions of land, "either a section or 640 acres may be used."

All sections, however, are not 640 acres. In Ontario, for example, sections also consisted of one thousand, 1,800 and 2,400 acres.

Much of the original surveying in Canada was done with the aid of "Gunter's Chain". This chain, so named after its inventor Edmund Gunter, (early 17th century) was generally used by the land surveyors. It is 66 ft. in length, containing 100 links each measuring 7.92 inches. It was very convenient when required to calculate areas in acres and decimals of an acre, since 10 square chains equal 1 acre; also when linear dimensions were required in miles and furlongs, since 10 chains equal 1 furlong, and 80 chains equal 1 mile.

The chain was a faulty instrument that suffered greatly in accuracy in use, since there were 198 points of wear in its links, the wearing of which lengthened the instrument. However, it was the only efficient long measuring instrument until technology made possible the manufacture of the steel tape, and later the invar tape. All of these have been supplemented by electronic measuring instruments.

Looked at any fences lately?

There are provincial statutes regulating the responsibility of maintenance and repair of fences marking the boundary between owners of adjoining lands.

For example, "The Line Fences Act" of Ontario applies "mutatis mutandis" to unoccupied land as well as to occupied land in any township in a county or district if the council of the township passes a by-law declaring that the Act so applies, and provides that:

(*a*) *The owners of adjoining occupied lands shall make, keep up and repair a just proportion of the fence that marks the boundary between them, or, if there is no fence, they shall make and keep up and repair the same proportion of a fence to mark such boundary.*

(*b*) *Owners of unoccupied land that adjoins occupied land, upon the unoccupied land becoming occupied, are liable to keep up and repair such proportion, and in that respect are in the same position as if their land had been occupied at the time of the original fencing.*

Where an owner of land desires fence-viewers to view and arbitrate as to what portion of such fence each owner shall make, keep up and repair, or as to the condition of an existing line fence and as to repairs being done to it:

(*a*) *Either owner may notify the other that he will cause three fence-viewers of the locality to arbitrate in the premises.*

(*b*) *The notices shall be in writing, and shall specify the time and place of meeting for the arbitration.*

(*c*) *An owner notified may object to any or all of the fence-viewers notified, and in such case, a judge shall name the fence-viewers.*

It is a very serious business. If, for example, an occupant who is not the owner of the property in question receives such notice of naming fence-viewers for arbitration and does not immediately notify the owner of the land, he shall be liable for all damages caused the owner.

The Act even tells about the responsibility of a tree falling across another's property. The owner of the land upon which the tree stood is responsible for making good any damage caused. If such tree owner neglects or refuses to remove the tree within 48 hours after notice in writing to do so, one may remove the tree, fix the fence, keep the remains of the tree for remuneration, and recover any further amount of damages beyond the value of the tree from the person liable to pay it.

Write the Queen's Printer in your province and obtain a copy of a fence-viewers act. It makes interesting reading.

What is a *Realtor?*

The application to register the name *"Realtor"* as a certification mark was filed by the Canadian Association of Real Estate Boards on July 15, 1958, alleging use in Canada by that agency since at least as early as the year 1921. The application asked for registration on the ground that the name *"Realtor"* had in the course of use throughout the intervening years come to be recognized as distinguishing those services offered to the public by members of the Real Estate Boards operating throughout British Columbia, Alberta, Saskatchewan, Manitoba, Ontario and Quebec.

Registration was awarded on March 18,1960, and recognized under Section 12 (2) of the Trade Marks Act covering services of:

Brokerage of real estate, industrial brokerage, farm brokerage, mortgage brokerage, in the appraisal of real estate, management of real estate, in the building of structures on real estate, in the subdivision of real estate properties, and for consultative and advisory services in community planning for the development of raw land and slum clearance areas.

The Canadian Association of Real Estate Boards (now the Canadian Real Estate Association), being the owner of the certification mark *"Realtor"*, authorizes its members to use the mark and advertise themselves as a Realtor.

An expression that is often found with reference to municipal real estate matters is: *Mutatis Mutandis*. Here is its meaning...

"With the necessary changes in points of detail meaning that matters or things are generally the same but to be altered when necessary as to names, offices and the like."

You figure it out.

A fast way to convert square feet to an acre is to multiply the number of square feet by 23 and take the answer back 6 decimal points. For example, take one acre to prove it:

$$43,560 \text{ sq. ft.}$$
$$\underline{23}$$
$$\overline{130,680}$$
$$871,200$$
$$\overline{1.001880 \text{ acres}}$$

It is not precise, but close enough for a fast pass at round figures:

1,000 s.f.	.023 acres (actually	.022956)
10,000 s.f.	.23 acres (actually	.229568)
100,000 s.f.	2.3 acres (actually	2.295684)
1,000,000 s.f.	23. acres (actually	22.956841)

Mill Rate: Mill: from the Latin, mille, a thousand. One mill in your tax bill is equal to 1/1,000 of the assessed value of property. Buildings and land are assessed separately.

If a house is assessed at $6,000 with a municipal mill rate of 70 for the current year, the taxes will be $\frac{6,000 \times 70}{1,000}$, or $420.

It is a quick way of looking at it, but it can get complicated. If you don't think it works in your case, go to your assessment office and ask for a detailed explanation.

———

Take advantage of an excellent service provided by Federal and Provincial Governments through the offices of the Queen's Printer, which is quite extensive and interesting if one wishes to know what the law has to say about a multitude of subjects.

For example, the Queen's Printer in Victoria, B.C. can provide not only copies of about 25 different titles to provincial statutes covering real estate subjects, but such diverse titles as *Dogwood, Rhododendron, and Trillium Protection Act!*

———

Six Times the Gross: One will often hear investors say they want to buy an investment property for something like six times the gross. What does it mean? Example . . .

Gross Income:	$100,000
Expenses:	40,000
Net Return:	$ 60,000

In this example the investor wants 10% return on his money. $60,000 is 10% of $600,000, which is 6 times the gross income of $100,000. In this case it also means that the investor wants to make an allowance of 40% of the gross income for the operating expenses.

No matter what the X times the gross, it can be immediately established what the allowances are for expenses: Examples . . .

5   × gross allows 50% of gross income for expenses
5½ × gross allows 45% of gross income for expenses
6   × gross allows 40% of gross income for expenses
6½ × gross allows 35% of gross income for expenses
7   × gross allows 30% of gross income for expenses

———

Here's a hot one: A broker received a letter written by somebody under an imposing letterhead in some Middle East country requesting information on investment properties listed with the broker, or known to him. The writer stated that a representative of a group of financial giants was visiting Canada shortly, and he wanted the details quickly so that they could go over them before arriving.

The same letter was mailed to several brokers, but what they all didn't know was that the information they mailed to the writer was promptly relayed to his pal in Canada who was a broker here, and who ended up knowing more about the investment properties for sale than anyone. The letterhead was a phony.

Some words that seem confusing at times are those that have the *ee* and the *or* on the end of them, as grantee, mortgagor, lessor, grantor, lessee, mortgagee, etc. To remember who's who, just remember that the word with the *or* on the end of it refers to the person who presently has title to the property. To illustrate:

Mortgagor: He gives an interest in his property as security for a loan.
Lessor: He gives an interest in his property by allowing somebody to occupy it.
Grantor: He gives an interest in his property for one of a number of reasons, such as selling his property, giving it to his wife, etc.

Expropriation: To illustrate a normal reaction to the receipt of a notice of expropriation, one could turn to a well-expressed and defined meaning of *Ugh* . . . "an expression of horror or recoil, usually accompanied by a shudder".

If you are not happy about the way your province handles the seizure of your lands, take heart. Newfoundland is showing the way, and their sense of fair play may some day be incorporated in *Your* provincial statutes.

The Newfoundland Family Home Expropriation Act ensures that the home owners will receive such compensation as will *At Current Costs and Prices*, put them in a position to acquire by *Purchase or Construction*, a home reasonably equivalent to the one being expropriated.

Sounds reasonable. Ontario has recently improved its image for expropriation compensation; remember that every property owner in Canada holds the land subject to the rights of the Crown.

Buy a Farm and Learn How to Relax . . . Summer cottage sites within a reasonable distance from urban areas are getting crowded, scarce, and expensive. And what have they to offer? A small piece of land, a frame building, and sometimes a bit of water.

Quite often, for the same money one of these small patches will cost you, one can buy *One Hundred Acres of Land*, complete with barn and house.

The last farm sold by the author was one hour's drive from Toronto. 100 acres. Big barn. House. Eighty-five acres leased to local farmer for $600 a year. Taxes $210.

     Price: $13,500.   What a buy! ! !

You can have wonderful weekends and holidays on a farm, especially if you own it. And the room!

     Think about it.

When agreeing to give a second mortgage (or third) to a vendor as part of the purchase price in buying real estate, insert a clause in the agreement whereby you, as the mortgagor, are to have the right of first refusal in the event that the mortgage is to be sold.

If it is sold, it will most likely be sold at a discount, and in the event that you are financially flush, you could save some money.

Highways??? The King's Highway, Controlled-Access Highway, Secondary Highway, Tertiary Road, Resources Road, Industrial Road, Development Road, Forced or Trespass Road, Quarter Sessions Road, Statute Labour Road, Provincial-Federal Resources Road, Mining Access Road, Connecting Link Road, Colonization Road, Streets on Subdivision Plans, Municipal By-law Road, Road Allowances and 5 per cent Reservation for Roads.

If you want to know what they all mean, write to your Provincial Department of Highways for definitions. And while you're at it, ask for a free road map.

A few centuries ago, an acre was considered to be the amount of land a man with a yoke of oxen could plow in a day.

The British Weights and Measures Act of 1878 defined it as containing 4,840 square yards (43,560 sq. ft.) and this "statute" acre was adopted by Canada and the United States. However, it is interesting to note that Scotland, Ireland, Wales and some English counties did not agree with it, and older land measurements of the acre are still to be found in these areas, and used.

The English, Canadian, and U.S.A. statute acres don't mean a thing in the rest of the world, as evidenced by the following land area measurements in a few examples:

Country	Unit	Size in Statute Acre
Argentina	Manzana	2.47 acres
Austria	Joch	1.42 ,,
Belgium	Hectare	2.47 ,,
Brazil	Cuarta	0.92 ,,
Cyprus	Donum	0.33 ,,
Denmark	Tonder land	1.36 ,,
Egypt	Feddan	1.04 ,,
Ireland	Acre	1.62 ,,
Russia	Dessiatine	2.70 ,,
Scotland	Acre	1.27 ,,
Wales	Erw	0.89 ,,
,,	Stang	0.67 ,,

There is always a buyer for a good piece of real estate, and Canada missed a dandy in Alaska: 586,400 squre miles to be exact.

United States treasury pay warrant No. 927, dated August 1st, 1868, for $7,000,000 closed the deal that had been made the previous year to buy Alaska from Russia, but a great many people thought the United States was mad at the time for paying that price for a "hunk of ice".

This could be a prime example of the importance of making an offer: it was since learned that Russia wanted to sell so badly that an offer of $5,000,000 would have been accepted. It could also illustrate the importance of time — the deal was made within a matter of *hours.*

It has often been claimed that the esplanade of Edinburgh Castle in Scotland is a part of Nova Scotia, but what happened is this:

The institution of the degree of Baronet of Scotland, contemplated by King James, was carried out by his successor Charles I, the object being to aid Sir William Alexander's scheme for the colonization of Nova Scotia (New Scotland).

Sir William was granted a Signature under the Great Seal for a charter of the lands lying between New England and Newfoundland for a furthering of his proposed Plantation on 10 September, 1621. With respect to the Order of Knights Baronets of Nova Scotia, all of Nova Scotia was for the one purpose of seisin (the act of taking possession) incorporated in the Kingdom of Scotland; apparently the earth and stone required for the ancient feudal ceremony could have been taken from any part of the Kingdom. It was taken from Castlehill because

Edinburgh was the capital and the castle the most eminent place in the Kingdom.

Some years ago the Province of Nova Scotia affixed a plaque to Edinburgh Castle to commemorate the historic connection between Old Scotland and New Scotland.

I know a man who borrowed $10,000. All the securities he had title to were assigned to the lender, with a reasonable market value of $43,000 but not immediately convertible to cash.

When pressing needs required more funds, the lender refused to increase the loan. No other lender would consider a loan because the security was tied up with the other guy.

Don't offer everything you have to one lender for security.

In the United States there is allowed as a deduction interest paid or accrued within the taxable year on indebtedness, which of course means that there are no restrictions on the deductions of mortgage interest, *including* one's own home. Think we'll all get that here? No way!

In 1941 there were 750,000 farms in Canada. Since then, nearly 400,000 have disappeared!

But not really. The acreage has remained fairly constant, which means that farmers are gobbling up the neighbour's land because small farms don't pay in today's streamlined production lines.

Andrew Carnegie said that "ninety per cent of all millionaires became so through owning real estate. More money has been made in real estate than in all industrial investments combined. The wise young man or wage earner of today invests his money in real estate."

You know, I think he's right. Go get yourself some real estate.

So you think a perch is a fish? Not in this book. A perch is a rod, 16½ feet, which was the length of the pole that was used to prod oxen. It is ¼ of a chain, and a chain is 66 feet; 80 chains to a mile. One square chain is one tenth of an acre. It's enough to drive you up the wall.

The chief disadvantages in the use of a compass for obtaining direction are that a compass needle will deflect in the presence of iron, and that magnetic north varies from time to time necessitating adjustments in bearings for any given period. It has been used very little in land surveys since 1900, and discontinued in 1909.

What is meant by a bank's "prime lending rate" and who qualifies for it?

To determine this, the following question was put to Canadian bank presidents, with the resulting answer:

Question: "I have never been quite clear as to the meaning of "best customer" where it relates to the bank's prime lending rate of interest.

For example, it would be reasonable to assume that a "best customer" would be the Federal Government of Canada. National Housing Act mortgages are guaranteed by the Federal Government. If a borrower asked for a current, prime rate loan with the Federal Government as co-signer, what would the bank's attitude be?"

Answer: "Generally speaking, the bank minimum lending rate is accorded to National concerns of undoubted credit standing where the degree of servicing is minimal and where the loan can be clearly identified as a current operating loan. A current or operating loan is usually considered to be one which is subject to annual renewal, which liquidates at periodic intervals and is accompanied by sufficient credit balances at least to provide for the cost in respect to the chequing and other activity in the account.

To the extent that a loan guaranteed by the Federal Government were to comply with these standards, that loan would normally be accorded at a rate no higher than the minimum lending rate. However, in the case of National Housing Act mortgages, these in no sense could be regarded as current loans. By definition, they are a type of long term loan and are subject to the interest rates in the market place for this type of loan. The banks are merely one of the institutional sources of mortgage funds and can never be too far out of line with the rates prevailing in the market place." End of quote.

Bank managers, take note.

The Veteran's Land Act, enacted in 1942 and broadened extensively in scope and financial provisions since then, is a measure to assist veterans of World War II and the Special Force (Korea) to settle in Canada as full-time farmers, part-time farmers (small holders) and commercial fishermen.

Assistance is also available to veterans who wish to act as their own contractors in the construction of their homes.

The advantages and benefits are many and varied; for example, certain loans may be obtained carrying interest rates from 3½ per cent to 7½ per cent. The deadline for making an application for financial assistance is March 31, 1974.

A 46-page clearly written summary of the Act may be obtained by writing to the Department of Veterans Affairs, Ottawa (K1A 0P4) Ontario. There are 27 regional offices from coast to coast.

Tax Sales: You've heard about them. Taxpayers don't pay taxes on the property which is auctioned by a municipality and supposedly snapped up at giveaway prices by the astute buyer.

It has happened, but with all the recent publicity given to this subject the bargains are getting scarce.

If you're curious, information about land to be auctioned for tax arrears will be found in your Provincial Gazette, a publication available from your Provincial Queen's Printer at nominal cost.

Good luck, but don't hold your breath . . .

Real Estate and Mortgage brokers are not required to obtain a license under the Federal Small Loans act to place funds secured by real property although they can be considered to be money-lenders under the act.

However, a recent ruling obtained by the author from the Federal Department of Insurance (which administers the Act) stipulates that mortgage loans not exceeding $1,500 may *not* carry a rate of interest higher than one per cent per month.

This raises an interesting point. One per cent per month is 12 per cent per annum, compounded monthly.

If the mortgage deed is to comply with the Federal Interest Act, it follows that to comply with the Department of Insurance ruling, the mortgage rate of interest would reflect a slightly higher rate than 12 per cent.

Remember, if you are going to obtain a mortgage loan for less than $1,500 don't pay more than 1 per cent per month!

Why are 99-year leases so common? Why not 89, or 104?

As early as the 16th century (in England) leases were commonly found to be of 21, 40, 90 and even 500 years! The British settled land Act, 1925, allowed building leases to extend for 999 years.

Research has decided that the 99 year lease originated many years ago when the term was often for three lives, the lessee, his wife, and son. It was considered that 99 years was a long enough period to cover the likely expectation of life of the parties concerned.

Don't be surprised if a bailiff demands payment of your current year's business tax before the end of the year.

For example, in Ontario, the tax rates imposed for any year "shall be deemed to have been imposed and to be due on and from the 1st day of January of such year unless otherwise expressly provided by the by-law by which they are imposed."

It is also provided in the legislation of the Province that when a ratepayer is in default of payment of any instalment by the day named for payment thereof, the subsequent instalment or instalments shall become forthwith payable.

In which case default on the first instalment would result in the other instalments becoming due immediately. Enter the bailiff!

What's the National Building Code of Canada?

It is an advisory document published by the National Research Council for use throughout Canada, essentially a set of minimum regulations to public health, fire protection, and structural sufficiency for buildings (but not intended for use with specialized civil engineering structures).

An advisory document only, having no legal standing until and unless it is adopted for specific use by a Provincial Government or Municipal administration, its essential purpose is the promotion of public safety through the use of desirable building standards throughout Canada.

It should be adopted from coast to coast without delay.

Adverse possession of real estate, sometimes called "squatter's rights", is something that still goes on, although it is seldom mentioned in the press.

There does not appear to be any simple set of rules about it. In Ontario, for example, it basically means that if one occupies and uses the land (unopposed) of another continuously for a period of ten years, then the person doing so may enter a claim to gain title to the property.

A farmer recently claimed adverse possession on the grounds that he had grazed his cattle, unopposed, on his neighbour's property for more than ten years. The claim was disallowed, probably due in part to a court judgment of 1894 which stated "To acquire title by "adverse possession" as against the patentee of land it is not sufficient merely to fence the land: some actual use and occupation of the fenced-in portion, not confined to casual acts of trespass such as the pasturing of cattle, must be shown."

It is interesting to note what other past court judgments have said in defining adverse possession:

(1911) "Merely fencing in land owned by another without putting it to some actual continuous use is insufficient to make the Statute of Limitations run so as to acquire possessory title to the land."

(1914) "One acquires title under the Statute of Limitations only to such land as he has had actual and visible possession by fencing or cultivating for the requisite period."

(1914) "The open, obvious, exclusive, and continuous possession of property necessary to bring a case within the Statute of Limitations is not destroyed simply because during the winter season the person acquiring title ceases to occupy the land.

"Occupation of an island suitable for fishing and summer residence by the erection of a house upon it, the exclusion of trespassers and the use of the island during the whole summer season for residence and fishing purposes and the leaving of personal belongings in the house during the winter is sufficient."

If the subject interests you, consult your Provincial Statutes of Limitations, and your lawyer . . .

Want to become a municipal assessor? A three-year correspondence course is offered by Queen's University, Kingston, Ontario. Also, local Community Colleges offer a 2-year course.

For further details write to: The Institute of Municipal Assessors, 9 Clintwood Gate, Don Mills, Ontario.

The Ford Motor Company of Canada does an absolutely superlative job in the way it illustrates and offers land for sale.

If you are lucky, Ford might let you have a sample. Its Canadian head office is in Oakville, Ontario.

Live in an apartment? Got some pals? Want to save money, get plenty of fresh air, exercise, enjoy yourself and learn something?

Then drive into the country, lease about one acre of land from a farmer and plant your own garden. Nice fresh vegetables and pretty flowers for everybody.

If you are ambitious and want to make money you might lease more than an acre, have the land plowed, and divide it into a number of 25 × 75 ft. gardens. Sublease these to city slickers for about $20 each. You'll get about 16 to the acre with plenty of elbow room.

However, tell the farmer about your plan, and ensure the municipal zoning won't spoil your fun (and profit).

Read your property listing agreement carefully. One broker had "inside information" that a highway was to be widened. He sent agents out to list as many properties as possible along the route, the listing price apparently being unimportant.

Why? Because the agreement signed by property owners stipulated that in the event of expropriation, the owner was to pay the broker a commission based on the expropriated price.

As an old smoothie once said, "keep your powder dry!"

Write to the Department of National Revenue, Ottawa, and ask to have your name placed on its mailing list for future copies of the "Interpretation Bulletins". Fascinating reading, and once in a while some good stuff about real estate.

It can cost less to borrow a hundred or two from a pawnbroker than it does from a finance (small loans) company, and is much more painless.

The finance company requires you to fill out an application then it checks your credit rating. If your loan for $300 or less is approved, you probably will be charged 2 per cent per month interest (24 per cent per annum, compounded monthly).

The pawnbroker, on the other hand, requires no application, no credit check, and gives you the instant cash (secured by a ring, watch, etc). The total annual charges in a test made by the author, in Toronto, amounted to less than 20 per cent, — it cost $14.60 to borrow $75.00 for one year on a ring I hocked.

What is a real estate *Consultant?*

A rare breed indeed. One that can be consulted and questioned on any and all aspects of real estate. If the consultant does not consider that he (or she) is fully qualified to handle the subject, he will get the answers for you from a fully qualified source.

Unfortunately, some agents, in their zealous efforts to generate business, will give you answers on any and all aspects of realty, sometimes without having the foggiest notion of what the subject is all about. This logically leads one to the question, "what're the guy's qualifications?"

If you want a recommendation for a consultant, write the author!

It appears to be an actuarial fact that over a period of any 20 years, 16 mortgagors (borrowers) in 100 will not live to complete the mortgage payments. The homeowner naturally would like to ensure that if the breadwinner is gone, his family will be left with a debt-free roof over its head.

Life insurance companies are ready to oblige, by providing term insurance (the cheapest life insurance one can buy) to cover the outstanding dollar balance owing on the mortgages. As the principal balance owing is reduced, the insurance coverage is reduced; the object being to have them both go down to a nil balance together.

Think about it, and do your best to fit its cost into your budget.

For a mortgage *lender*, title insurance is added protection to insure against loss that may be suffered because of concealed title defects that cannot possibly be discovered by lawers who examine the titles for real estate loans, such as:

— Forged deeds, releases, and so forth, in the chains of title to the properties on which money is loaned.

— False impersonations of former owners of the land.

— Instruments executed under fabricated or expired power of attorney.

— Undisclosed or missing heirs.

— Deeds not legally delivered in the lifetime of the grantor.

— Wills not probated.

— Deeds by minor or persons of unsound mind.

— Deeds by persons supposedly single, but secretly married.

— Marital rights of spouse supposedly, but not legally, divorced.

— Birth or adoption of children after date of will.

— Falsification of title records.

Title insurance is a definite insurance contract indemnifying the mortgagee, according to its terms, against financial loss of damage due to title defects.

Consumers' Association of Canada: Canada's foremost consumer watchdog. This non-profit, non-sectarian and non-government organization is your voice in consumer matters. It presents consumers' views to the federal, provincial and local governments, working for improved products, packaging and service and honest advertising.

Its bi-monthly publication, Canadian Consumer, contains a regular real estate question-and-answer feature.

Membership $4.00 a year, which includes the publication. Write: Consumers' Association of Canada, 100 Gloucester Street, Ottawa, Ontario.

Builders Financial Company Limited: An affiliate of the Royal Trust Company and U.S. Continental Illinois Corporation, it provides a service in making short and medium term interim financing loans. The loans consist primarily of construction loans which will be repaid from the proceeds of permanent financing. Typical loans will range from $500,000 up with terms of up to 3 years.

The rates are not unreasonable, the service prompt and the lender is of unquestioned strength in Canadian financing.

Mailing address: P.O. Box 367, Toronto-Dominion Centre, Toronto.

Financial Publishing Company: Just what it says it is. A publishing company strictly concerned with finance. This large American publisher has been supplying Canadians for many years with Canadian oriented tables of interest. Single copy prices and quantity discounts.

If you are a real estate and/or mortgage broker with a sales staff, it will interest you to know that you can obtain 25 copies of the pocket size monthly amortized mortgage payment tables, *with your name imprinted* for about one dollar each. All semi-annual compounding.

Write for its catalogue describing the publications available: Financial Publishing Company, 82 Brookline Avenue, Boston, Mass., U.S.A.

This bit is for the one who wants to (or must) rent a *house*. Here is a good method of determining if you are being asked to pay too much rent:

1. Establish the market value of the property.

2. Allow the owner a return of 8% on his investment.
3. Add the municipal taxes.

Example:

	Property market value:	$35,000
		8%
		$ 2,800
Taxes:		500
Annual Rent:		$ 3,300
Monthly Rent:		275

The tenant pays for all utilities (water, hydro, etc.).

In addition to the 8% (fair return) on his investment, the owner reaps the benefit of the financial appreciation of the property.

If you are being asked to pay more than the foregoing formulae indicates, think twice about it!

———————

There are more than 6,000,000 structurally separate sets of living quarters in Canada, each with a private entrance either from outside or from a common hall or stairway inside the building.

More than 500,000 of them don't have a bath or shower, and about 300,000 of them don't have a flush toilet.

Which means that a lot of people spend a lot of time running up and down the hall, or outside to the la la.

———————

Own a cottage? How close to the water do you think your land goes?

In Ontario, if somebody beaches a boat in front of your cottage, think twice before ordering him off "your" beach. The Provincial Government holds rights to a 66 foot strip of land along the shores of all lakes and rivers, and not only that, when such lands are incorporated into an organized municipality, the 66 foot strip does not pass to the municipality.

On islands of more than 15 acres, this 66 foot strip is also in effect, but if the island contains less than 15 acres, the 66 foot strip will be retained by the Crown for flood control purposes only.

The Crown strip of land is called a "one chain reserve". There are exceptions to it, but not many. The exceptions would be found in early land grant deeds, some of which went not only right to the water, but under it.

If your cottage is right next to the water, it is quite possible that it may be sitting on Crown land.

———————

The sanctity of the land boundary mark is ancient. The Romans even had a God called Terminus (The God of Landmarks).

Don't EVER remove a boundary mark. It is not only a lousy thing to do, it is against the law. In Ontario we take such a dim view of such an act that a judge can salt an offender away for five years.

Every book has an ending, but not this one. This book can be just the beginning for you, for the financial security of the future for you and your loved ones.

The older you get, the more you will appreciate the fact that true friends are few and far between, and therefore you will hopefully learn to financially look after your interests without leaning on, or crawling to, someone else for help.

If you are young, you are doubly fortunate. The opportunities for your future security are simply waiting for you to embrace them, and they could very well be in real estate. The basic secrets of real estate success are (1) know the ground rules, (2) buy wisely but not hastily, and (3) don't be greedy.

Get involved. Don't dream. Get a piece of the action — even a little piece. And to the 35,000 real estate agents in Canada who spend most of their time creating financial real estate success for others, while living on hopeful commissions, I have this piece of advice:

If *you* want to make it over the long haul, you'll very seldom do it on your commissions. You *must* get involved.

Richard Steacy

The author of this book, will be pleased to personally look after your real estate needs or interests.

All aspects of real property, including a consulting service.

BUYING
SELLING
LEASING
FINANCING

Let me help you get the top dollar for your property by listing it right!!

Associated with Chase & Taylor Limited, a foremost Toronto realtor, this knowledgeable and aggressive teamwork is at your service.

In Metropolitan Toronto
call me personally
Dick Steacy
493-5491
or
493-6037
or write c/o

Chase & Taylor Limited, 111 Ravel Rd., Willowdale, Ont.